CAKEWALK

CAKEWALK

A FULLY BAKED MEMOIR

SUSAN KATEIN
KATHY LANYON
&
CAROLE ALGIER

SHE WRITES PRESS

Published 2024
Printed in the United States of America
Print ISBN: 978-1-64742-746-7
E-ISBN: 978-1-64742-747-4
Library of Congress Control Number: 2024906803

For information, address:
She Writes Press
1569 Solano Ave #546
Berkeley, CA 94707

Interior design by Stacey Aaronson

She Writes Press is a division of SparkPoint Studio, LLC.

Names and identifying characteristics have been changed to protect the privacy of certain individuals.

For John, John, and Jack—the J Team

Tom & Helene for their unwavering support

Oh yeah, and Ralph, Beau, and Danielle
(because they're our kids)

Oh wait—also Jodi, our "new sister" who came into our lives to see to it that we told our story without screwing it up. Thank you, Jodi, we couldn't have done this without you!

Plus all the others who have so faithfully supported us
We treasure all of you.

FOREWORD

My journey with these three sisters—whose infectious enthusiasm, creativity, and, let's face it, booze transformed my pastry production kitchen into a realm of joy, laughter, and liquor-pumping fun—has been a delightful one. I was at that time a pastry chef-operator, product developer, wedding cake maker, and fellow dreamer, in addition to wearing many other hats, and I had the pleasure of witnessing and working in the whirlwind of excitement that Carole, Sue, and Kathy brought with them whenever they graced our doors.

Their arrival was always accompanied by an aura of spontaneity and a touch of disarray, yet amidst the chaos there gleamed a glimmer of unwavering determination and a shared vision for their dream cake business. It was this passion that fueled our collaboration and spurred me to pour my heart and soul into crafting confections that exceeded their expectations. Balancing the demands of quality and efficiency was no small feat, but with dedication and a sprinkle of ingenuity, we embarked on our quest to make their cake dreams a reality. Together, we navigated the intricate dance of flavors and textures, striving to strike the perfect harmony between delectable taste, seamless execution, and growth spurts.

Through countless trials and triumphs, Carole, Sue, and Kathy proved to be not only delightful companions but also resilient and steadfast allies in our pursuit of pastry perfection.

Their zest for life and unwavering commitment served as a constant reminder of the profound joy that comes from pursuing one's passions with unflagging fervor. It is with a sense of pride and nostalgia that we honor the cherished memories we created together—and what better way to celebrate this enduring bond than with this sweet account of our shared journey.

So here's to Carole, Sue, and Kathy, whose indomitable spirits and infectious laughter are a continuing inspiration to us all. May their story serve as a reminder that life is indeed a "cake walk," especially when accompanied by a generous serving of Amaretto cake. Indulge in and savor the sweetness of this heartwarming tale, for it is a testament to the timeless joy that comes from following your dreams and believing in the power of pastry.

Sweet Regards,
Chad A. Durkin
Owner of Porco's Porchetteria, Small Oven Pastry Shop,
and Breezy's Deli

FIRST THINGS FIRST

Once again, while sipping martinis and enjoying bites of our fabulous amaretto liqueur-infused cake, we sit around the table trying to decide the best way to tell our story. Should we take turns narrating? Should we bounce back and forth in time? Should we be *really* honest? Should we swear? Then my two sisters—partners, troublemakers, and comedians, they are—just start launching stories from the bottomless pits of creativity that are their brains. The stories roll out easily—starting with our often preposterous childhood—then move through romantic joys and foibles and march right into the cake years, those glorious cake years that keep coming. And I type. This pretty much describes our process. These two tell me I'm a decent writer, and I believe them. In fact, tepid as the compliment is, I grab and eat this praise as if it's the last piece of limoncello cake and there are four hungry football players just a fork away. It cements my role as the one who will do most of the writing work. They applaud this decision loudly and regularly.

Looking at our lives from three different perspectives—but for most of this book from one melded perspective—will help us explain not only our differences but how genuinely alike we are.

I'm Sue, your narrator (for now). I'm three years younger than Carole and three years older than Kathy, so my perspective on, well, everything related to this clan has something of a mediating, moderating, middle-ish flavor to it. For most of my life, Kathy and Carole have been my dearest friends and mentors, and together we've woven this tale of our beginnings, our big ideas, our failures, and our countless hours spent laughing. The other two will jump in as narrators to let you look into their closets, if you will, and then for the rest of the book, I'll tell the tales. But be assured it's three brains, one keyboard. And as is the case when we craft a recipe, we're going to load this book with all the best ingredients. We want this story to be as delicious as a slice of our obscenely moist amaretto cake flipped on one side, then the other, in a frying pan shiny with dancing hot butter.

This is the story of three sisters who crawled through the rubble of a wildly unstable childhood, stood up straight, and learned to fly.

CHAPTER ONE

Our beginnings were a bit of a circus, so let's start with the ring leaders. Bill Yoder, the person who would eventually become our dad, was a handsome, charismatic, self-centered man who stood about six foot four and dazzled the ladies with his thick head of brown hair. And his warm brown eyes that drew females in at first glance. He grew up the favorite child of his Irish mother, our Grandma Yoder, who was a generally unhealthy woman. She had a weak heart due to a bout of rheumatic fever during her childhood and remained sickly into the early years of her marriage, which relegated her to a lot of bed rest and therefore a chronic cluelessness about what was going on in her own house.

The eldest of four, Bill was a skilled manipulator who often blamed his mishaps on his younger siblings. He was the kind of guy who would break a milk glass, then point the finger at a younger brother who would be punished for it. I'm guessing the younger kids grew up thinking their big brother was a colossal shithead. But maybe that's just me insinuating myself (and so soon!).

"Tell them how we know all this," interrupts Carole.

"Yeah," says Kathy, "you want to be a reliable narrator, don't you?"

Get a load of those two. I'm not two paragraphs in, and already they start peanut gallery-ing. Okay, fair enough. We pieced together this history of our parents, those messed-up, star-crossed "lovers," with help from Aunt Diggie, who might have been helped by vodka—a terrific truth serum.

Shall I continue?

"I'll allow it," says Carole.

"Proceed," says Kathy.

Do you see what I deal with?

Bill was an enterprising hustler, who made the most of being his mother's pet, and she smothered him with unearned adoration, probably because it beat focusing on her marriage to a philandering drinker. Her husband, the person who would eventually become our grandfather, wasn't even sneaky about the philandering part. When he *could* be bothered to show up for his family, he'd take his side piece to family functions and introduce her as his "friend."

Well, as is often the case, the son learned from the father. Apparently, young Bill grew to understand that most if not all married men had female "friends." And his mother did little to redirect the burgeoning morality of her boy. Because some people interpret silence as acceptance, young Bill apparently internalized the idea that wives are generally okay with this setup. So the cheating man example provided by his father plus the "Number One Son, you can do no wrong" training provided by his mother worked in concert to create a young man so overflowing with misogyny and entitlement he saw no reason not to become a philanderer himself.

But let's not get ahead of ourselves. Before our father could cheat on our mother, they had to meet.

Anne, our mother, was a beautiful, brown-eyed, shapely girl with wavy black hair and a flawless complexion. She was the daughter of a large, bossy Italian woman and a medium-sized Italian man who never told his wife to "zip it." Mom's mom, whom we called "Nana," was the drill sergeant of the family, and as you know if you have military experience or have watched *An Officer and a Gentleman*, if you talk back to a drill sergeant, your life is going to soon include very unsavory meals, unpleasant sleeping quarters, and extra sit-ups. Also, with Nana there was a lot of hitting. She espoused many classic parenting platitudes of the day, like "Children should be seen, not heard" and "I'll give you something to cry about."

Nana's children weren't the only unlucky recipients of her soldier ways. She also treated her husband as if he were her underling, barking orders for how to clean and cook. The man was a trained chef, for God's sake, but Nana probably sucked all the joy out of his time in the kitchen. He didn't speak much—muttered mostly. Nana didn't mind smacking him on the back of the head either. But in her defense, Nana worked in a factory as an auto parts assembler, and how much fun could that have been?

So no, our mom didn't have an easy childhood, and from those parents she certainly didn't learn about healthy relationships or the idea that she had the right to expect respect or affection from a marriage. She was the youngest of four and had been the Cinderella of her household, assigned the tasks of mopping floors, folding laundry, washing dishes—that kind of crazy, girlhood fun. And she was constantly being manipulated by her older siblings, who ordered her to do *their* chores as well as hers.

Anne read a lot of fairy tales to help her forget about her lousy life, and as a product of such fantasy literature, she spent a lot of time dreaming of the day she'd find a Prince Charming who would whisk her away to a better place. She genuinely believed a man was the answer, the escape, the road to some semblance of happiness for the first time in her life.

Sigh. This is by no means the only part of our parents' histories that weighs heavily on our hearts. It really hurts to learn that during Mom's childhood, nobody was on her side, *in her own home.* Oh, how it hurts that we can't go back and help her, can't teach her how to stand up for herself and craft a future that isn't dependent on a man. Alas, we cannot. So, for now, let's see what there is to be learned from her journey.

Cut to a stereotypical East Coast high school, circa 1947. Bill, both a very popular basketball player and his school's very handsome prom king, had all the ladies batting their eyelashes and bending over *just so* to pick up a dropped book whenever he was near. One day, the beautiful Italian gal, Anne Cimino, caught Bill's eye as she sashayed into the local high school hangout, the soda shop/burger joint where the Norristown High School kids gathered after class. Even though Bill had already graduated, he still paid plenty of attention to the girls at that local hangout; several of them would be graduating the following year, which meant before long, the market would be flooded with lots more sweet young things of legal age. Or close enough.

Ugh, does that remind anybody else of Matt McConaughey in *Dazed and Confused*? He plays that creepy, twenty-something guy who long ago graduated from the local high school but keeps smarming around to leer at teenaged girls.

"Who could forget?" says Kathy.

"'That's what I love about these high school girls, man,'" Carole mimics. "'I get older—they stay the same age.' *Ewww*."

All right, all right, all right—let's move on.

Bill's movie star looks and cheesy-movie-dialogue charm—and surely his letter sweater, which he wore regularly to attract the younger set—captivated Anne, the girl who spent inordinate amounts of time daydreaming about running off with a handsome cowboy . . . or duke . . . or earl . . . or who knows—*some* good-looking guy on a horse. And here he was, right there in the flesh, looking just like the guys she'd been dreaming about. This Bill guy was going to be the prince, the happily-ever-after she longed for! He was going to be her ticket out of a life of misery and servitude! Now she just needed to lock this thing down.

Their romance began in secret, with most "dates" consisting of back-seat sex and a milkshake, always at least one town over so Bill's other prospects wouldn't think he was off the market. Also, Bill's Irish mother would never have approved of her golden seed of male perfection lowering himself to consort with some broad from the House of Swarthy Italians. God, no. Just imagine the strange words that would emanate from such a house, the dark traditions, the murky food smells!

Anne was happy to play in the shadows if it meant she got to be the handpicked filly who was to be seen (if only in semi-secret) on the arm of a yummy Gary Cooper meets John Wayne meets Henry Fonda. Wide-eyed and gullible, she was willing to do anything this prince asked of her, including "parking," during which outings she'd perform all the sex things he pushed for, even when she thought doing so was wrong and might jeopardize her reputation. This was a guy who'd been taught to treat women like property, and Anne was a girl who'd been taught that only a man could save her from a miserable future. They were a match made in hell.

Well, one backseat romp led to another, and *Voila!* Anne found herself pregnant just one year after graduating from high school. Despite surely being a mortified basket case of panic, she rationalized that the pregnancy wasn't necessarily a bad thing. *This guy told me I'm the love of his life*, she surely thought. *This might be okay! We're going to be married! Right? We're going to be married. Right*?

Anne broke the big news to Bill, and he responded with a quick, "I'm leaving for the navy in two months. What do you want *me* to do?" (Don't see much of *that* kind of dialogue in ye olde fairy tales, do we ladies?)

Of course, Anne knew Bill had been planning to become a navy man. She also knew two months was plenty of time to whip up a little old wedding. But rather than get down on one knee and continue his pledges of true love, he simply offered to send her some meager amount of money now and then "for the kid."

When it was almost time for Bill to shove off, he and Anne knew they'd have to tell their parents what was, um, *cooking*. To no one's surprise, the news of an impending O'Bambino wasn't met with a hallelujah chorus. All four parents made it clear that no kids of theirs were going to be the source of community embarrassment. Both the Italian and Irish camps decreed that these two screwups were going to tie the knot and tie it tight. So with that romantic stroke of fate, Anne got her wish—a husband. And one in a naval uniform, no less!

We three sisters—only a percentage of the loving children who eventually sprang from that charmed union—have often reflected on our mother's choice to marry a guy who couldn't be bothered, *even during their courtship,* to keep his hands on her alone. If the granting of our wish wouldn't warrant us nonexistent, we'd wish for our mother something far better than marriage to that brand of "prince." Like maybe a pony or a new Edsel. Or steak knives.

Despite a lot of family moaning and pearl clutching, the young parents-to-be were married in a full-blown Italian/Irish Catholic wedding with all the trimmings and traditions, including standard American wedding fare, like $1 dances, which bought the male guests the right to three minutes of pawing the bride; a garter belt slid down the bridal leg and tossed into a sweaty mob of single guys; and of course, the bouquet toss for the hopeful single gals!

By the way, I'd love to know who came up with that one. You, the bride, turn your back to a crowd of young, pretty, happy females, heave the bouquet backward over your head, then turn around fast to watch them lunge and claw as they try to snatch a bunch of flowers in a gesture symbolizing that being the next to call yourself "Mrs." is worth knocking some of your best friends off their party heels.

The bride wore a magnificent, flowing, satin-and-silk wedding gown dusted with tiny pearl beads, and her bridesmaids wore pink. Bill and his groomsmen were dapper in their black tuxedos with ruffled shirts and pink bowties. Anne considered it a fairy-tale wedding.

The newlyweds skipped right over the honeymoon (surprise!) and moved into the drafty, third-floor bedroom of Bill's childhood home, a bedroom almost as cold as the reception Anne received from her in-laws. It was a dingy, dark space filled with old family junk and the ghosts of shitty relationships. For Anne, it was like being relegated to an attic in a Brontë novel. Bill's punitive mother, who apparently missed the lecture about how babies are made, spent her days slinking around with a surly expression, paying almost no attention to the little guinea harlot who had immaculately conceived using Bill's sperm.

Only two weeks after their nuptials, Bill took off for the navy, and Anne was left essentially alone in a loveless house, much like the one she'd just escaped. She spent her days writing letters to her new husband and dreaming of his homecoming when they could start their life together. But Bill rarely wrote back. And any money he earned from the navy he sent to his mother to pay for Anne's room and board instead of to Anne to build their nest egg.

While Bill traveled the world and played basketball for the navy, Anne did her best to survive in the dismal, third-floor bedroom, suffering through aching loneliness and countless first-time pregnancy fears. She even had to carry buckets of water up three flights to bathe and clean her tiny excuse for a room.

When I think of our mother in that horrible situation, I feel immense sadness. When I was a teenager, she told me stories of how she spent most nights crying and wondering why her life was so tortured.

In my imagination, she's small and frail in a tiny room "decorated" with old wooden furniture that splinters and creaks. I picture her as lonely as a person has ever felt, and if I think about it too long, I can feel my blood pressure start to rise.

Carole, Kathy, and I have often thought about traveling

back in time and shaking her sane. We want to teach her about independence and women's rights and self-respect. We want her to benefit from all the extraordinary progress made for women in the decades that followed her girlhood. We want her free. But that would involve all kinds of tinkering with the time/space continuum and, well, we're pretty busy, you know, with the cake business and all. And again, such an intervention would lead to our not existing. Crap.

Anne kept believing Bill would soon come home and save her, that it was only a matter of time before he'd be stateside and thus they would begin their happy love story. While she waited, our mother received her little miracle: Michael, her first son. She gave birth feeling quite alone in a small, local hospital and shortly afterward returned to the sad place she called home. But at least now she had a companion.

As the story goes, Michael's birth was no simple event. He showed up twenty-seven inches long, weighing fourteen pounds. *Fourteen pounds?* For the love of God, that's a Thanksgiving turkey. Mom was alone in the house when her labor started, nary a helpful mother-in-law in sight, so she called a cab to take her to the hospital. Four hours later, she expelled that enormous infant. Our mother had stood a wee five feet, four inches and weighed around 110 pounds when she got pregnant (but a whopping 170 just before delivery), so we find it shocking that the trauma of her first go at pregnancy and childbirth didn't convince her to stop producing babies. Nope. She signed up for six more. You'll see.

The day Michael was born, his father was squeaking around a basketball court far across the world, so the arrival of their first child didn't lead to the family unity Anne hungered for. But at least now she could focus on the joys of motherhood. In the days that followed Michael's birth, she passed many hours telling her baby boy fantastical stories of the special times she and Bill had spent together and how he'd promised to save her from her horrible mother and sisters after he finished doing his part for Uncle Sam. *Great* content for baby stories, am I right? But Anne would also make up other stories for her little boy, stories of princes and princesses who lived in happy splendor inside enormous, beautiful castles. Castles on vast estates soaked in sunlight and surrounded by miles of rolling hills, where they could play and laugh and frolic with the bunnies and deer that lived in the nearby forest. Anne found solace in such stories, and it was during this troubled time she realized she had not only the strength of a Siberian musk ox but the heart of a writer. She filled page after page with poems and short stories about love and galas and all the things she dreamed of, and the writing soothed her weary soul.

By the time Bill came home from the navy and met his son for the first time, little Michael was already eighteen months old. Bill took one look at his frazzled, desperately lonely young wife, then at his toddler son, and said, "He looks just like you, a dumb dago."

Gifted with an astonishing ability to filter vile remarks from narcissists, Anne wasn't dissuaded. To prove to her sailor she was worthy of his respect and love, she devised new and creative ways to please him, mostly with sexual favors she'd read about in escapist love stories. (I know, *ew.*) Apparently, her sexual tricks hit the spot, if you will, because Bill stuck around—more or less—and for a time did seem to enjoy parading his beautiful young wife for his friends. Her long, shiny black hair, which was always styled like a movie star's, fell perfectly across her narrow shoulders and contrasted beautifully with her ivory skin. With her big brown eyes, she would gaze at him adoringly, and by launching a constant stream of compliments, she'd fluff his paper-thin ego. Anne was very careful to keep her eye on the prize, which wasn't so much Bill himself as an escape from his creepy mother and that miserable attic.

Around the time Anne convinced Bill they needed to buy and move into their own home, she discovered she was pregnant again. Thanks to training he'd gotten while in the navy, Bill was able to secure a job as a welder, and with financial help from Bill's Aunt Diggie and Uncle Dixie, Anne and Bill bought a home in Collegeville, a town about twelve miles from her childhood home.

Moving out of her in-laws' den of despair gave Anne a sense that she was now at the beginning. The beginning of what, though? With this guy for a husband, what could Anne be sure of?

Enter Carole, baby number two. For a while after little Carole was born, Bill doted on his daughter, but he soon became bored and started spending a lot of time in bars, where he acquired a number of girlfriends. And although he didn't actually flaunt his indiscretions, being married didn't deter him from having them. So as it turned out, neither the addition of children nor the purchase of a new house offered Anne the feeling of home she wanted more than anything.

Although Anne didn't make friends easily, she did try to connect with some of the women at the town park where she would take her little ones for fresh air. Those local gals didn't mind telling her they'd seen her husband on the town with other women, nor did they mind sharing stories of how Anne's husband had flirted with *each of them*. So much for making friends in Collegeville.

When our mother told us about this phase in her life, we winced. Bill knew he was hurting and embarrassing her with his very public affairs, but he kept at it.

We still can't imagine how, why, *how* our father rationalized continuing to hurt his wife, the mother of his children. What kind of empty vessel neglects his new family and in the face of his wife's anguish over his betrayals shows no remorse, no contrition—offers not so much as an "I'm sorry" let alone a sentiment like, "I love you and our family. I'll change"?

Alas, that's probably an exploration for a (highly qualified) therapist. As the daughters of this damsel in despair, these stories are difficult to revisit. At the same time, they make us ferocious; we want to snatch that young lady by the collar and drag her into an "I Am Woman, Hear Me Roar" immersion program. But for now, we're just your storytellers, so we'll hang back here with you and watch Anne make her own choices.

Each time Anne heard another tawdry tale about her husband, she confronted him with the rumor, and like the seasoned cheater he'd become, he'd bat the ball back using one of a number of diversionary devices, like gaslighting ("You're imagining this! You need more to occupy your mind."), false flattery ("You're a beauty. Why would I need more than you?"), and the ever-tedious envy angle ("Those girls are just jealous because you have the guy *they* want!"). Seriously, he had the bloated ego of a pop diva multiplied by three Kardashians.

From what Mom told us, the ladies at the park referred to Dad as "the town male-whore." I've never understood the need to add "male" to that moniker, but I digress. It's difficult to imagine how our mother could have been so gullible—or so needy—that she could have rationalized away the gossip, even sometimes telling herself her husband was the innocent target of lascivious women who simply spread rumors because he'd rejected them. How did she rationalize his utterly flimsy excuses for not coming home to his family? Those mysteries remain unanswered, although I suspect having two little kids and no career had something to do with it. According to Mom, as time went on, he stopped trying to hide his partying and cheating and *even* explained it was okay for a man to cheat, that it was just the way of the world. Imagine how proud he must have felt for being so honest about his dishonesty. He was dishonest as hell but not too busy to do his part to keep the baby train rolling.

CHAPTER TWO

Bill was a sports enthusiast, which is what finally led him to build a relationship with little Michael but only after the lad passed his fifth birthday. As Bill taught Michael baseball, basketball, and other sports, Anne began to think that maybe—just maybe—her prince was finally emerging. Maybe her husband was going to embrace fatherhood! So as naïve young women often do, she decided the best way to help a lousy father become a decent father was to give him another kid. Enter child number three, girl number two, Sue!

The next two-plus years went relatively smoothly as Bill appeared to be settling down a bit. He actually came home right after work, shared a cocktail with his wife, and ate dinner with his family. Now and then he'd even take his kids for a piggyback ride or read a bedtime story. But, of course, he soon grew restless again.

Bill also tired of being a helmet-wearing welder who took direction from engineers, so he dedicated himself to working his way up the engineering ladder. He worked hard, read whatever he could about engineering, and was promoted to architectural engineer for a local steel company. For a while, the home life was relatively content as Anne felt Bill was concentrating on his family, so she followed her recipe for family harmony and got herself another bun in the oven. Then Debbie was born. Mom continued to believe that if it ain't broke, don't fix it, so eleven months later came Kathy. That's right. *Eleven* months later. For those of you readers who knocked out a kid within a year of knocking out a kid, please explain by writing to us at bewilderedsisters@holyhellwerentyoustillsore?.com.

But it gets crazier!

Eighteen months after the arrival of Kathy, the family got itself a Charlotte. What the bloody hell? But wait! *There's more*! Ten months later, David showed up. *Ten* months! Anne was clearly taking the insanity of "performing the same action but expecting a different result" to a new level. She seemed to think she was in some kind of competitive reproduction tournament, and dammit if she wasn't going to take home the trophy. Maybe she was so tired of being lonely, she decided to create her own crowd. With seven kids under the age of ten, who has time to feel bad about a rotten marriage?

And this should surprise no one: Word is that Bill didn't show up at the hospital for the arrivals of any of his offspring.

His routine was to drop our contracting mother at the hospital, then make a beeline to the house of the mother-in-law he despised, pick her up, and then dump her at our house to take care of the resident crowd of small people until our sore and exhausted mom came home to resume her duties. Also, it was no surprise that Dad bragged about being the creator of the brood. I can just hear him.

"*I* did all that. They're all mine."

Barf. If you think I'm being hard on him, keep reading.

Mom's return from the hospital was always met with little fanfare except for some internal cheers from us older siblings who were thrilled to once again be rid of our nana, a frosty taskmaster. We were thrilled to have her gone and our mother back, even though Mom always returned with yet another pink, screaming defecation machine.

With seven children and two adults under one roof, the young family's once cozy three-bedroom house now felt more bloated than any one of us after the Tropicana's all-you-can-eat ravioli night. As we grew older, the five girls shared one bedroom that featured one set of bunk beds and a double bed that had to sleep three, kind of *Cheaper by the Dozen* style. Only Carole and I, the oldest girls, got to sleep alone, each in our own bunk bed. Luxury. The two boys shared the other bedroom, which was actually a closet that fit only one twin bed, which they both slept in—at the same time. That was some real Charles Dickens crap going on there.

In that first house, our family didn't have a television, so Mom did her best to get a peek at the outside world by reading hand-me-down copies of *Life Magazine* and occasionally sneaking off to see a movie, the latter requiring that *her* mother feel generous enough to babysit for a few hours. As you read, Nana wasn't particularly fond of her grandchildren and probably not too keen on helping her daughter, the baby factory, solve her self-imposed domestic problems. But on occasion she agreed to watch us, probably to piss off her son-in-law. She knew he hated having her in the house. Unfortunately for the health of the growing family, whenever Nana was at the house, Dad would take off to escape the great stresses of family life, and I think we all know that for Daddy-O that didn't mean a thought-clearing stroll around a lake.

Toxic as my parents' marriage was and damaged as our family dynamic was by Dad's affairs, we kids did manage to have a lot of fun. Outside, we played kickball, baseball, hopscotch, and hide-n-seek until the sun went down, sometimes until after it had gone way down. The outdoors was high and wide and gave us a lot more opportunity to breathe, so we spent a lot of time breathing it in, and the games we played took our minds off the cracks and fissures that glared in all those indoor spaces.

The house was a "twin home," which shared a center wall and looked like two identical houses with a backyard that stretched back about two hundred yards. In the other side of the house lived a sweet old woman named Mrs. Reifsnyder, who often tried to help Mom manage her flock of children. Our back property had seven tall maple trees, which were good for climbing, and a little pond that housed our ducks. Playing in our backyard was like going to a modern-day obstacle course with piles of discarded wood from Dad's projects that went unfinished because he wasn't home long enough to finish anything. The other quirky feature of our backyard was that it opened to a swampy wetland we wouldn't play on because we were sure that after one or two steps in, we'd sink to the depths of muck and be grabbed by the creature from the black lagoon (who, of course, would have been visiting our neighborhood that day). Because we never so much as stuck a toe in that murk, the swamp served as a constant source of mystery and child control. All one of us olders had to say to freak out one of the youngers was, "You see that ripple? That's *him*. And he's hungry."

Siblings are siblings, and we three eldest were shits to the younger kids, even during game time, and there was one game of hide-n-seek that nicely illustrates our shitheadery.

"Okay, guys!" shouted Carole like a summer camp counselor trying to fire up a bunch of bored kids tired of playing dumb camp games. "Hands over your eyes and count to twenty-five. Nice and slow to give us time to hide out here!"

I thought it was a nice touch adding the "out here." Sly.

The four little ones gathered in a circle like puppies around a bowl of kibble and started to count out loud.

"Slower!" yelled Carole. "You smarties are way too fast for us!" Then the three of us thrashed shrubs and crunched over gravel to make our little siblings think we were scurrying off to hide behind trees or under bushes, then we hustled through the side doorway and up to the girls' bedroom where we stationed ourselves at the edge of the window to watch. Down on the lawn, the kids finished counting, flung their hands from their faces, and took off in four directions toward every bush or car or piece of big country junk on the property. Up in the bedroom, we giggled like idiots as we watched them dash around like ants on pavement.

About three minutes into the giggle fest, Kathy and Debbie ran into the house, and about three minutes after that, Mom came storming through the bedroom door.

"You're supposed to be watching them, not torturing them!" she shrieked. "Get back downstairs and take care of your brothers and sisters!" Then she stormed out.

Mike waited until her footsteps had faded and said, "Let's go play paratrooper."

"Okay," we said, then scrambled down the stairs and out the front door.

Playing paratrooper was one of our favorite warm-weather activities. It involved climbing high into trees, then dropping ourselves to the ground like paratroopers as we screamed commands like, "Take the hill!" or "They're not getting me alive!" In the early days of paratrooper, we jumped while holding bedsheets or umbrellas, Mary Poppins style, over our heads, but those accessories never once delayed the inevitable *thump* on the ground, so we switched to jumping commando—using no gear of any kind, just a naked leap to the ground. We kept this up, jump after jump, climbing and dropping from higher and higher, until one of us sprained the hell out of an ankle or ripped a tendon, which halted our paramilitary games until we forgot about the consequences and started climbing again.

Our house sat on the edge of a small street that served as a throughway between two towns, so the traffic was usually pretty heavy. The cars whizzed by so fast you'd have thought the drivers were headed to the lottery office clutching a ten-million-dollar winner. One summer afternoon, a big red truck raced down the street and blew a tire that flew across the yard and hit our front porch.

Mom ran to the trucker and screamed, "You could have killed one of my children! You need to slow the hell down!"

Our mother didn't usually yell at anyone but her kids, so a bunch of us watched from the window and cheered as the driver faced the wrath of Anne Yoder. Can't say we ever saw that red truck on our road again.

Along the backside of the house was the door to the basement, and in front of the door was an *open* cesspool.

For those who have never seen nor perhaps even heard of such a thing, let me help. A cesspool is like a septic tank in that it collects all the foul, disgusting fluids and solids that flow from inside humans into sinks and toilets. This slimy, fetid stew lives in an enormous soup can—a container about six feet across and five feet down—that gradually lets all the putrid glop, which smells like the inside of a rotting hippo's lower intestine, leach out into the land all around it.

It's actually not strange that we had one of these swill tanks in our backyard—houses all around our town disposed of their inner sewage the same way; what's strange is that ours didn't have a lid. Because children don't tend to question the *what's what* relative to things like plumbing, electricity, sewage disposal, etc., none of us asked what the deal was with the gaping hole in the backyard, which was clearly the portal to Satan's outhouse. But why our parents didn't mind a potentially deadly in-ground cylinder full of terrifying crud-slime to sit uncovered just outside the door to the home of their seven children is a question for the ages. We kids simply steered clear of it.

In our backyard, there were no swings or jungle gyms or other play structures, which motivated us to wander off the property. To prevent such roaming, Mom had to be creative, as she was with her infamous clothesline strategy. She tied a rope around each of our waists (not Prince Mike's of course), and looped each rope on the clothesline. Then, like spaniels on a dog run, all six tethered kids ran up and down the yard without Mom having to worry about us straying into the street. By today's standards, this safety device might be deemed . . . um . . . inappropriate? Abusive? Illegal? Hey, I don't blame her; it was seven against one. Crafty as Mom was, she wasn't clever enough to restrain notorious escapist Carole, who one day disconnected her rope from its tether and, still roped, sprinted across the yard. Apparently, the kid was so focused on what she was escaping, she didn't notice where she was headed. Her blind run for freedom was precisely in the direction of that gigantic, unsealed can of human waste.

Thrilled to have escaped the dog run, Carole ran and ran, again and again looking back over her shoulder—probably to confirm no one was after her, and then sure as shit, *sploosh*—in she went!

Mom and Mike heard the rest of us screaming, then came running out of the house and made a beeline for that shit soup with a Carole crouton. Thanks to Mom, Carole was already rigged and ready to yank, so Mom and Mike grabbed the part of the rope that lay on the ground, dug their feet in, leaned back, and pulled like two champions in a tug-o-war to the death.

Carole had never been a particularly tidy kid. She rarely brushed her hair and would wear the same clothes for days, plus all our goofing around the backyard usually led to every one of us ending the day smeared and smelly. But when *that* girl was hoisted out of the in-ground poop pot, it was an astonishing thing to witness. The five of us who remained tethered watched in awe as they pulled what looked like some kind of feral forest nymph from the decrepit cave of muck where she'd been eating dragon carcasses all her unwashed life. She was covered in sludge from face to feet, and even from ten feet away, we could smell her. She stank worse than the backside of a buffalo on a bean diet. There were big lumpy chunks of feces in her hair, and she was such a complete walking poop smear we couldn't even tell what color her clothes had been.

Each time she discovered another piece of poop hanging from her clothes or hair, she shrieked, "I'm full of shit! Get it off!" The five of us who remained fastened to the dog cable stood transfixed, alternating between astonished silence and squeals of joyous disbelief.

The most fun of all was watching Michael hose Carole down with an icy-cold jet spray that pretty much knocked her to the ground, where she wriggled and writhed until, like magic, she began to resemble a human child again.

To this day that girl won't step within ten yards of a Porta-Potty.

"Tell them about Collegeville," says Kathy, as she wistfully watches the swaying branches of the maple trees out the window of the dining room where we've come together to record more of our story. "Tell them about its Norman Rockwell-ness. Tell them about all the cute little one-story shops and Dewane's—remember—buying a pop for five cents and getting a penny back when we returned the bottle. And what about Mr. Ludwig in his grocery store, cruising back and forth along the shelves on that rolling ladder? How Norman Rockwell is *that*? What about Lutz's and that other drugstore for vanilla and root beer floats? Oh man, I want one of those right now. And tell them about all the American flags made at Collegeville Flag Company."

"Anything else?" I ask her.

"That we were always called the Collegeville Goofy Seven," she adds, "because we were always seen together."

"Yes, I know why we were called that. Anything else?"

"The creek. Of course. The creek."

"Yes, I'll tell them about the creek."

Carole says, "Like that time, remember at the creek that time when the thing happened?"

"Yes, Carole," I reply. "I'll tell them about that time and the thing."

What would I do without these two raconteurs by my side? The "thing" is the time we were all ice skating and playing hockey on the creek.

Our only puck went flying to the lower edge and big brother Mike sent Carole to retrieve it. Carole skated over to it and heard the ice crackling.

"Hey!" she yelled. "I can't reach it, and the ice is cracking here!"

Mike yelled back, "Don't be a baby! Use your stick and drag it back. Hurry up!"

Carole kept going, grabbed the puck, and then plunged through the ice and started thrashing and screaming. Yes, once again Carole had plunged into something she shouldn't have.We all skated as close to her as we could, and soon everybody was screaming.

Mike yelled, "Calm down! Grab my stick!"

Within seconds, we realized the water at the creek's edge was only about a foot deep, so we all erupted into laughter. And so were the days of our childhood.

Anyway, as Kathy already rambled . . . er . . . illustrated, all in all, Collegeville was a dreamy place for kids to grow up. We spent countless summer hours in fields and parks and floating on or jumping in some body of water. On winter days, we built snow forts with walls big enough to protect the seven of us during neighborhood snowball fights. We built tunnels through to the back of the fort so we could escape if we were losing a battle.

When we weren't sledding or ice skating on neighborhood ponds, we were playing on the big beautiful Perkiomen Creek. Not sure whose idea it was to call it a creek rather than a river—it was thirty-eight miles long and wide enough for an army of canoes to cruise it side by side. But creek, river, or whatever it was, it was plenty deep enough, fast enough, and wild enough to serve as the site of many our youthful adventures, like swinging out over the water holding a rope we'd tied to a thick tree branch or sitting in the water in front of the creek's dam and watching an arch of water soar over our heads.

As we kids busied ourselves with kid things, our parents' relationship—if it could be called that—was unraveling. Dad disappeared for days, even months at a time.

"Mom, where's Dad?" I often asked, surely articulating the confusion of seven kids."Why doesn't he live here very much?"

"Your father is away on business," Mom would answer.

"Why is he gone so much?"

Mom usually sighed. "Because his business calls for it."

"What's his business?"

"Wash your hands for dinner."

Those kinds of answers must have been confusing for the younger ones, but Mike, Carole, and I were beginning to understand there was a dark cloud hovering above our home. We often heard our mother crying on the other side of a closed door.

A crying mother is a very painful thing for a child.

As far as we kids knew, couples in our little town didn't split up. Most everybody's family had a mother and a father, and most of the fathers were easy to spot—showing up at baseball games or taking their families to dinner in town. We knew our family was different from those households, but we couldn't yet piece together what that meant. We just accepted that our family ran as it ran, and we tried our best to make our mother's life easier by obeying and being helpful around the house. Whenever Dad disappeared for days, we all prayed he'd come home and make Mom smile again.

Our dad's Aunt Diggie and his sister, Aunt Mary Louise, were like guardian angels who did their best to watch over our family. They brought meals and treats to the house, directed us toward household chores, and tried to distract us from our mother's misery. As much as we loved being around our aunties, we older kids knew that when they were around a lot, it was a bad sign. By the time I was ten, Mom would stay in her room for hours, and Mike, Carole, and I had a pretty good idea that the stress of a seven-kid house along with the pain caused by our father's cheating, drinking, and disappearing was destroying our exhausted mother.

One horrible summer evening a tall, husky man banged on our front door and yelled, "Get out here, you bastard! Sleep with my wife—I'll kick your ass!"

As we kids watched from hidden places, Dad opened the door, the big guy leaped on him, and the two of them fell into the front yard wrestling and punching each other. I couldn't make out everything the other guy said, but I heard him blurt "wife," "cheat," and "scumbag," along with a lot of curse words. Within a minute or so, Mom ran out on the lawn and tried to pull the guy off our dad while yelling, "Go talk to your wife! You don't bring this mess around my children!" The guy didn't let our dad out of a headlock, so Mom screamed, "I'm calling the police!"

That did it. He stood up, brushed himself off, and walked

back to his car. There was no follow-up fight between my parents, and neither of them said a word about it to us. Shortly afterward, Dad left for the bar and wasn't seen again for several weeks. I think that's when Mom began the fast slide toward her first nervous breakdown.

I remember clearly the day Mom snapped. She just couldn't get out of bed. As she lay on her side with a blanket pulled over her head, she told Carole and me to keep the younger kids busy, so we grabbed the Candy Land game and tried to amuse our siblings.

Now and then I knocked on Mom's door. "Mom?" I called softly. No reply. "Mom? What's going on? We're getting scared." No answer.

That's when Carole and I decided it was time to call the aunts.

Aunt Mary Louise said, "Tell Mike to call an ambulance. I'll be right there." She arrived several minutes later, and about a minute after that, a terrifying red ambulance screeched into the driveway. Two big guys in uniforms threw open the back doors of the vehicle and ran into the house. Then we kids stood on the porch in silence as we watched our limp mother carried out on a stretcher and loaded into the ambulance, which then disappeared down the street.

Mike said, "Don't worry. Everything will be okay." I couldn't imagine where he was getting that idea, but I thought I might as well try to trust him.

Soon Aunt Diggie arrived, and our two aunties made us dinner. Aunt Mary Louise said,"Your mom will be home in a couple days. She just needs time to rest."

That didn't sound likely to me.

"Your mother has a very bad cold," said Aunt Mary Louise.

A cold? Seriously? I knew my aunts were doing their best not to let the situation scare the hell out of us, but an ambulance, two paramedics, and a stretcher because of a cold? Even four-year-old Kathy saw the BS in that one.

She said, "Mom didn't take hankies. How will she blow her nose?"

For the next two weeks, Aunt Mary Louise ran our household, doing her best to keep us clean, fed, and distracted with card games like Go Fish and Old Maid. Every night at bedtime, she kissed each of us goodnight, not only the boys, and every day while we were in school, she visited Mom at the hospital and reported back that Mom missed us and loved us and would be home soon. But she didn't come home soon.

In the meantime, the aunts tracked down our deadbeat father and convinced him to show up for his family. For about three weeks, he did some of the things decent fathers do, like actually come home every evening. He'd also make us dinner, which consisted of canned tomato soup with stale saltines. To this day, I can't touch tomato soup, not even if it's gourmet, not even if it's being served with a world-class grilled cheese. For me, tomato soup tastes like ambulances and abandonment.

For thirty days Mom was hospitalized, and the only updates we received were from Aunt Mary Louise who told us each night as she tucked us in bed that Mom was thinking of us and would be home soon.

Then one afternoon, Dad called us into the living room and said, "Your mother is feeling better, so she's coming home tomorrow. You all need to be good, clean your rooms, and not bother her."

Little Kathy said, "She's been resting for a while. I think she'll want to play with us. She misses us, you know."

He didn't know what to do with that brand of honesty, so he simply said, "Just don't get in her way."

The next day, with Aunt Mary Louise's arm around her shoulder, Mom ambled through our front door. All seven of us greeted her with hugs and kisses, and nobody asked any questions.

For about a week, we kids tiptoed around her and tried to let her rest as much as she wanted to, but then things started to resemble the old days. Dad went out at night and disappeared for days at a time. Mom cooked dinner, but Carole and I did all the laundry and cleaning without a word of complaint. We were just so grateful to have our mother back.

Since those torn-up years, Kathy, Carole, and I have talked many times about how some of our memories are fuzzy, but that by 1960, it was pretty clear we were fending for ourselves. It's not uncommon in big families to lean on the older kids for help taking care of the younger ones, but what a rip-off for the three of us who were born first. We weren't ready to help raise kids. We didn't want to raise kids. We wanted to be kids. Being asked to bathe, dress, and feed our younger siblings and keep them safe from household dangers like poisons and knives and predators—that was a lot. And it wasn't fair.

Anyway, hang on—we're not quite finished telling you about our childhood. Nobody gets out that easily.

CHAPTER THREE

Across the street from our house of dysfunction lived Mr. and Mrs. Castle, a sweet, elderly couple who were the opposite of "get off my lawn" old folks. They actually let us play in their side yard, which was an open field with lots of space for us to play baseball. Unlike some of our other playtime settings, their yard was free of rocks and trees, so an afternoon at the Castle's led to far less bleeding than we were used to.

At that time, Carole was the most outgoing in our group of seven, so one day some of us talked her into asking the Castles if we could goof around on that empty field.

"Sure," she said, "be right back."

She walked up to their door and knocked. After several minutes, little old Mrs. Castle opened the door, invited Carole in, and closed the door behind them. The rest of us sat on the grass and waited. And we waited.

Ten minutes passed. "How long does it take to say, 'Can we use the side yard?'" askedKathy.

"Maybe she's chained up in the basement," said Mike.

"Maybe," I answered.

Several more minutes passed. "What the heck is she doing in there?" asked Kathy. "Should one of us check on her? Should we tell Mom?"

After about thirty minutes, the front door opened, and Carole walked out with a big, dumb grin on her face. She joined us on the lawn and said Mrs. Castle had just finished baking peanut butter cookies and insisted Carole enjoy several of them with a big glass of milk. Salivating like a pack of scrawny coyotes, we asked Carole the obvious question.

"*Why* didn't you tell her we're out here?"

She wiped a few crumbs from the edge of her mouth and said, "You guys made me knock on their door. I thought I should be the one rewarded."

Kathy scrunched up her face. "You rat!"

Even worse, Carole had failed to ask if we could use the field! Like a group of street urchins, we gathered on the Castle's porch and knocked. Again, Mrs. Castle opened the door.

"Mrs. Castle," I asked, "do you mind if we play on the side of your house?"

Apparently, Carole had stuffed all or most of the peanut butter cookies into her enterprising mouth because we weren't offered even one of those baked delights, but Mrs. Castle did make us an offer.

"If you nice kids will help Mr. Castle and me with milk delivery, you may help yourselves to the field."

Every Saturday, the milkman dropped milk at the entrance to their property, which was about fifty yards from their front door. The Castles were getting frail in their old age, and all we had to do was lug the milk to their front door. We quickly agreed to carry in the milk and to perform any other tasks they needed, which led to our shopping for their weekly groceries at the local little store, taking out their trash, and helping keep their yard free of weeds.

Much of the time, Mrs. Castle was almost bedridden, so she'd give us a quarter to carry her dirty clothes to the laundry room and to help Mr. Castle fold it when it was clean. We appreciated the money, and we would have been happy to do the work for free, but she insisted on paying us. And sometimes—when she had the energy to bake—we were also rewarded with a batch of her delicious cookies.

What eye-openers these lovely people were for us kids—thanks to the lousy draw we'd had in the grandparent lottery, we'd always been under the impression that old people were cranky grumblers and drill sergeants. But as the months passed, we got to know the Castles more personally, and they left an indelible impression on each of us.

One summer afternoon as we all sat on the Castle's front porch eating cookies, Mr. Castle examined a peanut butter cookie and said, "When I was in the army, we ate uncooked beans from a can."

"Yuk," said Kathy.

"You had to eat what you had," he said. "The army taught a fella to be tough."

I wondered what the navy taught a fella. From what I could tell, it was how to take a lot of business trips.

"Tough like how?" asked Mike.

"Well, for one, we had to make ourselves into pigs in the mud," Mr. Castle said.

A few of us giggled.

"Yeah, it sounds funny, but it sure wasn't. We'd lay flat in the mud until the enemy got close enough to shoot. Flat, like pigs in mud."

Wow, shooting enemies, I thought. Had Mr. Castle ever killed anybody? I was too embarrassed to ask. But he went on to tell us all about how he'd had traveled all over the world "protecting us and protecting those in turmoil." We may not have fully grasped what he meant, but it made us feel safe knowing that good men like Mr. Castle were standing up for us. Until that day, we'd all thought military service was about playing basketball in foreign countries.

Mrs. Castle never interrupted when Mr. Castle was talking. She always watched and listened and nodded as he spoke. When he finished telling us war stories, she told us that while Mr. Castle was "over there fighting the war," she was working in a weapons factory as a line assembler.

"That's right," she said. "With the men away, we wives had to do our part for the war effort."

I had a hard time picturing Mrs. Castle assembling anything bigger than a bullet, but I believed her stories. She said the wives worked ten to twelve hours a day, which we found fascinating because we didn't know women could have jobs. We thought all women who had children stayed home and made dinner.

At the end of their stories, Mr. and Mrs. Castle always smiled and kissed each other, and that made me feel so good I wanted to cry.

Absent as our father was, he did value the Castles and the lessons we were learning by helping them.

"Gather round, kids," he said one day before dinner. "Mr.

and Mrs. Castle are getting old, so they're going to need more of our help."

He assigned specific tasks to each of us. Every day during the summer months, two of us were in charge of taking the Castles a meal, washing their dishes, and tidying their house. During the school months, Mom did most of that work for them. And all year round, she sent us running to their front door with delicious prepared meals, like French toast, tuna fish sandwiches, roast beef with mashed potatoes and carrots, and all kinds of desserts.

We all pitched in to clean their laundry, wash their dishes, dust and sweep their house, and cut their lawn. Although we probably didn't know it at the time, we were learning about the importance of giving of yourself and taking care of people even though there may be no return. We were also building self-esteem, which we came to understand is one of the lovely byproducts of simply being a good person. We felt valued. We felt important. Even though we were just kids, we were improving the lives of adults. It was powerful stuff, and we didn't even mind doing all those chores. Something about the loveliness of the Castles made it not feel like work.

Over a period of about four years, we watched as our dear elderly friends' health declined and they became incapacitated to the point that Mom would stay with them most of the day and send one of us over after school to just sit with them until Mom would come back to help get them to bed. One evening, Mr. Castle tried to go downstairs but tripped and fell. Mom called an ambulance, and they took him to the hospital while I stayed with Mrs. Castle. The next day we all heard Mom tell Dad Mr. Castle had died in the night. It was the first death of someone I'd known, and for the five of us who had taken care of him, it was devastating. When we heard the news, we hugged Mom and just cried and cried. Mrs. Castle died two days later.

Mom explained that Mrs. Castle had died from the heart-break of losing her cherished partner of sixty-plus years. She said the Castles would always look out for us from heaven, because we had showed them so much respect and love.

Then came their miraculous act of generosity. In their last will and testament, Mr. and Mrs. Castle left to our family their *entire* five-acre property. All of it—the house with everything in it and the barn. Most of the furniture was pretty old and beaten up, but when we heard they'd left us the property, everyone in our family was thrilled. We kids just knew our good deeds had led to a great reward for our parents as well as for us. And wow, the space we had to play on now! Five acres that included, of course, our treasured playfield. But there was one little problem: the house was practically falling down. Dad decided to knock it all the way down and build a new house. For that we'd need money, and he thought the best path to cash was through a cornfield.

The three acres of land next to the Castle's house had just the right kind of soil for planting corn, so that's what Dad decided we were going to do. Of course, as we've all learned from reading social studies books, when it comes to an agricultural endeavor, there's nothing better than having a workforce already living on your property. Have a gaggle of kids because eventually, *they'll* do all the farming!

Under our father's direction, all seven of us planted, plowed, and harvested three acres of corn. Luckily, Dad had a friend willing to plow the three acres we were going to plant, and as soon as the soil was ready, Mike used a hoe to carve the lines into which we younger ones dropped and covered the seeds. The work was utterly exhausting and even sometimes dangerous for our chain gang of youngins that by then ranged in age from five to fifteen; we battled insect armies and went to war with cornstalks as sharp as bayonets. When rain was scarce, it was the girls' job to drag twenty connected hoses from our house over to the cornfield, which was about fifty yards away and stretched about one hundred yards.

June through August 1963 was the "summer of corn." We ate corn at every meal and in every way imaginable: corn fritters, corn soup, corn sandwiches, corn bread, and of course, corn on the cob. Thank God Dad didn't have us growing cauliflower. Or lima beans. Or liver.

Our labors resulted in an impressive profit. We, the unpaid staff of children, worked not only as planters, tenders, and harvesters—we were also the sales force. We picked the corn, rain or shine, loaded it into baskets, plucked out the bugs, and then hauled it back to the table set up in front of our house, where we sold the harvest to the countless people who pulled over to the side of the road to buy our fresh corn on the cob for fifty cents a dozen.

One summer morning, a man from a local grocery store pulled up to our stand and said to me, "I hear this is the best corn in town. I'll need three hundred ears. Can you do it, little lady?" I must have looked stunned because he said, "Maybe I should talk to your mom or dad."

Kathy and I were on duty that day, and Kathy, who was now seven years old, immediately responded. "No, you can talk to us. And to pick up an order that large, you'll have to come back later."

The man raised his eyebrows and replied, "Well aren't you the little corn boss. And *how* much are you charging?"

I said, "The sign says fifty cents per dozen."

Up went the eyebrows again. "Don't I get a volume discount? Maybe you should ask your mom and dad?"

Kathy said, "No discounts. We still have to pick every ear and load it all into your truck."

When he saw neither of us was about to budge, he agreed to the price and said he'd be back at 1:00 p.m. to pick up his order.

First thing we did was run to tell Mom. I blurted the story of our big sale and added, "We have five hours to do it!"

Kathy said, "He asked for a better price, but we told him to forget it."

Mom smiled and said, "Your father would be proud. Good job, girls." I glanced over at Kathy, and we both smiled.

Because Kathy and I were the deal brokers, we got to "man the stand" and watch for other customers, which left Mike, Carole, and Debbie to pick three hundred ears of corn. It took them about two hours, and I'm pretty sure they grumbled all the way through it. Later that day when the grocery store guy returned for his three hundred ears, Dad showed up from work and thanked him for the order.

The man said, "You have some very smart, hard-working kids here. They're doing a great job. You should be proud."

Kathy and I looked at each other and beamed. He was right, and we felt mighty proud. Until our father opened his mouth again.

"Thank you," Dad said. "Yes, even the girls do a pretty good job."

What a weasel, trying to burst our bubble. He did let some air out of it, but by those days, several of us kids had already gotten good at steeling ourselves against the words of the only father we knew of in our town who had to be yanked out of bars by children.

During that summer, we sold thousands and thousands of ears of corn, which meant not only were we able to start building our new house, we were able to afford a family vacation! And we were going to spend it in what sounded like the most exciting place in all the world: Atlantic City, New Jersey!

Yep, we were going to the beach! We were going to a place where none of us was going to have to clean, cook, or make our own beds!

Dad actually said, "You've all done such a good job with the corn, you deserve this treat."

I can honestly say that's the only praise I ever remember hearing from my father.

On a bright, sunny summer day, our family of nine piled into our green, 1960s, seat belt-optional station wagon and headed east to see the ocean—for most of us it would be the first time. Crowded in the back sections of that old car, we kids buzzed with excitement.

"My friends say the beach is the greatest place on earth!"

"I think they have French fries all over Atlantic City!"

"And rides! And ice cream!

"I heard the ocean is really warm, and the sand is so hot you have to wear shoes!"

It was the happiest we seven had been in a very long time.

That evening when we finally hopped out of the car at the water's edge, we were mesmerized. The ocean was enormous! It looked so blue and so deep—and so wavy! We were thrilled just to stand there and smell the salt and watch the massive, magical body of water, mysterious and exotic. To this day, none of us has forgotten what it felt like to see the mighty Atlantic for the first time.

What followed was a week-long vacation that turned out to be a feast for the eyes and the stomach. First, we pulled into our home away from home, the Lollipop Hotel, a delightfully whimsical place with pink and purple lollipop-shaped chairs. As we walked into the lobby, a receptionist treated each of us to a giant lollipop and then directed us to our rooms—a pink room for the five girls, a blue room for the two boys, and a yellow room for Mom and Dad. Every bed had lollipops painted on their headboards and colored bedspreads to match the walls. It was like sleeping in Candy Land.

Then it was time to dive into the carnival of Atlantic City—a thrilling place that exploded with colors and was loaded with fascinating characters, like soldiers on leave, finely dressed couples strolling arm in arm, and women walking with their children who appeared to be bound by dog leashes. To country kids like us, it was as if we'd landed on an alien planet, and we wanted to get a good look at every weird creature living there.

We went to the beach every day, frolicked in the ocean, collected seashells, and spent the nights on the boardwalk playing games, riding the Ferris wheel, the merry-go-round, and the spinning saucers, and being treated to Atlantic City's countless edible goodies: ice cream, French fries, fudge, and saltwater taffy. Carole and Kathy were crazy for the ice cream stands, and Mom had to start declaring rules.

"You can have only *one* ice cream once per night on the

boardwalk, so pick your favorite place. We're not stopping at all of them."

Occasionally, Dad wandered off, and I heard Mom say to him, "If you leave us here, I will never forgive you. For once, think of the kids."

But other than some restrictions and an occasional warning by Mom, the entire trip was joyful. We spent the entire time wide-eyed and deliriously happy in that wonderland of fun unlike any place we'd ever seen. Carole, the most artistic one of us kids, seemed to be particularly charged by the sights and sounds of Atlantic City.

At night as we flopped onto the fluffy mattresses at the Lollipop Hotel, Carole said, "We've fallen into a magical world, and I'm storing all of it in my mind so—when we get home, I can paint it."

Something about the idea of this magical place somehow following us home made me tingle with excitement.

Eventually, the week ended, and we drove home, this time in a much quieter station wagon. It was the only family vacation the nine of us would ever take.

When we look back on that trip, we reflect on one of the few life lessons Dad ever taught us. During that getaway, he reminded us, "Kids, it was all your hard work in the cornfield that made this vacation possible. Don't forget that." It's a lesson we took to heart and have talked about many times since those days.

One thing the seven of us have in common is our earnest work ethic. Sure, some of us are more ferocious battlers than others, but all seven of us went on to be hard workers dedicated to our chosen careers, and the work ethic responsible for our professional successes was born in a tiny town, then harvested in a cornfield.

In 1964, the new house was completed. It was a lovely 3,500-square foot, fieldstone front Cape Cod with green cedar shingles; a red front door; a giant, front, bowed window; four bedrooms; two bathrooms; an enormous eat-in kitchen; a full-wall stone fireplace; and beautiful hardwood floors . . . in other words, a mansion! We were going from a 1,200-square-foot duplex with junky, old furniture, three hobbit-sized bedrooms, and one measly bathroom to a veritable palace loaded with new furniture. It was thrilling, and we felt like newborn royalty . . . sort of. Still, grand as the new house was, it had only two bathrooms. Design a house with only one bathroom per every 4.5 people? *Why*? Even as kids, Kathy, Carole, and I didn't understand the miserly planning, the bad math, the intentional ignoring of the inconvenience, fighting, and discomfort that had been caused by our not having enough bathroom access in the other house. But as usual, nobody asked us.

The girls' bedrooms were upstairs and were painted purple, which delighted us even though I don't remember anyone asking us what color we wanted. The boys' bedroom was downstairs next to our parents' room and was painted green because the boys actually got to choose their color. The basement was large and housed the laundry room, a freezer, Dad's drafting table, and our old, cast-off couch and chair. For kids with relatively low standards, this space would work beautifully as a party room, and rather quickly it occurred to us if we were going to have friends over all the time, we'd need refreshments. *What to do, what to do*?

Right about move-in time, Dad heard about a trash dump near a pig farm where a local soda manufacturer often threw out dented (but still full!) cans of soda that had been deemed "unsafe for sale." Well, we weren't planning to buy them.

Seven kids plus all their friends adds up to a lot of need for soda, so Mike decided to work like a team (of pirates) to pillage as many cans of dented soda as we could.

Dad loaded us five oldest into the station wagon with a pile of large cardboard boxes, which we would drag up the trash mound and fill with the dented cans. Carole, Debbie, and I would climb first, fill our boxes with cans, and then slide the full boxes down to Kathy and Mike, who would put them in the station wagon until we filled the back of the wagon. We ended up with about four hundred cans of assorted sodas.

After the success of that maiden diving voyage, we spent many hot summer days scaling walls of slimy, disgusting dumpsters, navigating our way around trash-nesting rats, and dodging trash-scrounging pigs. We then hauled it all home and down to the basement where we washed the cans and lined them up on a shelf, ready for our little downstairs gatherings.

But wait, there's more! The money we earned for turning the cans in at the recycling center earned us cash to buy snacks *and* a used pool table, both of which helped us become popular with kids around town who looked forward to hanging out in our party pit.

You probably won't be surprised to read that our father took a cut of the money we made from returning cans.

"Finder's fee," he said.

Sigh. Ah well, we wrote it off to another solid lesson in entrepreneurship. Looking back now, we realize the basement party project taught us important business principles, like making the most of available materials and the importance of delegating. Score another point for Dad and another hundred thousand points for us kids for doing every bit of the work.

Because we were a household of nine hungry mouths, mealtime required a lot of organization—usually by Mom. Family dinners in particular could be complex, but Mom did her best to make the most of this nightly ritual that represented the only time each day when we were all in the same place at the same time. We ate meals on a wooden picnic table in the middle of our kitchen. There were benches on either side and two chairs at each end.

At dinner, there was a seating arrangement. Dad sat at the head of the table with me directly to his left, Debbie to my left, Mike to her left, David at the other end of the table, Kathy to his left, Charlotte next, Carole to her left, and Mom at Dad's right. If you mapped that lineup in your mind just now, you probably noted that, no, Mom didn't sit at the other "head" of the table. That spot was given to a male. Mom didn't even get to sit on the roomy bench; there were four on her side, three on ours.

Family dinners offered a chance to review the day and update Dad on each kid's schoolwork, but sometimes those dinners didn't start until as late as 9:00 p.m. because Mom insisted that before her children be allowed to eat, her husband would have to be home from the bar. He usually wasn't in any hurry to be under the same roof with the woman he married or the children he sired. Dad would linger at his local pub, doing and saying who knows what with who knows who, but—we can only assume—fully aware that by 9:00 p.m., some of his children would be so hungry they'd practically be tipping their heads back like baby birds desperate for a helping of regurgitated worms. We usually waited patiently for Dad to arrive, but I also bit my nails. I was always on edge that this would be the night our father would disappear again, and unfortunate for me, my father's routine of being missing in action planted the early seeds for my becoming a consummate worrier.

When Dad was in town, our parents often fought about his coming home late because he was hanging at the local bar. Many times, Mike, Carole, or I were sent there to beg him to come home for supper. At ten years old, I was on a father retrieval assignment—a task I dreaded immensely because it was never a pleasant job to beg your father to come home while the other drunks laughed and sneered at me.

On countless occasions, one of the drunks would slap me on the back and ask, "You here to pick up your daddy?"

Before I could say a word, my dad said, "Ever touch my kid again and you'll be very sorry."

I didn't know what to make of the strange sensation I had of feeling both protected and embarrassed by my father. How twisted it seems that the only memory I have of feeling taken care of by him is my recollection of that night when I stood in the middle of a bunch of drinkers as they giggled about a kid having to drag her old man out of a bar.

Whenever Dad came home stumbling, slurring his words, and smelling like the bottom of a whiskey barrel, we knew it meant we'd have to navigate the stormy waters of his drunken unpredictability.

"What the hell is that hat?" he snarled at Carole at one late-night dinner. She cast her eyes down and adjusted her beloved red beret on her head. Dad stared at her. "Take it off! Go to your room!"

With her eyes cast downward, Carole slipped the beret off her head, swung her legs over the picnic table bench, and headed upstairs.

Her offense was wearing something on her head. Her offense was daring to own something that made her happy, and the punishment was being sent to bed without food. The same punishment landed on any of us who dared to wear a sweater at the dinner table, so if anybody forgot that idiotic rule and showed up in a turtleneck or cardigan, he'd send us to bed with no dinner, too. Meanwhile, Mom said nothing.

Dad demanded I sit directly next to him because I was so often plotting something. I'm not sure what my sitting next to him at dinner time was supposed to accomplish relative to all my delinquent behaviors at all hours, but, again, there was no talking back to Dad. I certainly did get into my share of trouble in those days: smoking at school, staying out late with my friends, garden-variety teen stuff. Sometimes my indiscretions would land me in house jail for up to four months, but I couldn't be contained. I sneaked out my second-floor window at least three times a week by tying two bed sheets together and sliding down, James Bond style. It was an escape method that not only served its purpose beautifully but also made me feel extremely cool. Then one of my sisters ratted me out. One of those nights, as I quietly and slowly slid down the sheet to the ground below, I could feel something was wrong, like maybe my timing was off . . . something.

As I thumped on the ground ready to make my getaway, I turned around to find my father standing behind me bellowing, "Just *where the hell* do you think you're going?"

Back into the house I went. He probably grounded me for an

extra month; when there are so many punishments, who can keep them straight?

I later found out that Kathy, upset I'd refused to take her out with my crew, had run to Daddy.

"I don't remember it that way," interrupts Kathy, who's shaking her head.

"You don't remember it that way?" I parrot.

"I don't think I was a tattletale."

"You don't think you were a tattletale?"

"Stop that."

"Stop that."

"Knock it off, you infants," says Carole.

"I know you are, but what am I?" I respond.

"I'm rubber, you're glue," says Kathy.

"Jesus," says Carole, "I'm going to have a martini—alone. Clearly, neither of you is of drinking age."

Kathy shouts after her, "Whatever you say bounces off me and sticks to you . . . *infinity*!"

When I found out it was Kathy who had turned me in, I felt like sending her out the window without a bed sheet, but eventually I realized her tattletale tendencies were probably just a desperate attempt to gain some of Dad's approval.

When a family is overrun by kids, any one child's chance of getting quality time alone with a father is limited—even when the father gives a damn. But given our father's relatively rare appearances in our home life, he relegated his children to acting like city park pigeons scrapping over a piece of popcorn.

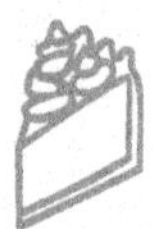

CHAPTER FOUR

On the rare occasions when Dad made it home for dinner at a decent hour, we kids knew it was because he was plotting another idea that would mean calling on child labor . . . *again*. Each time he explained a new money-making scheme, he delegated all the duties involved, and if any one of us rolled our eyes or groaned, that kid was saddled with one of the worst of the scheme's tasks, like scrubbing garbage cans or ironing Dad's shirts or the boys' clothes.

One evening in late spring, when we were wound up and happy about the end of the school year about to lead into a summer of freedom, Dad announced his latest brainstorm. He sat up in his chair and spread his arms wide as if he was about to present the greatest show on earth.

"Everybody, I have an announcement—"

Before he could reveal the idea that would surely ruin our summer, Michael blurted, "Whatever it is, count me out. I have baseball every day." And with that, the little prince designated himself a free man. The rest of us usually weren't quick enough to spit out a Michael-style draft deferment, so without further delay, Dad revealed the big plan.

"Kids," he said, "we're going into the catering business!"

There wasn't a word from any of us, and Mike didn't even seem to hear him. He just kept his head down and shoveled mashed potatoes into his mouth.

Then Mom spoke up. "You can't do this to the kids. Let them enjoy their summer."

"What's not to enjoy about making money?" answered our loving father.

Mom tried a different direction. "We don't know *anything* about catering!"

Without pausing for a breath, Dad said, "You've been catering to these bums forever. You know how to feed and serve groups. Just take charge, woman!"

Then he blabbered on about summer parties and simple recipes and everybody pitching in, like he was lecturing to attendees of a free seminar on how to make a quick buck. He sounded like a street urchin hawking fake watches to tourists.

This might be an opportune time to point out that Dad wasn't a cook. No one in the family could have been genuinely considered "a cook," certainly not one with skills that promised success at the commercial level. Mom could whip up a mean cupcake, and of course she managed to keep our small army fed and growing, mostly with meat and potatoes. Most dinners consisted of pork chops with mashed potatoes and corn or meat loaf with mashed potatoes and corn. On Friday, dinner was always fish sticks.

As was the case with most of Bill Yoder's schemes, the summer of catering went forward. Most of the events we catered were large-scale picnics for Dad's drinking buddies, and those meals were almost always clambakes. On a busy day, we prepared up to *five hundred* clambake meals at a time, which included making fifty-plus pounds of potato salad and cooking hundreds of ears of corn on the cob. But before all the prep started, somebody had to buy the food and drag it all into the house for the Friday-to-Saturday production. As usual, Dad was nowhere to be found, so everything landed on Mom. One Friday afternoon before a typical clambake, Mom loaded four of us girls into the old green station wagon for a trip to the grocery store, while Mike was left home to watch the two youngest kids.

In the store, Mom handed us lists on torn pieces of paper.

"Carole and Kathy—you'll get corn (too bad we only planted corn that one year), celery, onions, potatoes, and carrots. Sue and Debbie, read your list carefully—you're getting the oils and butters and all the paper products. Ask for help if you can't find the netting."

We dashed around the store with our arms full of food and supplies like we were trying to win a competition. Then we all waited quietly in line alongside three grocery carts practically spilling over with everything we needed for this project none of us wanted anything to do with. Waiting for our turn to check out, I watched Mom's face. It was pinched and twitching, as if there was an uncomfortable conversation going on inside her head.

After what felt like an hour of standing and waiting for our turn to check out, Mom paid, and we loaded everything in the car. We were hot and getting cranky, and now the car was so packed, there was no room to allow any space between us packed in the back seat. If this was a look at the summer ahead, we were headed for misery.

I watched Mom's face in the rearview mirror. She still looked weary and pinched, but then smiled as she veered the car onto an exit and drove to a little ice cream shop on a dusty road. None of us could believe it! It was close to dinner time, we had a carload full of food that was getting warm, and only God knew what would await us if Dad made it home before we did. She pulled in front of the ice cream shop, switched off the ignition, and turned toward us with her arm across the back of the bench seat.

"Come on, girls" she said with a wink. "I want you to know how much I appreciate all your help." Then she held her finger to her lips and said, "*Shhh*. It's our little secret."

But we couldn't *shhh*. We all squealed and leapt out of the car and ran into the ice cream shop. Debbie and I ordered double-dipped vanilla cones. Carole and Kathy chose black raspberry double-dipped cones, and Mom ordered her favorite, a bowl of butter pecan. We licked it up so fast it didn't even have a chance to drip onto the ground.

Our memory of that day is extremely vivid, probably because such a thing rarely happened. That afternoon we weren't the daughters of abusive man or an abused woman, nor did we feel like abused child laborers. We were just Mom's girls.

Once we were back home, the real work began. We had to put together clambakes for an afternoon party of two hundred people. With the grace of an orchestra conductor and the regimentation of a platoon leader, Mom gave us assignments and supervised our work, while she was also busy cooking the eggs, potatoes, and the many pounds of chicken we'd be adding to each clambake.

"Okay, girls, let's go," she said, scuttling around the kitchen. "Carole, you'll start. Grab a net and put a half-cob of corn into each one. Then slide it down to Debbie and Kathy . . . you two add a potato and a carrot. Sue, you'll add the clams—six if they're small, four if they're large. You'll get the hang of it—just keep each serving balanced. I'll add the chicken and tie the net closed. Debbie, keep the work spaces as clean as you can by putting all the egg shells and peelings in the garbage. Let Charlotte help you."

As I watched her breeze from station to station, slicing, chopping, measuring, and stirring, I wondered how she knew how to do all this.

After suffering and sweating through so many long Friday nights and the following Saturdays of being packed in the kitchen working our young tails off to make our father's latest scheme a success, we ended up with damned-sharpened kitchen skills. Eventually, Kathy became a masterful potato peeler. She could peel five pounds of potatoes in fifteen minutes. Carole learned to shuck corn like a pro—she could clean two dozen ears in only a few minutes. I shelled eggs for potato salad with the expertise of Lucy on the candy line.

"Wait," I hear, as Carole interrupts my storytelling, "is that *good*? Lucy on the candy line?"

"Yeah," adds Kathy, "the whole thing got away from her. The candy started coming at her so fast, she had to stuff a lot of it in her mouth."

I stare at them blankly.

Kathy continues, "Might not be the efficiency comparison you want. Just sayin."

With my usual grace and open-mindedness, I accept their critique and promise to reconsider my choice. Then I frisbee-fling a molasses cookie at each of their heads.

I recommend snacking while typing—it helps.

As I mentioned, I shelled the eggs for potato salad with the efficiency of a Detroit assembly worker constructing Corvette bodies. I had a method: I rolled the boiled eggs along the counter so the shells cracked and then peeled right off.

After we filled and tied about two hundred clambakes, we hauled them all downstairs to store them in giant refrigerators in the basement. We practically crawled into bed at around 10:00 p.m. exhausted. With our necks and backs and legs aching, we walked like mini Frankensteins to our beds where we crash-landed on the mattresses. Then we set our alarms for 5:00 a.m., so we could drag ourselves up and get right back to work.

Dad had bought enormous, commercial-size stockpots in which we boiled the netted clams on the stoves in both the kitchen and basement. Boiling took about forty-five minutes, and after the food was steamed, we loaded everything into our pretty, mint-green catering wagon (which was just a van with shelves in the back) that Dad had won in a card game. Dad then drove off to deliver the entire shmear to the club or park where the function was being held.

But after Dad pulled away in the wagon, there was still no rest in sight. Nope, we females piled into the family station wagon and headed to the event, where we served all that food to the mostly drunken picnic partiers. We did our best to conduct ourselves like swift waitstaff—very little conversation or even eye contact—because the alcohol-soaked hooligans apparently thought it was always open season on young girls. These picnics were basically big beer-swilling clambakes for gun clubs and other men's gatherings. We were the unpaid help, sent there to serve and clean up. And when it was over, we had to pick up trash, clean the park, and pack all the equipment back into the station wagon. By then, Dad would have been long gone in the catering wagon, off to his evening activities. But the drunks liked to hang around until the very end.

"Come on back over here, sweetharrrt," one of the drunks slurred after I passed his picnic table to collect trash. "Yougonnagimme a nice, cole beer?"

Eyes ahead. Keep it moving.

"Whaaasamatta sweet thing? You no speakie Englie? I got lotsa time ta teacha!" Then he practically collapsed in his own laughter.

For two years, that's how we spent our summer weekends as our friends swam, fished, and fell in love while floating on the river and swinging off ropes into a lake. We didn't go to the river or the lake. We were always tired. And we were so, so frustrated. We knew how grossly unfair it was that we were being robbed of our young summers, but we knew how much Mom needed us, and we would have done anything for her.

Exhausting as it was, Dad's catering business gave us great training for our future endeavors. Watching Mom calculate exactly what she needed for each event, observing as she organized her staff of five, watching her delegate and keep everybody focused and productive—we've put those lessons to good use for many years. But you couldn't have told us that back then.

Dad wasn't shy about pricing—he believed a good product deserved a relatively bold price tag—so the party enterprise did quite well financially. So well that shortly after we served our last clam, Dad was flush and ready to drag us all into his next hustle.

The family that owned Rocco's, an Italian eatery known for great pizza and for having a hotel attached, was ready to hang up their aprons, and they made Dad an offer he couldn't refuse. So our family became the proprietors of Collegeville Commercial Hotel. Dad thought the name would help attract college students from the local Ursinus College to head our way to eat, drink, and even stay overnight. As usual, Dad's plan was to make his wife and his female offspring do almost all the work, so just like that we became hotelier/restaurateurs.

Around this time, Carole (sixteen), Kathy (ten), and I (thirteen), sensed we were becoming more than sisters to each other. We were the three kids who most helped Mom run the kitchen and the restaurant while she was also busy booking *and* cleaning the hotel rooms while we were at school. After a few months, Dad hired a waitress and a couple of young college guys to keep the bar stocked, refill the beer barrels, and pick up and deliver the bar's supplies, like bar mixers and garnishes, potato chips, pretzels, nuts, and miscellaneous other goodies every bar needs. But most of the work fell to Mom and us. Mom did most of the cooking, Carole and I waited tables with the help of the hired waitress (when she could be bothered to show up), and Kathy kept the tables clean. The "waitress" was the wife of a friend of Dad's from the bar, and no matter how useless she was, he wouldn't fire her, which we figured was because he wanted to look like a good guy to strangers and bar flies. Instead, he let his wife and daughters take on even more work, and fortunately for us three daughters, we worked together beautifully.

We never argued or wrangled over who was doing what or whether one of us had been burdened more than the other two. We just did what had to be done. For all the tedium and fatigue that job caused us—and all the time it stole from our being able to do fun girl things—we look back fondly on that phase in our lives because back then we were creating a bond that only grew stronger with time. The hard part was knowing that our friends were going to dances, parties, and football games and hanging at the local drugstore, while we existed as prisoners of another of our father's schemes. We resented him for saddling us with the burden, but once again, we weren't about to quit because our mother was working herself to near collapse. And we knew that without us, she would definitely collapse. So we put our heads down and made the best of it.

But while the restaurant side of things was challenging and frustrating, the hotel side was dangerous and disgusting.

The two-story building that became our Collegeville Commercial Hotel had been constructed in the late '30s and needed countless upgrades. The building's paint was faded and peeling inside and out, the old wallpaper was curling off the hallways and rooms, and the furniture and linens were tattered. The hotel's décor was kind of an early-American-grimy meets haunted-attic-chic. This place was *creepy*. Whenever we dared to scramble around the dilapidated second floor, we expected at any moment we might be visited by the ghost of Lizzie Borden. Or maybe just regular Lizzie Borden. But Dad wasn't willing to pay to update any of it.

No amount of whining or reasoning was going to get Dad to spruce up that dump because Dad was *all* about the bar—that's where the action was—so he spent most of his time down there, tending bar and being charming. Pouring drinks and bullshitting with customers was the only part of the business he could be bothered with, and the locals loved him because he gave away more shots and beers than he charged for. He probably thought this largesse made him look like a big man, but it turned him into a poor man. When Dad did the math on his bar business and factored in that no respectable human being would rent the grungy, old rooms upstairs, he came up with yet another business brainstorm.

For those of you readers who consider yourselves child advocates—or just responsible adults with ethics, decency, general horse sense—you might want to brace yourselves for what's coming next.

To cover the hefty mortgage on this new enterprise, father of the century decided he should move his seven kids and wife into the cruddy rooms on the derelict second floor of the hotel so he could rent the shiny new house to strangers! Yep, he figured we—his *family*—deserved junky, outdated, and maybe even unsafe accommodations while college students, who we had no connection to, should be comfortable.

When our family of nine packed up and moved back in time to the 1930s, I was pretty sure we were getting a look at life during the Depression. Think of the hotel in *The Shining* but with less light and optimism. Across creaking, squeaking floors, we dragged suitcases full of our clothes up to our rooms while dodging spider webs and kicking hallway trash into abandoned bedrooms.

While we were settling into the nightmare on Main Street, our beautiful home was becoming the new residence of several Ursinus college students *and their donkeys*. Yes, donkeys. Dad migrated his own family to a ramshackle dump worthy of condemnation but rented our lovely home, fully furnished—the place where, for the first time in their lives, his wife and children had been able to live in comfort—to a bunch of nineteen-year-olds and their basketball-playing donkeys. On a standard basketball court, people ride on the backs of donkeys while trying to shoot a basketball into basketball hoops. For two years, our father actually let the donkeys live in our home. Apparently, it was less expensive than paying to board them in a barn.

When the students were at class, the donkeys were allowed to roam our new house all day, which left them free to kick holes in the walls and scratch up the beautiful hardwood floors. Donkeys don't use litter boxes, so yeah, you can imagine. After two years of that, those kids and animals moved out, but by then the damage they'd done to our house was dramatic. So for two more years, the house stayed empty except for when Kathy and I were sent there to try to clean the place in preparation for what we hoped would be our return to our real home.

"You can't make this crap up," says Kathy.

I reply, "You know, I used to think that, too, but it's kind of an insult to good writers."

"Good point," she says.

Carole adds, "Yeah, of course you can make this crap up. But isn't it just so much more compelling and outrageous and despicable and sad when it's true?"

The three of us sit for a moment letting that sink in.

In the hotel dump, we lived across the hall from our parents in the equivalent of a three-room bunkhouse that had no living room and no kitchen. Seven kids had to share one disgusting bathroom with a stained toilet, a sink that dripped, and a mildew-infested shower. We also had no privacy or security.

Whenever one of us showered, somebody had to watch the door because the bathroom had no lock, and the bar patrons were free to wander upstairs into our "home" anytime they liked.

Our bedrooms were so small and had so little closet space we were allowed to bring with us only what we needed to wear to school; play clothes weren't necessary anymore because all we ever did was work. The boys were given one room; Kathy, Debbie, and Charlotte were in another; and Carole and I roomed together in the third. We all slept in bunk beds. Mom and Dad slept in the two-room/one bath apartment across the hall. There were three additional rooms one floor up that were rented regularly by two of the town drunks so they could "sleep it off" and our restaurant's chef, who also spent most of his time drunk and needed a place to lay his lazy head. Strangely, the guy we called our chef rarely cooked. He spent most of his "work" time sitting at the bar, so we guessed he got the gig because our father had lost to him in a poker game or because the guy had some dirt on the old man. Mom was relegated to acting as sous chef to this clown until about a month in, when she'd had enough.

One evening in the restaurant's kitchen, I watched her in conversation with the chef, and her bright red face and flailing hands told me something big was about to happen. She threw down her meat tenderizer and yelled, "You're incompetent, and you're fired!"

Then she turned and walked out to the bar as Dad stared in disbelief. For a second, it looked like he was going to stand up and push back, maybe tell her she wasn't the one who made management decisions, but I think he might have seen what I saw in her eyes, and he stayed glued to the bar stool.

Mom shouted at him anyway. "I am *not* taking orders from a

drunk, particularly one who has *no* idea how to run a kitchen." Then she turned and pointed back toward the kitchen. "I have seven kids who could strap on blindfolds and still do a better job than this guy." For good measure, just in case the guy wasn't clear where he stood, she yelled again. "You! Are! Fired!"

Carole, Kathy, and I watched with our mouths open. We'd never seen our mother stand up for herself like that. For a second, I felt like clapping. And for once, Dad knew when to keep his mouth shut.

Later we learned the chef had responded, "I could destroy your marriage with what I know about your husband, and that includes some serious gambling debts."

The dismissal was even more impressive when she replied, "Go screw yourself."

Bravo, *madre.*

When we weren't in school, Carole and I helped with the restaurant's cooking. Kathy and Debbie cleaned tables and served meals. They weren't dream years for us girls who had no free time and were constantly working near drunk old men who gawked at us. We also didn't need our childhoods tarnished by the frequent sight of the guilty-looking men and women who rented the hotel's cruddy rooms for an hour at a time. We pretty much knew what all that was about, and we also had a creepy sense it wasn't the kind of foot traffic kids should have to negotiate *in their own home.* These people prowled around all the time, and with our mother working herself to exhaustion and our father rarely around, we were unsupervised, so we learned quickly that safety was on our own shoulders.

The bedroom Carole and I shared had no lock on it. One Friday night, we were awakened by a rumble at our door, which turned out to be a drunk guy who mistook our room for his. He stumbled in and felt his way around in the dark. Carole and I slept with hairbrushes under our pillows, always ready to take a swing at one of these bumbling drunks. As this boozer clunked his way through our dark room, we both jumped out of bed and beat him with the flat side of our big brushes. He flailed around blindly in the dark shouting, "What the hell!?" and quickly dashed to the door and out of our room.

When we told Dad about a drunk man stumbling into his daughters' bedroom in the middle of the night, he said, "Push a chair against your door."

As was the norm, we were once again shown there was no point turning to our father for help or care, so after several nights during which we attacked interlopers with our brushes, Carole and I started sleeping with baseball bats.

Since the only route to the other three kids' bedrooms was through Carole's and my room, we served as guards for the youngers, and we took that responsibility seriously. During our four years in that shitty, old hotel, Carole and I had plenty of sleepless nights, but we always knew we had each other. Young as we were—we lived there until she was eighteen and I was sixteen—we had a strong sense that together we could take on just about anybody.

It's a wonderful thing to have that much faith in a sibling, to feel that strong of a bond of support and loyalty so early in life. But what a sorry reason for girls to bond.

Meanwhile, Mom was saving the restaurant. Because the sorry excuse for a chef Dad hired was a sorry excuse for a chef,

Mom worked exhausting hours to create new dishes, like her delicious clams casino, fresh pasta specials, and delicious desserts, including eclairs and cream puffs. Thanks to her, the restaurant's reputation stayed in good shape. But running the restaurant's kitchen wasn't all that kept her busy in that place. Because Dad was still regularly disappearing for nights at a time with this or that "friend," Mom often had to act not only as executive chef but bartender. As a result, our mother wasn't available for much child supervision. We weren't particularly aware of being neglected at the time, but looking back, we don't remember hearing questions like, "Have you brushed your teeth?" "Where's your report card?" or "Are you hungry?" As a result, we figured things out for ourselves. The only parental guidance we remember getting during that four-year period involved our mother telling us how to cook, clean, and serve customers. That's when we realized that to remain part of our household would mean being entrenched in a life of servitude.

We each plotted our escapes.

CHAPTER FIVE

Michael was the first to break out. He was a shy, quiet, good-looking athlete who didn't date until he was a senior in high school. And then, just a year after graduation, he married the first girl he dated. It wasn't even a shotgun wedding. Nope, he simply wanted the hell away from that hotel and the hell away from our messed-up family. But first, before we were in the hotel, he had to introduce his betrothed to his six siblings and his parents. Before bringing her home, Mike spent a week warning us that if we didn't behave, he'd tell every guy we ever dated we were out of our minds.

On introduction day, Mike and his girl walked through the front door, and the rest of us stood quietly in a kind of receiving line in the living room. The tension was thicker than cold peanut butter as we all said some super polite form of "hi." It was like we were meeting the queen of England and didn't want to be hauled away by one of those guys in the big fur hats. Then, within minutes of the last introduction, we all went back to our usual brand of lunacy, which on that night included running through the house, fighting over which TV show to watch, and knocking over bowls of popcorn. That seemed to scare the nice girl away forever . . . away from our rowdy mob, that is. She later married Mike, but she didn't seem to like us much, so we never really got to know her. We weren't even invited to the wedding, but we were happy Mike had escaped.

Next in birth order and next to break out was Carole, while still in the hotel, who married the year after she graduated high school. Carole had been seeing her beau in secret, and as soon as Dad found out Carole had a boyfriend who never came to the house, he said, "You bring him here to meet me or say goodbye to car privileges." No car meant no more slipping out to see the boyfriend, so she agreed to bring him around.

I don't think any of us liked him, least of all Dad, who could surely see Larry was a young Bill Yoder in training. In that first meeting, Larry didn't offer to shake Dad's hand, didn't look Dad in the eye, and didn't act as if Carole was anything special. He just offered clipped answers to the family's questions and seemed generally perturbed he had to be there. Most of us could see he was kind of a jackass, but Carole wanted her freedom from our house of pain, so she married Larry to get it.

Thanks to Michael and Carole skipping town, the family labor pool shrunk, so the hotel-restaurant enterprise began to fall apart. There were now only five unpaid child workers left to keep the business afloat. Dad was disappearing more and more and for longer and longer, which meant Mom had to cover the bar (which surely ticked off the bar flies who were used to Dad's freebies), as well as slog through the kitchen and hotel work she'd been doing all along. Even with Kathy, Debbie, and me helping as much as we could, it was too much. Things didn't look good for the future of the Collegeville Commercial Hotel.

Before long, Dad decided the way to break free of the financial albatross he'd shoved around all our necks was to claim bankruptcy, which meant we were going to lose our beautiful home. Even though he had no idea where he'd house his own children and wife if a bank took our home away, he proceeded with the plan to declare us bankrupt. *Bankrupt*. What a perfect word to describe anything related to the man who fathered seven kids he made no time for, the man who did nothing to show care or love for the woman he married.

The future looked miserable, so we lived in constant state of anxiety about where we'd be sleeping next. Then once again, our family was kissed by an angel.

A wealthy town leader named Mrs. Wismer had paid attention to our family since the day she'd met Mom at the restaurant. She often dined alone and quietly observed us as we raced around. One night, Mrs. Wismer waited forty-five minutes for us to make and serve the pasta dish she ordered. She was patient and sweet, and when I was finally able to serve her dinner, I said, "I'm so sorry, Mrs. Wismer. We're terribly short-staffed tonight."

"Oh, not to worry, dear," she said, "but is your mother okay?"

Where to start?

"Mom is okay, I guess," I said, "but I know she's tired. She doesn't get much rest. We try to help her as much as we can, but Dad disappears a lot, which leaves Mom to work the bar alone because we're not old enough."

Mrs. Wismer shook her head, then said, "She must be so proud to have children with such lovely manners and such a great work ethic."

I thanked her and hustled back to the kitchen.

A week later, she came back for dinner and asked Kathy if

she could have a word with Mom after things had settled down. When most of the diners had cleared out, Mom sat at Mrs. Wismer's table. Kathy and I tried to eavesdrop through the kitchen door but could pick up only a few words.

"He hasn't been around . . . bankruptcy."

Then Mom covered her face in her hands and began to sob. Loud and clear, we heard her say, "It's my fault. I let him treat me this way," and "I can't keep letting my children go on living like this."

Mrs. Wismer let Mom calm down and then asked, "If the bank takes your home, where will you go?"

We heard Mom answer, "I just don't know. I just don't know."

In the kitchen, Kathy and I looked at each other but said nothing.

A week later, a banker stuck a sign on the door of the hotel: Closed for Bankruptcy.

Dad said, "Pack your clothes. We're moving out this week."

When we asked where we were going, he said, "Don't worry about it. You'll know when we get there."

We were four girls and a young boy who had no idea what was next for our family, where we would go, or how our parents could let this happen to us. We couldn't move in with Mike or Carole; neither of them had room. Nana wasn't an option because she hated Dad.

We were all worried sick but too afraid to ask questions for fear of upsetting Mom even more. Then, as we packed our clothes in battered, old suitcases, we heard a knock in the hallway and jumped up to peek. There stood Mrs. Wismer. Mom opened her apartment door, saw the kind lady standing in front of her, and broke down in sobs. They stepped into the apartment and closed the door behind them, then we kids nearly went crazy trying to figure out what the two of them could have been talking about. Even our best eavesdropping offered little more than a reminder of how torn up Mom was.

We heard her cry, "I just don't know how this happened. My kids, my poor kids." Then about two hours after she arrived, we heard Mrs. Wismer step out of the apartment and walk away down the hall.

We kids sat quietly on our ratty hotel beds next to our packed bags. Then Mom walked in and, strangely, didn't look miserable.

"Kids," she said, "Mrs. Wismer has done something extraordinary. Grab your bags. We're going home."

On our way home, Mom explained that Mrs. Wismer had proposed a miracle. After hearing we were about to be tossed onto the street, she volunteered to pay our house's mortgage in exchange for a simple promise: our parents had to agree they wouldn't sell our home as long as even one of us kids was still living in it. There were tears in Mom's eyes as she gave us the news.

Years later, she told me, "I'll never get over what that generous woman did for us. Not one of my own relatives offered to help us, not even in the smallest ways, and here a stranger swooped in and saved our home."

Mrs. Wismer saved much more than our home; she saved our dignity.

"That's an understatement," says Kathy. "Who knows what people were saying behind our backs. Can you imagine?"

"I *can* imagine," says Carole. "Deadbeat father, long-suffering mother, and a bunch of unwashed kids headed for the gutter."

"Ah, yes," Kathy adds, "but two Castles and a Wismer equal a thousand of those snipey, small-minded shits."

"Here's to Mrs. Wismer," I say, though I'm not holding a drink, for which I blame Kathy. "God, it felt good to move out of that rat trap and into a decent place with real beds and no grabby drunks."

We were able to move back into our home thanks to all the cleanup work Mom, Kathy, and I had been doing since the renters and donkeys moved out. The place was still pretty wrecked, thanks to those disrespectful heathens—holes in the walls, deep scratches in the hardwood floors, tears in the curtains—but we didn't care. We'd fix all that. We were just so happy to be home again.

"Yeah, but remember after we ditched the hotel and moved home, Mom could barely get out of bed for the next two months?" Carole says. "I'd stop by to visit, and sometimes she wouldn't even try to wake herself up."

"She must have been sooo depressed," says Kathy.

"I think we were all depressed," I say. "We didn't have a name for it. Or meds, of course. Or help of any kind. We were just supposed to count our blessings and suck it up."

"I wouldn't go back to those days for all the vodka in Poland," Kathy says.

"Oh, God, me neither," I say.

Carole raises her eyebrows. "Poland?"

"Yeah, Poland. Or all the vodka in Sweden. Or France. Or even Texas. But screw Russia."

"Sassy," says Carole.

We raise our glasses, and Carole says, "To the Wismers and Castles of the world. Long may they reign."

After four brutal years in the Collegeville Carnal Hotel, Mom, five kids, and Dad—sort of—moved back into the house just around the time I was graduating from high school. Being back under that roof gave us the chance to relax and feel safe again in our bedrooms. Dear God. The kinds of fear and astonishingly inappropriate conditions we were subjected to . . . and all we could do was endure it. At some point, every one of us probably thought about running away but to where? With a lot of uninterested relatives and no connections or network beyond our little town, there was no place for any of us to run.

It's difficult to express the relief we felt being out of that hotel, and it seemed no one needed to recover more than our mother. For the first few months after our return to the house, she slept most days, spoke very little to any of us, and rarely left the house. So while it was a relief to be home again, it looked like Mom was spiraling toward another breakdown, and the idea terrified those of us old enough to remember the first one. We tried to make her life easier by preparing dinners, keeping the house clean, and doing everything we could to bring Mom back to us.

We were terribly overtaxed kids. Beyond attending school, doing our homework, going to sports practices and games, and working to exhaustion to keep our household running, we bit our nails every day thinking today might be the day Mom would go over the edge and the big ambulance would pull up the driveway. What would become of us then?

We were starved for attention, love, and something resembling security. Our father had never nurtured us, never protected us, or made us feel safe in any way, so we turned to our mother like a wriggling litter of hungry puppies. But she was completely burned out and crippled with sadness. She had almost nothing left to give, and even then—after years of neglect and abuse from the man she called "husband"—what she had she usually reserved for our father, a master of self-absorption and a black hole of need.

Mom didn't say much about Dad's absences, and whenever he was around, they usually fought, mainly about money. Sometimes, we had the pleasure of hearing our almost-always absent father belittle our mother's parenting. One evening when Mom was suffering worse than usual and had been in bed all day, Dad came home, went to their bedroom, and railed, "You should be more involved with these kids!"

This from the man who probably hadn't noticed that two of his children had already moved out. He went on to suggest she should start watching Debbie, Kathy, Charlotte, and David play sports at school. Interesting point of focus, I thought; not a word about the messed-up condition of the house or the fact that his wife could barely lift her head from the pillow. No, what Mom needed, according to this wise, sensitive man, was more time sitting on bleachers.

Ever obedient, Mom did start attending the sports events of her youngest four kids, and she actually started to find joy in watching them play high school hockey, basketball, and football. She cheered and clapped and jumped up and down in the stands, yelling "That's my daughter!" and "That's my boy!" It was an almost miraculous transformation. Had it really been set off by her listening to our deadbeat dad? Or was it just about finding purpose again, taking simple steps to make herself remember what it meant to feel like a mother?

Six months after moving home from the hotel, Mom felt good enough to start baking again, so after school every day we came home to the glorious smell of fresh-baked cinnamon buns, donuts, pies, cakes, or cookies and were free to grab a glass of milk, sit, relax, and enjoy a baked treat. That one change in our home life did wonders for morale among the kids who remained in the house. Something about seeing Mom in the kitchen, wearing an apron dusted with flour, baking ingredients all over . . . it felt like a home.

Although Mom had developed lots of interesting and sometimes even sophisticated dishes for the catering business and the hotel, she wasn't a very motivated cook at home. Breakfast was usually cereal, lunch was almost always canned soup and peanut butter and jelly sandwiches, and dinners consisted of burgers, chicken, roast beef, or pork chops with potatoes or corn or peas. On very rare occasions, we'd see a leafy, green vegetable. Nutrition didn't appear to be her focus, but back then society wasn't exactly riding a wave of nutritional awareness. Families were devouring canned ravioli, Twinkies, and spreadable margarine. I was old enough to drive before I learned fish could be eaten in forms other than breaded "sticks."

Mom's primary goal for our dinners was to get something edible on the table to keep the engines inside her kids running. After the hotel years, we ate dinners at a decent hour, no longer waiting for the missing father to show up. And, thanks to Dad's not being involved anymore, dinnertime became a relatively peaceful experience. Oh, how excited we always were for dessert. Every dessert Mom made was delicious, but she had a real talent for custardy creams, so whenever she whipped up a filled dessert, we could barely wait to get our forks into it.

After we moved back into the house, Mom started to open up to me about her and Dad. I was almost eighteen and the oldest kid left in the house, so maybe she started to view me as a girlfriend. I worked two jobs—one at a nursing home, another as a waitress in a diner—so I was able to help pay for minor expenses and food. I felt like the other parent in the house, helping the family survive and easing our mother's stress, and though I was exhausted a lot of the time, my ability to contribute that way made me proud.

On a sunny afternoon, Mom and I were relaxing on the front porch sipping lemonade when she said, "I don't have women in my life."

I didn't know what to say. She continued, "Life for a woman without other women around is a very hard thing."

I asked, "What happened to your sisters? We never see them."

"We were never close," she said. "And I was the Cinderella of the family."

It wasn't the first time she'd referred to herself that way. When I was younger, I'd pictured her in a tattered cotton dress and torn shoes, sweeping and carrying baskets that overflowed with laundry.

"And they never liked your father, so that made it even easier for them to distance themselves."

I could hardly fault them for disliking Dad, but why did they have to shut out a family member who needed so much help? It was always clear to my siblings and me that we were the outcasts of Mom's family. We were rarely invited to family gatherings, with the excuse being there were too many of us.

Not only did Mom have no sisters to lean on, she had no girlfriends. She never devoted time to developing even one, real, female friendship. Even though she was friendly with our neighbor, Mrs. Smith, they both had so many kids (thirteen between them) there wasn't much time to do anything for themselves. Occasionally, they'd have coffee after the kids had gone to school, but other than that, Mom's life was relatively devoid of friendship. I became her confidante, and together we spent many hours sitting with coffee or tea talking about countless personal subjects. At first, it felt awkward to hear about the inside of my own parents' marriage, but the discomfort was soon overruled by my curiosity and desire to ease her life any way I could.

As she rolled out story after feeling after lament after regret, I was stunned she could still love my father.

"I've done everything he's ever asked of me," she sighed, "and still he strays."

I felt honored Mom confided in me. It made me feel like an adult, but I was definitely a biased one. I squirmed in my chair, unable to look her in the eye as she whined and ached over a despicable man who had never taken care of her in any perceivable way. Nor had he shown me love of any kind. I'd grown up fatherless, and now I was close to heading out into the world without a shred of evidence that my father loved me or saw any value in me at all. But I did my best to listen as my mother spoke of him, as if I was just a woman listening to a friend vent about her difficult life.

But when Mom said, "I'm sorry I haven't been there for you kids," I looked into her eyes and cried. It was too much. Even the youngest of our gang must have known Mom had given her best, had done more to hold our family together than many would have been capable of. She couldn't possibly think she'd been a bad mother, could she?

She stared at the floor and dabbed the corners of her eyes with a tissue, and the words tumbled from my lips in rapid-fire stream of consciousness. "*Mom,* you've been there every bit as much as you could, as much as any human could. What example did you have to follow? Your dreams were crushed before you had a chance to take even one step in their direction! All your kids love you, and, yes, it's been gut-wrenching for us to watch you be treated like he's treated you. Do you know how it's been for us to be the kids of the town drunk? Do you know how many times I've wanted to slap the hell out of that man? Do you know how much I've wanted to change the locks? But we don't blame *you.* You're the only one who took care of us, even as it completely exhausted you. Listen, Mom, you need to know this: You'll always have us. You'll never be alone."

She blotted her tears, trying to smile. Then I blurted the question I'd wanted to ask for as long as I could remember. I checked the tone of my voice, making sure my question didn't sound too aggressive.

"How can you let a man treat you like he does? He neglects, he cheats, he steals, he abuses, he leaves. *Why*, Mom? Why does someone get to pull that kind of shit and still keep his family?"

She blew her nose into a tissue and looked out across the yard. Then she said something I didn't expect. "I pray you never fall in love so hard that you forget you deserve more."

Wow. My mother was admitting to being deeply in love with my father. In love with a complete louse who had brought to her life insult, embarrassment, disrespect, betrayal, and utter exhaustion. A guy who probably hadn't given a second thought to what his unrelenting abuse was doing to the physical or mental health of his wife and seven children.

At the time I wasn't equipped to dive too far into that pool of psychology, so I asked, "Mom, why don't you divorce him?"

"Because I have seven children who need their father."

"*What* father? He hasn't been a father to any of us. We're seven kids *with no father*. Forget about him. It's time for you to think of yourself."

She didn't say anything, but at least she wasn't silent anymore.

"Mom, please try to find something to make you happy."

After a few seconds, she cleared her throat and said, "Maybe I'll get a part-time job."

A tingling rush washed through my body, and I think I felt more like an adult than I had in all my life. I'd given an adult advice, and it seemed she was going to take it.

Mom got a part-time job at the local pharmacy as a check-out girl, and she loved spending hours every day talking to co-workers and customers and earning her own money. She found she was really good at dealing with the public, a task infinitely more manageable in an environment free of the kind of hell she put up with during the hotel years. Then she took another part-time job at a local pizzeria, where she felt very much at home running a kitchen. She helped the owners immensely thanks to her experience as a chef and her ability to estimate how much product would be needed to keep on hand to always be ready for the crowds. The restaurant owners loved her. She felt valued.

At home, we felt the change in the air. Life started to feel comfortable again and maybe even kind of stable. Dad wasn't around much, and with my support, Mom was able to buy food and other necessities, so eventually we barely needed his meager financial contributions.

I consider "the cherry pie afternoon" to be the turning point, the day my father's reign ended. After being absent for the better part of a week, Dad walked into the kitchen while five of us were enjoying one of Mom's magnificent cherry pies. As we chatted and laughed about our day, he stood there, waiting for us to greet or acknowledge him—something. But nobody said a word to him. After several seconds, he nearly shouted, "Well I guess nobody missed me!"

We all glanced at him, and Mom said, "That would be correct." Then we turned back to our conversation around the table.

He stood there for several more speechless seconds, then walked out the front door. I got up and stood by the window to the front yard and saw him looking back at the house with a hurt expression.

Mom had stopped asking him not to leave, and his children were no longer interested in where he went or whether he was ever coming back. His power was gone.

By this time, I had graduated high school and was desperate to get out of the house and onto the next phase of my life. Turned out Dad's power hadn't completely eroded yet. That destructive creep crushed my early dreams of independence, which I'll tell you about, along with my young marriage and pregnancy, but for now I'll just say that, yes, like Michael and Carole before me, I took the marriage escape route.

Dad was now mostly out of our lives, three kids had moved out—leaving only four at home—and Mom was content with her jobs. A kind of peace settled over the battered family. Then disaster struck.

CHAPTER SIX

One very hot August afternoon, I arrived at my little house in Collegeville that I shared with my new husband, thinking only about how much I couldn't wait to peel off my shoes and bra and relax in my air-conditioned living room. I was sweating through my fourth month of pregnancy in the heat of a brutally humid Pennsylvania summer, and I made a mental note that next time I'd try to *get* pregnant in summer.

As I opened my front door, I heard the phone ringing, and I ran into the kitchen to answer it. On the other end of the call was a gruff voice. "Hello, is this Susan O'Neil?"

"Yes, who is this?"

"My name is Officer Terrence, and I have your name and number listed here as the person to call in an emergency for Anne Yoder."

My heart began thundering so hard, it seemed to be trying to pound its way out of my body."Is she all right?" I gasped. "What happened?"

"Mrs. Yoder was in a car accident and was thrown from the car on Mile Hill in Collegeville. She's at Montgomery Hospital and needs surgery immediately. Can you get here right away to give the approval?"

"I'll be there in twenty minutes!" I hung up the phone and raced to the hospital.

In the emergency room, a lovely nurse who told me to call her Linda spoke in a soft voice. "Your mother was driving down a steep hill in the rain and hit a bald spot in the road."

I pictured Mom in the garbage 1955 Chevy Bel Air Dad had won in a card game, veering out of control, turning left and right trying to correct the swerving old junk box that probably hadn't been properly serviced since the day our good-for-nothing father had handed her the keys.

"Is she going to be okay?" I gasped.

"We're going to do everything we can for her. She's in rough shape right now because the car hit a road sign, and your mother was thrown from the car. We'll need to get her into surgery as soon as possible."

I felt myself becoming hysterical. "I'm here! *I'm* the emergency contact! Where do I sign?"

Nurse Linda's voice stayed calm. "I'm afraid that's for contact and communication, that sort of thing. But your father's is the name of record for insurance coverage, so he has to give the approval for surgery."

I could hardly believe what I was hearing. *That* guy? The guy responsible for so much of my mother's suffering was in control of whether she could now have a potentially life-saving surgery?

Linda led me to a phone, and I called Dad's office number. Surprise, surprise, there was no answer, no answering machine. At that moment, I realized he wasn't working there or probably anywhere else, so all I could think to do was find him at one of his regular bar stops. I didn't even think about calling one of my siblings because I was completely focused on finding the person who could get my mother's surgery underway.

I said to Linda, "I need a phone book right now!" Then I dialed all the bars I knew my father wasted his life in and asked whoever answered the phone, "Is Bill Yoder in there? Really tall, brown hair, probably in a suit. Look for a drunk who's completely full of shit." After about ten panicked minutes of calling bar after bar, I found him in one mercifully close to the hospital. The bartender handed him the phone.

"Dad!" I screamed. "Get to Montgomery hospital right now! Mom's been in an accident and needs surgery that only you can sign for. Get here right now!"

He surprised me by not asking a bunch of dumb questions. He said, "I'll be right there." From the few words he spoke, I couldn't tell how drunk he was, but I prayed he could drive well at high speeds. I wanted him to arrive safely only for Mom's sake. Aside from that, he could wrap himself around a tree for all I cared.

As I paced the hospital floor waiting for my father to show up, I thought about how despicably unfair life was. Our deadbeat father went through life without a scratch, and my mother, only forty-six years old, had already suffered more than most people experience in a lifetime. I pictured Mom on a stretcher being rushed away from a mangled car and shoved into yet another ambulance. Had she been conscious when they found her? Was she terrified? Was she in a hospital bed right now worrying about her kids? I prayed she wasn't in pain. I prayed she knew help was on the way. I prayed she'd be okay and that this would be only a minor setback for a wonderful woman who was just starting to turn her life around.

After about twenty minutes, Dad hustled into the hospital waiting room and blurted, "What the hell was she doing speeding on a wet road? She was always a lousy driver."

I wanted to slap him across the face and pound him with my fists. "This isn't about *you!*" I screamed and pointed toward the desk where Nurse Linda was waiting with papers in her hand. "Sign the consent form *right now!*"

He grabbed a pen from his suit pocket and signed the papers Linda had slid in front of him. Then Linda looked at me and said, "She's in the best hands" and dashed away.

Dad turned back toward me and said, "Why did they call you instead of me?"

"Are you kidding me?" I said, trying to keep my voice down. "Why would *anybody* list *you* as an emergency contact? Nobody ever knows where you are or when you'll ever show up again! How does it feel that your daughter knew the place to find you was in a seedy bar? Rough day at the office, Dad?"

He didn't have a reply for any of that, so I continued to let it rip. "While I've been pacing here, alone in a hospital, waiting for my father to pry himself off a bar stool, I've learned more details about my mother's devastating accident. She was thrown from that piece of shit car you couldn't be bothered to replace, and she skidded fifty yards down the highway on her back. She has broken ribs, a broken pelvis, and collapsed lungs. And she might lose her spleen. Wonder why she lost control of the car? You're a gambler—what do you suppose the odds are it's because those shit tires are bald as a baby's ass?"

He looked at me as if trying to figure out where he knew me from.

"Nothing to say, Dad? Okay, tell you what. I'm going to call my brothers and sisters, and we'll take it from here. Why don't you head back to that busy office you work in every day? Oh wait, there's no such place. Back to the bar, then." I turned around and headed toward Linda's desk so I could start calling my siblings.

Mike was home and said he'd jump in the car, pick up the kids, and get them to the hospital; Debbie, Kathy, Charlotte, and David were just home from school, so I told them the gentlest version of the story I could and said Mike was on his way; Carole was vacationing in Puerto Rico, so we had no idea how to reach her.

Dad didn't shuffle off to the bar right away. Nurse Linda directed him upstairs where he had more paperwork to deal with. I sat alone in the waiting room, and Linda handed me a glass of water. She rested her hand on my shoulder and said, "This is a lot of stress for a pregnant woman. Sip some water and try to calm down. Your mother has an excellent surgeon." I appreciated her kind words, but I needed my siblings.

Mike and the kids showed up within the hour and all of us, including Dad, sat and waited.

After six excruciating hours, a surgeon decked out in scrubs and other doctor gear walked into the waiting room, and we all jumped out of our seats.

He said, "Yoder family? Hello folks. Anne is a tough lady. Her lungs collapsed, she has four broken ribs and a broken hip and pelvis. We had to remove her spleen, but that's an organ you can live without. She's doing okay, but she's been through a lot, and we'll probably keep her here for a month or more." He waited for questions, but we were in shock. Then he added, "We'll continue to give her our best effort, and she'll work through some intensive rehab. Folks, you should know that we won't know for a bit whether she'll be able to walk again."

That did it. Kathy started crying.

The doctor continued, "We're likely to keep her in intensive care for several days. She should be out of surgery soon, and then off to ICU. Can I answer any questions?"

I have no idea if anybody asked questions. My mind was a ferocious swirl of fear and grief. The surgeon went back to wherever he'd come from, and Mike said it was time to get the kids home. He and Dad shuffled them all out to the parking lot, and I sat down, alone again in the waiting room. I couldn't leave until I saw my mother. After another two hours, Nurse Linda directed me to Mom's room, and I tiptoed in. Because her face hadn't been cut or bruised, she looked strangely okay. If it hadn't been for all the tubes and beeping machines, I might have just thought she was peacefully sleeping.

With tears streaming down my cheeks, I leaned over her bed, kissed her forehead, and whispered, "Keep fighting, Mom. We all love you, and we need you." Then I stood up, wiped my eyes, turned toward the door, and blacked out.

The next thing I knew, I woke up on the floor of my mother's hospital room. I checked myself for pain and bleeding, but I seemed fine. It appeared I'd crumpled down into a kind of napping position, and because no one had found me, I assumed I hadn't been out for long. I chalked the collapse up to stress, exhaustion, dehydration, and all the oxygen in Mom's room. But I couldn't bear to be in that hospital another minute. Convinced my unborn baby and I were fine, I stood up, took a few deep breaths, walked slowly out of the hospital, then got in my car and drove home more carefully than I'd ever driven.

I took a week off from my job at a local loan company and moved back into the family house to help keep the kids' lives as normal as possible. Several nights a week, I took them to visit Mom in the hospital. She couldn't walk yet, but she was talking, and during every visit, the kids spoke to her in voices so gentle, it was as if they were afraid of breaking something.

Debbie and Kathy were seniors in high school, so after I returned to my own house, they kept the household running, but I stopped every day after work, took them to see Mom, and made sure they ate, did their homework, and kept the house in order. Carole went to help every weekend, and Mike visited Mom at the hospital a few times a week.

Where was our father in all this? The husband of the devastated patient, father of the terrified children, the adult who should have been taking care of things was, as usual, useless. He showed up at the hospital once a week but almost never checked in on what was happening at home. At this point, I considered him a completely worthless human being. I despised him more by the day.

We also saw no help from any of Mom's side of the family. Mom's sisters and mother knew all about our recent tragedy but did nothing to help any of us. We received not so much as a casserole or an offer to shop or clean or even visit Mom's bedside. As usual, Dad's sisters Aunt Mary Louise and Aunt Diggie were the ones who showed up for us. They made sure there was food in the house, and they were the reason Dad bothered to visit Mom at all.

Thirty-six days after her accident, I picked Mom up from the hospital, drove her home, and settled her into her bed. And so began a very long recovery that we knew might never give our mother back to us. Thanks to time and physical therapy, Mom could now walk with a cane, but she was still in a lot of pain because of the broken pelvis and ribs. Her doctor prescribed Percocet. Although I didn't make it my business to monitor her meds, it seemed to me there were a lot of pills going into her mouth. It appeared that addiction was being added to Mom's list of problems. Day after day she lay in bed watching TV, getting up only if Dad stopped by, and as a result, she became weaker and weaker until she could barely walk at all. Our mother seemed to be headed to a very dark place, and not one of us kids knew how to help her.

Mercifully, she decided to help herself. She stopped taking the pills and little by little started building her strength back until she could walk on her own again.

One afternoon, Mom told Kathy, "I died on the operating table and had an afterlife experience."

"How do I describe Mom's expression when she said it?" says Kathy. "She looked both bewildered and peaceful, if that makes any sense. It was like watching Dorothy describe the first time she saw Glinda and the munchkins."

I laugh. "Wouldn't it have been great if a house had landed on a certain someone?"

"I remember when she snapped out of the funk," Carole says. "God, that was like a miracle. Just before she started talking about the afterlife, I thought we were going to lose her."

Kathy continues, "She said she was on the operating table heading up toward some white light but also watching the surgeons try to save her life—like with the paddles and all the drama, lights flashing, people scrambling. She said she wanted to just float up into the light but knew her children needed her, so she came back."

"That was such a strange time," I add. "She was so depressed, wouldn't get out of bed, was popping Percocet like candy—"

"Remember she could barely walk by then? She had zero lower-body strength," says Carole.

"And then, boom, she was back, thanks to all that passion about reincarnation. It was like she had some spiritual awakening," I say.

"Would that be considered irony?" Kathy asks. "She gets all hyped up about life after death, and that's the thing that brings her back to life *before* death. That's ironic, right?"

Carole says, "Look at you. Resident English professor."

Mom started reading everything she could about reincarnation. She believed she'd come back to life to be there for Debbie, Kathy, Charlotte, and Dave; and she kicked the pills on her own, cold turkey; and made it bearable by smoking lots and lots of cigarettes and eating hard candy by the bag.

Eventually, Mom was able to walk again without a cane, but because of her physical limitations, she never returned to the jobs she loved. As the months went on, Mom and I heard the usual reports of Dad with other women in bars, and in time, Mom cared less and less about whether he showed up at home. The few times I was around when he came home, she barely reacted to his arrival. She didn't hug him or greet him in any noticeable way. But I felt a burn in my heart seeing the sadness in her eyes when she looked at him. It was as if she still had hope.

Two years after Mom's accident, Kathy escaped down Marriage Road, and Debbie headed off to college, which left only Charlotte and David still living in the family home. The three of them had all the space they could want, and with Dad almost never around, their lives were relatively peaceful.

Then, in keeping with his total lack of character, integrity, or empathy of any kind, the man who fathered us entered into an agreement that would once again uproot his children.

He'd been approached by a well-known land developer who wanted to buy our house and the acreage that went with it. So with the usual dollar signs in his eyes, Dad agreed to a deal that would effectively launch his wife and kids out of the house. The developer wanted the parcel of land our house was on to expand his shopping center, so he offered Dad a nice chunk of money to buy another home and property elsewhere. Mom adamantly refused because she loved that house, and she was fortified by Mrs. Wismer's directive that the house couldn't be sold as long as even one of her kids was still living in it. But our father, who had mastered the skills characteristic of sneaks and cheats, negotiated a secret deal with the developer. Dad proposed that our house could be moved two acres away and dropped on a little piece of land he'd included in the deal. So *technically*, the kids would still be living in the house, just not in its original location. So *technically*, he wouldn't be violating the Wismer agreement.

Before the company moved the house, the guy in charge explained we could leave all our belongings and nothing would be damaged. He said all the dishes, furniture, files, memories, and keepsakes should stay right where they were. To demonstrate how steadily they were going to move our house, he set a glass of water on a table and said not a drop would spill. Sure enough, after the home was moved to its new location, we were allowed to step inside to have a look. Everything was still in place, even the glass of water. But they wouldn't be allowed to move in for another two months.

First they'd have to secure permits, finish the septic system, wire the electric, blah blah blah. Mom, Dad, and David moved into a furnished apartment about eight miles from our home, and Charlotte moved in with her boyfriend.

"Just take your clothes," Dad told David and Charlotte, "because in no time you'll be back in your own rooms with all your things in place."

That never happened. No one from our family ever moved back into the house.

One night, shortly before Mom, Dad, David, and Charlotte were supposedly moving back home again, Bill Yoder went out to buy a gallon of milk and never returned. Of course, we didn't know right away that "never returned" was part of the deal this time. He'd been the disappearing father and husband for three decades, so how were we to know this departure wasn't just another of his usual, selfish, sleazy, despicable self-serving stunts and he wouldn't be back in his usual five to seven days?

But that time he did actually take off for good. Not, however, before pulling his most despicable maneuver of all.

The sixty-day lease on the apartment was almost up, and no one had heard from Dad in weeks. Prior to his disappearance, he'd repeatedly said, "Everything is going great with the house relocation. There's nothing to see, though, so don't bother going down there."

Eventually, it began to feel very strange that we hadn't heard any updates about the family home. Mom and I decided to head to the site to ask the contractor what was taking so long. I picked her up, and we drove back to our old neighborhood, excited to get the answers that would let everyone move forward.

As we pulled up to the location where the house had been moved, we stood frozen in disbelief. The land was completely empty. Flat. There was no house. There was no sign that there had ever been a house on that spot.

As we stood there in utter shock, trying to process what we were looking at, Mom and I broke down and cried. Had that heinous piece of human garbage sold our home and everything in it?

Once Mom and I calmed down, I urged her to go to the police, but she said, "No, let's go to the township and see what they can tell us."

I was disgusted by what I could tell she was still thinking, that maybe, *somehow* this wasn't his doing but was just some kind of crazy miscommunication; that our house was somewhere nearby, and her husband wasn't the devil. Biting my tongue nearly bloody, I drove us to the township building.

The gentleman at the office seemed confused by our ignorance. Checking the paperwork in front of him two or three times, he looked up and said, "The house on that site was demolished two days ago." When he saw how broken up we both must have looked, he said gently, "I hate to be the bearer of bad news, but that house was sold to the developers expanding the strip mall, and they wanted it removed immediately."

"*I* was one of the owners of that property," Mom gasped. "How was my house sold without my permission?"

The clerk said, "If I were you, I'd go to the county courthouse right now."

Mom was so quiet, I thought she might melt into a puddle of pain, but she said, "Yes, the courthouse. I need to know what he's done." Then she looked at me and said, "Take me there *now*."

At the courthouse, we were directed to public records and told how to find the recent transactions for our house. There it was in black and white, literally. He did it. He sold our house to developers whose plan was to immediately demolish it. On the deed to our house were two signatures, one was Dad's and the other was a forgery. Someone had signed my mother's name.

Mom looked at me with a blank stare and then fell to the floor. Lying there she moaned, "How could he have done this to us? How could he have done this to me?"

My mother was as broken as I'd ever seen her. She was reduced to a curled-up ball on the floor of a government building. The courthouse workers stood there, speechless, watching her writhe, their eyes heavy with sympathy. I sat down next to her and rested my hand on her back, crying quietly as I absorbed yet another round of emotional brutality rendered by the man who fathered me.

After about fifteen minutes, Mom stopped crying and slowly rose to her feet. She breathed deeply, and I watched as her expression shifted from anguish to fury. To no one in particular, she screamed, "*I did not sign this!* This is a forgery! Somebody help me!"

A compassionate woman behind the counter said, "You can't let this happen. You have options. You need to hire a lawyer and get to the bottom of this."

I assured Mom we'd find a lawyer, that we'd find out where

Dad had taken off to and would get some justice. We left the courthouse and headed to the apartment where I settled Mom on the couch and made her a cup of tea, hoping it would help her decompress. She sat there and quietly cried and cried. Now and then, she'd cry out some expression of angst or disbelief.

"After all the years of abuse, now he's taken my home!

"My home, my children's home!

"This is the worst thing he's ever done!"

As difficult as it was to watch my mother go through the agony, I felt optimistic that now maybe she was getting angry . . . really angry. Maybe now she'd do something about it and deliver him some of the retribution he'd earned.

But no.

She calmed down and said, "Forget it. I just can't hunt him down and watch him lie to me one more time. I hope he enjoys his blood money."

I wanted to shake her. I wanted to demand she take action, get a lawyer, and make him accountable for his despicable—even illegal—actions. But she wouldn't budge, and I had to let it go. And I was grateful Mrs. Wismer had passed away a few years earlier, so she'd never know what had become of her extraordinary, selfless gesture.

I can't think about that day without crying. As the three of us sit around Kathy's dining table revisiting the God-awfulness of what that man did to all of us, we're all crying. He took everything a man can take from a woman . . . and she let him.

"Why didn't we push her to go after him?" Carole asks. "I

don't remember why we let it go. How could we have left it at that? No justice, no punishment, no retribution? What happened there?"

"I don't know," Kathy says, dabbing her eyes with tissue. "We tried, right? We did our best without flat out ganging up on her."

I say, "I think we didn't push harder because we didn't want to add to her pain. She was so fragile. We were all afraid she'd have another breakdown and end up back in a hospital."

"It's strange how different people are," says Carole. "If that were me, there would have been no peace until there was justice. If some creep bastard had done that to me, there wouldn't have been a day of rest until we all sat in front of a judge and I got to watch my lawyer rip him to pieces."

"Same," I say.

"Same here," says Kathy. "Then again, if it had been up to me, he would have been in pieces before he could make it to a courthouse."

"In pieces and buried under a new mall development," I add, feeling not an ounce of guilt.

A little research revealed that Dad had found a woman to impersonate our mother and cosign the papers required to sell the property our house had been moved to. The price for selling the land out from under the feet of his children was $100,000. Then he disappeared. It was emotional cruelty at its worst, and we were all ravaged by it. Because our mother was so weak and broken, so geared to hope for some version of a fairy-tale life no matter how much bloody evidence to the contrary rained down on her life, she refused to legally pursue the matter. Then Mom admitted to me she worried that a court fight would diminish the chances her husband would return to her.

Those were very rough days for me. I was constantly torn between my anger at my father and my utter frustration that my mother still acted like a sniveling girl with a crush on the school bad boy who wouldn't stop slapping her around. It's not easy to try to unconditionally love a parent who won't let go of her fairy-tale dreams and stand up for herself. But I did my best.

We all did our best despite our family home being knocked down with all our personal belongings in it. Everything gone. Luckily when Mike, Carole, Kathy, and I had moved out, we each took lots of our childhood pictures with us, so we still have plenty of those memories preserved in albums. But Carole lost her precious art portfolio and most of her art supplies. Carole and I lost our wedding dresses. All seven of us lost every crafty thing we'd made or built or drawn as children.

As our hearts broke more and more with each realization of what had been taken from us, we did our best to support our mother. By this time, Debbie was away at college, Kathy had gotten married (more on that, shortly), and Charlotte was living with friends. I had recently divorced (more on that, too), so Mom came to live with me in my apartment.

After graduating college, Debbie and Mom moved into their own apartment near mine.

We kids continued to search for Dad, but Mom refused to be involved with our search; she still refused to admit that he'd actually left. She believed he might return even after the detective we hired told us he was alive and *remarried*, not to the mom imposter who had forged her signature but to a woman about ten years his senior. The detective told us he'd moved to Ohio, married this woman, started some type of engineering business, and became the *church deacon.*

Dad had neglected to divorce Mom before remarrying, so he was a bigamist. This super-fun family fact eventually became a great icebreaker at parties. If there's ever a lull in the conversation or, say, a whiner complaining about how his boss is a pain in his ass or that his roofer never shows up on time, one of us chimes in with, "Yeah? My dad went out for a gallon of milk, committed forgery to steal my family home, and then became a bigamist. *Waaaa.*"

As we were all trying to move on with our lives, Dad filed for divorce from Mom because he feared his new wife would realize he was never divorced. When she received the summons to appear in court, she sank into a deep depression. Then she started talking about the upcoming day in court, which seemed to snap her right out of her sadness. Why? She was looking forward to seeing him. She even insisted she have her hair done before the court date. I'd like to say I was dumbfounded, but by then nothing surprised me.

I took Mom to the hearing and actually was dumbfounded as I listened to our father claim, "I have always taken care of Annie and sent money to ensure she had everything she needed."

Of course, he couldn't show a shred of proof of that lie, and now Mom had her big chance to refute his bullshit. While Mom was on the stand, the judge asked, "Did Mr. Yoder support you financially during his absence?"

She answered like a beauty contest contender, demure and feminine. "He didn't send money, but I believed he was coming back until our house was destroyed. That was when I realized there was nothing left of our marriage, and I wanted nothing from him."

She was also asked if she wanted to press charges for his illegal marriage. She said, "No, just let him go."

And that was it. Sitting there in a court of law and directly asked if the sleazebag she married should suffer any repercussions for bigamy, she said, "Do nothing."

I want to say I was angry at her for letting him off the hook, but I was partially relieved she was going to let it go. She had her seven devoted children, and I hoped that would be enough to help her finally move beyond the painful, terrible life she'd led.

Fourteen years later, at the age of sixty-one, Mom passed away from leukemia. For at least two years, she suffered in silence, never divulging how sick she really was. Even though several of us took turns taking her to her many doctor appointments, she never let the doctors tell us what was actually going on. She told us her "iron level was low" and that she was just getting "iron transfusions." Then on her deathbed, she explained her position had been that we'd all suffered enough, and she didn't want to burden us with any more pain she could prevent.

Mom said she wanted to be cremated so she could be with us always and still be part of our joyous parties. So, year after year, we siblings passed her ashes between us for safe keeping. We believe she was very happy on those mantels in a position to see so clearly how we've stuck together as a family, notably her girls, and even more notably, Carole, Kathy, Debbie, and me.

We love our siblings—truly love them all—but this sister cluster has stayed particularly close.

Several years after Mom died, Dad dropped dead of an aneurysm on a sidewalk in northern Pennsylvania, his illegal wife by his side. Hearing the news of this death from our Uncle Charlie was like reading a newspaper clipping about the passing of some incompetent math teacher we'd once hated and now barely remembered.

We kept Mom's ashes in a beautiful walnut box that Kathy's husband Jack built of wood taken from a walnut tree from our childhood backyard. And for many more years, Mom "joined us" for every holiday and family celebration. For special occasions, we dressed her resting place in pretty bows. Whoever kept Mom for the year tended to have a year of good luck, like the year Carole was offered a new business venture and the year Kathy received a big promotion. Good luck aside, twenty-five years after our mother's death, we siblings decided to bury her ashes so our children wouldn't be saddled with that responsibility.

Mom had always told us she dreamed of going to Hawaii. So on her eighty-sixth birthday, all seven of us got together, cooked Hawaiian food, wore leis, and had a going-away party for our mother; the woman who had suffered so much, given so much, tried so hard, and had surely done the best she could.

It was a windy, cold November day, and we stood near the hole we'd dug to bury her ashes in the backyard of Debbie's home, where Mom had lived for five years. The wind whipped through the trees, and we wrapped our coats around us. Then, as I began to read a poem we'd collectively written for Mom's sixtieth birthday, the wind suddenly stopped, and the air became mysteriously still. All around us, the world seemed to go silent. It was a beautiful experience that made the moment feel magical for all of us. It was as if Mom was letting us know it was okay to say goodbye, that she was in a better place and would watch over all of us. Her belief in reincarnation had given her some peace, and on that day, it gave the seven of us peace.

Then the wind began to gently pick up again, and we felt she was right there, whispering her love.

CHAPTER SEVEN

Carole, the Artist

Carole here. I wasn't the firstborn, but I was the first girl. In some families that means you've just answered your parents' dreams. You're responsible for creating the perfect foursome; now they have "one of each." Of course, I had no idea that eventually this sweet little family would grow into a mob of seven, and I'd end up in charge of five little people I never asked for.

Year after year, as my parents continued to reproduce, my older brother remained the little prince of the family while I remained relegated to nanny goat. As the second of seven born to middle-class, 1950s parents, it was all but guaranteed that in time I'd be used as second-tier mother, untrained housekeeper, and obscenely overworked-but-never-paid employee. The cleaning responsibilities—which included dusting, vacuuming, washing dishes, doing laundry, and making the beds—were somehow both exhausting and tedious, but the childcare responsibilities were worse. Wrangling those five small banshees was like trying to lasso a snake using a piece of dental floss. They were slick and slippery, always dividing and hiding, and it seemed their daily goal was to drain every bit of energy I had.

It cracks me up today when I hear about parents looking for babysitters who have been trained in CPR, first aid, water safety, and infant care. Huh? Water safety in my family consisted of trying not to land in a cesspool during a garden-hose fight. It's startling to me we all managed to make it out of childhood with our eyesight and limbs intact.

During those babysitting years, I realized I wasn't into taking care of kids, nor did I want any of my own. Maybe I had the spirit of childcare burned out of me by parents who saddled me with responsibilities no kid should be saddled with. I realize now their making me responsible for five little kids was actually a form of child abuse. It should never have been my job.

My outlet was art. It was my escape and my way to dream myself a future beyond the troubled walls of our family life. I think I was nine when I first recognized the presence of art in the natural world. With no money for art supplies, I used a red colored pencil to draw flowers, trees, and clouds on a brown paper bag. Every few days, I sneaked to the neighbors' precious rose garden to snip a bloom or two to use as models and then slipped away to a tree behind our house, where I could sketch in privacy and dream of the day I'd have a real canvas, a set of paints, and maybe even an easel. I thought I was smart hiding them under the crumbling cement steps behind the house, but one day Dad shoved one of my brown bags in my face and sneered, "This is how you spend your time? This shit is useless. Art is useless. Concentrate on your homework so you can get a real job." He crumpled my beautiful brown bag and threw it in the trash.

For having the audacity to spend some of my childhood time drawing in the quiet of nature, I was assigned the extra chores of washing windows and cleaning the oven, tasks my parents knew I despised.

But I wasn't dissuaded. I continued to cut clippings of flowers, herbs, weeds, grasses, branches, and anything else I could find growing. I sneaked the clippings into my room and drew them fresh from the garden, then drew them again as they began to wilt, then drew them again in their most dried out stages of deathliness. I saw beauty and art everywhere I looked.

High school art classes were my refuge from the subjects that held no interest for me, like math, English, and history. My eyes grew wide when my art teachers told us about all the ways someone could both be an artist and make money; there were ceramicists, muralists, portrait painters, graphic artists, art directors in ad agencies, interior designers—all careers that called for artistic ability. And the wider my eyes grew, the stronger my resolve grew to stand up against my father.

At least I had Mom. She complimented everything I showed her. The day I brought home a clay bust I'd sculpted, Mom said, "Oh, Carole, this is so lifelike! I can't believe you did this with your very own hands!" I told her my art teacher was submitting it in the high school art show, and she said, "I'm so proud of you, but don't tell your father. He doesn't see the point of art, so let's keep it to ourselves."

Why, Mom? *Why* keep it to ourselves? Of course, I knew it was to keep peace with Dad.

Early in December, my art teacher, Mr. Hale, told me my bust had won first place in the art show and that part of the prize was art supplies. I thought my heart would burst! I dashed home and told Mom the thrilling news.

She pulled me into a big hug and said, "You're so talented,

Carole! Can you make me some of those resin ornaments for our Christmas tree?"

I got right to it, proud to have been commissioned by my mother. But as she was hanging them on our tree, Dad walked into the room and said, "We're not putting that junk on our tree. We have real ornaments."

"Bill, I asked Carole to make them for me," my mother replied. "I think she could even sell these and pay for some of the materials she needs."

"Well, it's official," he said. "You're as dumb as she is. That stuff is crap."

As usual, Mom didn't stand up to him, and I slunk away to my room as he threw them all in the trash.

One day, my seven-year-old brother, David, presented our father with a simple, childlike picture he'd painted of a tree. The old man's face lit up, and he said, "Very good, David! Keep painting, and maybe someday you'll become a famous artist."

That day, I realized my father was a flaming misogynist, and the realization was a gift. From then on, I did everything I could to stay away from him.

When I was in ninth grade, I landed my first job, working after school and on Saturdays for Mr. Noller, a kind, German man who owned a bakery. As I walked in to apply for the job, I smelled the intoxicating aroma of freshly baked *everything!* After I filled out the application, he read it quickly, handed me a big sugar cookie, and asked, "What's your favorite dessert? There's no wrong answer." As I paused to consider the question, he said, "No fears, honey, everything we make here will become your favorite. You're hired."

Wow, so this is what a decent man sounded like. Mr. Noller

welcomed every customer with a bright, charming comment like, “I have lots of sweet and delicious treats just for you. Take your pick, and this little girl here will wrap it up to keep it nice and fresh. Thanks for coming in and have a sunny day!”

He specialized in iced cinnamon buns, which he called “prosperity buns,” and Springerle cookies, anise-flavored treats he pressed with an embossed design. During the holidays, people came from faraway towns to buy his prosperity buns, and it gave me joy to be part of a team that made so many people’s holidays more delightful. Mr. Noller was a generous man who often sent me home with leftover pies and prosperity buns to share with my siblings. I gave most of my earnings to Mom to help with the family’s expenses but always kept enough to buy art supplies. Meanwhile, I developed my art skills.

During my senior year, still in the fleabag hotel, I wondered which road would lead me out of the hellscape of my family life. I knew it would be through art in some form, so I continued to investigate options that might lead to a career. I also believed the road to independence began with college, so I committed to getting into college, then becoming an artist and entrepreneur. I told Mr. Hale about those dreams, and he encouraged me to apply to the Tyler School of Art in Philadelphia. He submitted a recommendation, which led to an invitation to present my portfolio in an admissions interview.

After I begged for weeks, my father agreed to drive me to the interview. The inside of the car all the way to Philadelphia was as quiet as a mausoleum, and I just knew he was quietly muttering that this was a waste of everyone’s time. I tried to focus on the interview that might change my life. As much as I tried to fill my head with positive thoughts, insecurity welled in my stomach.

Maybe my father was right. Maybe my wanting to be an artist was a silly dream.

We pulled onto the school's campus, where we were directed to the interview office and told to wait until I was called. My foot tapped as I waited.

A gray-haired woman stepped into the room and said, "Carole Yoder, we're ready for you. Bring your portfolio and follow me."

I followed her into a room where a panel of six art professors sat facing me like a firing squad. But the moment I opened my portfolio in front of those professors, my fears faded. I showed them my sketches, collages, flower paintings, and my favorite glass sculptures. I explained I'd also delved in glass blowing and enjoyed working with glass even more than I liked painting a canvas, but that I was open to all the possibilities. The interviewers were very pleasant and said positive things about my work, and then one of them showed me to the door.

"You'll receive a letter to let you know if you've been accepted."

When I walked out of the interview, my heart fluttered with joy as I imagined life beyond Collegeville. I pictured myself heading an art exhibition in New York. I visualized my creations becoming the newest art crazes. I saw my life away from a toxic household. I could see my future, and it looked glorious.

Every day for the next few months, I ran home from school and flung open the mailbox door, hoping to receive the letter of admission that would mark the first day of the rest of my life. Every time I pulled out another bill or PennySaver or real estate flier, my heart dropped into my stomach.

I told my father I was going to ask Mr. Hale to check on my application, but Dad said, "That's not his job. I'll call them." The next day he said, "I contacted them, and they assured me they'd be in touch."

Then after three more agonizing months of waiting, my father delivered the news about my future.

"I heard from the school today," he said in a voice devoid of expression. "You didn't get in."

I froze. This made no sense—the interview had gone so well. But before I could ask any questions, he followed with, "I told you you're not that good. I told you there's no future in what *you* call art. Let's be done with this crap. Now you can concentrate on getting a real job."

I rushed to my room sobbing. Sue tried to reassure me I really was talented and shouldn't listen to Dad—about this or anything. After a few minutes, our father slithered into my room holding my portfolio and lectured me on what was wrong with each of the pieces.

"This one here, you see," he said, holding up my favorite ink sketch, a drawing of a peaceful island surrounded by water and sloping palm trees, "this one is just plain stupid."

Sue said, "You just gave her bad news. Why don't you leave her alone?"

He snapped back, "You're just as stupid as she is. Get the hell out of here. I'm teaching your sister how the real world works." Sue left the room, and my father pulled out my glass sculpture and started banging it against my desk.

He said, "Do you really think anybody wants to buy something so asinine?" He banged it harder and harder until it smashed into shards.

That night I cried myself to sleep, and in the days that followed, I cried myself exhausted. I was now a high school graduate with no future, no plan. But with the help of my Aunt Diggie, I secured a job in the secretarial pool at Montgomery County Community College.

On my first day, I walked into the tiny, two-room office and was greeted by Linda, a lovely woman just a couple of years older than me, and Mary, an older woman who said she'd worked at the school for years.

Mary said, "Welcome, honey. Are you here as a career secretary or is this just a stepping stone to what you want to be?"

This was an honest question, so I gave an honest answer. I told them I hoped this was just a stop on my way to my dreams. I wanted passionately to become a professional artist. Linda and Mary listened and from that moment forward never stopped being my champions for independence. They always pumped me up by reminding me, "You can use every job as a step toward building the life you really want," and "Believe in yourself. You'll get there—just keep believing and don't give up."

Those women demonstrated a kind of strength I'd never seen because I'd been raised by a subservient mother. They never stopped pushing me, and they're greatly responsible for what happened next.

To those fabulous women from the secretarial pool of Montgomery County Community College from 1968 to 1970, if you're reading this, please know you helped save my life. You told me I could reach any goal I worked for, and you made me believe it. What a gift. I'd like to raise a martini glass to you and give you a whole lot of cake.

Even though I punched a clock as a secretary from Monday through Friday, I was still an artist at heart, so after a year of working nine to five, I enrolled in evening art classes at the

Moore School of Art in Philadelphia. I'd been saving my money to move out of the house, but I used all my savings to pay for a year of classes, so I had to stay home for a little while longer.

My first day of school was indeed the first day of the rest of my life. I walked into my art theory class, took a seat, and watched the other students stroll in—people who carried art portfolios, had ink-stained fingers, and wore paint-stained jeans. It felt like I'd finally found my people.

As the semester went on, I made friends. My classmates and I were budding, struggling artists, and the energy of that was exhilarating. After several weeks in my new art program, my optimism for life was fully percolating, and at the end of the semester, I joined some of my classmates at a pub to celebrate completing our first leg of our art education.

Almost immediately after entering the crowded bar, I locked eyes with a quintessential Mr. Tall, Dark, and Handsome. He flashed a little smile my way, and my heart thundered, but I stayed on my side of the bar with my artist friends. Then after about an hour of eye-and-smile flirting, the handsome stranger bought a beer and had the waitress deliver it to me. Feeling bold, I sauntered over to him and introduced myself.

"Well, here I am," I said. "What are your other two wishes?"

He smiled and said, "I'll tell you one of them—you dump your friends and sit with me." I agreed and spent the rest of the evening with him. He listened closely, saying very little as I rambled about my artistic ideas and dreams. I felt immediately drawn to him because he just wanted to hear about me. *Me.*

After a few hours of letting me tell him all about myself, he said, "I think we've both found something worth exploring, so my second wish is to take you on a proper date."

Oh my. These weren't the words of a boy. This wasn't the confidence of a boy. This guy was a man. I couldn't say "Yes!" fast enough.

We started dating the following week. Larry lived in West Chester, PA, about forty-five minutes from Collegeville where I still lived. He was rarely willing to make the trip to visit me in my hometown, and as much of a red flag as that was, I took great satisfaction in secretly sticking it to my dad by going on dates he didn't know about.

For a year, I continued to ignore flaming red flags, like his almost never being willing to drive to see me or the fact that every time we went on a date in a restaurant or movie theater, I paid. Then came Larry's half-assed proposal.

"Now that I've graduated from college, I figure it's time to settle down. Do you want to get married?"

Who could resist a proposition so romantic? Clearly not this product of a loveless marriage. I married Larry eight months later on Valentine's Day.

Sue was my maid of honor, and Linda, an art school buddy, was a bridesmaid. There was music but no dancing, and no typical wedding traditions. I was pretty sure that more than half the guests assumed I was pregnant. But I was finally making my escape! Even my new mother-in-law didn't dampen my optimism when she showed up dressed for a funeral . . . black dress, black gloves, and a black veil. Oh man, this did not bode well for my romantic future.

Waving goodbye to our guests—the most notable one looking like a bereaved widow out of *The Godfather*—we shoved off for our honeymoon in St. Thomas. Although only four days long, our getaway offered a classic, tropical honeymoon experience, including beautiful beaches, sexy hot tubs, umbrella drinks, and lots of romantic music playing in the background. Larry was sweet and attentive, so it was a very happy few days. They were the only happy days of the marriage.

On the plane back to Pennsylvania, Larry revealed he'd planned a short honeymoon because we needed to get back to help move his mother into *our* apartment. He added that promising her a place in our home was the only way he'd gotten her to attend our wedding. I chose not to fight about this unwelcome news. I was still glowing from a delightful time with my new husband on that beautiful island. Maybe his mother wouldn't stay long.

Her complaining started immediately. She criticized everything I did. Apparently, my cooking sucked, I didn't clean well enough, and I just didn't do a good enough job of serving her son by having his dinner and a cocktail waiting as he came through the door each night. Even though this woman had no job, she sat around all day waiting for me to get home and make dinner, clean the house, and wash and iron her clothes.

This was *not* going to be my life, so after three weeks of living with the mother-in-law, I gave Larry an ultimatum. "Your mother is selfish and lazy. I didn't marry her, and I *never* agreed to live with her. If you want to stay married, she's out. As in *right now*."

To my surprise, he simply replied, "You're right. I'll find her an apartment."

Within a week, his mother was out of our home, but Larry made me pay for it. He became surly and bitter and even threw things at me. During our early quarrels, which were usually about his mother or money or something I'd done that pissed him off, Larry slapped me. As time went on, he closed his fist. I think the worst of it was that after he hit me, *I* apologized to calm him down. Before long, I came to the sick realization I'd married a man just like my father. Both had been coddled by their self-centered, controlling mothers, who had taught them nothing about how to be a good man. Larry seemed to have studied from my father's playbook.

"Okay, I think I have to stop us here," says Kathy. "Carole, why do you think you chose a guy like that? You're one of the strongest women I've ever known. What do you think made you put up with all that shit even as long as you did? Or were there no signs of his assholeness until after the wedding?"

"Well—"

Sue cuts in. "Of course there were signs, like how he wouldn't pick her up. She always had to go to him. And he never took her on any dates, only to parties. He had to have things his way all the time. Bad signs!"

"Of course there were signs," I say. "Who's ever looked back on a lousy relationship and not seen the red flags that were there all along?"

"True," Sue adds. "Then we talk ourselves out of them. We rationalize them away."

"That's right," I tell her. "Larry was my ticket out of hell house, and there's no way I was going to let red flags get in the way of it."

Kathy says, "I just wish you hadn't had to go through hell to get out of hell."

"Thanks, honey. I know you do."

ℓ·ℓ·ℓ

As many abusive control freaks do with the women in their lives, Larry isolated me from the people I cared about. He'd almost never join me to see my family, and he had countless reasons why I shouldn't drive to Collegeville to see them: gas was too expensive, the weather made the drive dangerous, or I'd promised he and I would spend more time together.

Also, as many abusive control freaks do, Larry tried to crush my dreams of having a career in art. When we were dating, he'd said my artistic nature was what he loved most about me. Fast forward to married life, and suddenly I had "no talent." He refused to help pay for art school, so I had to find a full-time job. I concentrated on finding a position where I could utilize my artistic skills, and luckily I was hired as an apprentice for McGraw-Hill Publishing as an illustrator for children's books. The job didn't pay well, but it was my first time being paid to be creative, which was a genuine step in the direction of my dreams.

In June 1970, Larry and I had been unhappily married for a little more than a year. Larry was working for an engineering company as a surveyor, and he wanted desperately to advance to the position of engineer. He was constantly passed over for promotions, but then the army stepped in and saved him from further embarrassment. Larry was drafted, and we were told we'd be moving to Fort Bragg, North Carolina. He convinced me that in the South, we'd have a fresh start. For me, that "fresh start" meant leaving my family, friends, and a creative job I adored for the hot South, where I knew no one and would be marooned with a miserable husband who didn't like me.

In North Carolina, I took a job as a bank teller on the military base. The work was dull, but it spared me eight hours a day of Larry. I adopted a sweet sheepdog after she'd been dumped out of a moving van, which was leaving the army base. I named her Fudge, and even Larry grew to love her, so I was allowed to keep her.

For the first year, life in North Carolina was tedious but relatively free of verbal and physical abuse, and I was convinced there was something about the presence of the dog that kept Larry from acting on his violent impulses. I wasn't happy, but I wasn't desperately unhappy, either.

One day at the bank, a group of guys posing as soldiers stuck guns in my face and demanded all the money I could reach. As I'd been taught in training, I handed over all the cash in my drawer, then dropped to the floor. That was enough military-style excitement for me. I quit the job, which, of course, infuriated my husband. He showed no protectiveness or sympathy for what I'd gone through. Instead, he called me "a weakling and a coward."

Now that I'd left one of the few available jobs on the base, money became tighter and tighter, and Larry's moods grew darker and darker. I searched all day for a job but had to be home with dinner ready when he returned from work.

Usually his first words were, "Find a job today? Of course, you didn't—you're too stupid to do anything but paint pretty little pictures."

"I love painting," I said. "That's what I should be doing. I belong in art classes and working as an artist."

"That's not going to put food on this table, is it? What good are you?"

His words were cutting and painfully familiar, and I began to sink into depression. I'd made no friends, and aside from my walks with Fudge, there was nothing I looked forward to.

Sue called relatively often, and every time we spoke, she'd say something like, "I'm worried. You don't sound right. What's going on? Tell me the truth."

I always responded with, "I just miss you and home. Don't worry."

One rainy afternoon, as I was dusting the living room, Larry told me to sit down because we had something to talk about. My stomach surged with dread. Was he going to try to move his mother back in?

"Have a seat, Carole," he said. "I have an idea."

I sat and waited for something negative to come out of his mouth.

"In four months, my Fort Bragg commitment will be done."

Oh God, I thought. What other godforsaken place is he going to drag me to?

He said, "I think you should head back to West Chester before me and get us settled before I get there."

What had I just heard? I couldn't have been happier if he'd handed me an acceptance letter offering a scholarship to the Sorbonne!

I pretended to consider what he'd just said. The last thing I wanted to do was show him how joyful I felt about the idea.

"Well, I guess that makes sense," I said quietly. "If you think it's the best plan, that's what I'll do."

I packed in what felt like minutes, and within a week, Fudge and I were back in Pennsylvania. I found a simple secretarial job with an employment agency and enjoyed quiet nights at home, just Fudge and me. For four months, the air I breathed was entirely free of the miserable man I'd married. Then Larry was discharged, and he moved back into our apartment.

To get away from him again, I'd meet up with my friend Trish who Larry approved of my spending time with because she was married to Artie, one of his college friends. But he didn't know that during my outings with Trish for lunch or cocktails, we were plotting my escape.

One morning in April, almost four years after I'd married a terrible man I barely knew, I waited until Larry left for work, packed a suitcase with as much of my clothing as I could smash into it; boxed my favorite cooking and art supplies, family pictures, and some knick-knacks; grabbed my baby Fudge; jumped into my car; and drove to Trish and Artie's house, where I could breathe and plan my next move. I left behind everything that had anything to do with Larry, including every picture I had of him. I wanted no reminders, and I knew he'd understand once he took inventory of what I'd left behind.

Had I been ready to pack up and leave him because I was now back within range of my support system? Did I wake up that day feeling especially courageous? Or was it just the day a battered woman decided she'd been pushed too far? Whatever had clicked inside me, it clicked hard, and I took off at full speed toward self-sufficiency.

Larry didn't even put up a fight other than threatening to take Fudge away from me, but he didn't put any effort into that threat. He faded into the background, and it was almost shocking how easy he was to forget.

I took a job with an engineering company and, over the next year, spent time with my brothers and sisters. I also worked to reconnect with friends I'd neglected. The strengthening of those relationships fortified me to start trying to repair my relationship with myself. Relieved as I was to be free of the chokehold of a horrible marriage, I was sad and disappointed in myself. After growing up in a house of hell wrought by an oppressive, selfish man, how could I have married someone exactly like him?

I started by reading books about self-awareness and self-respect and became a sponge for any advice that could help me learn to believe in and love myself again. After a quick divorce, I was officially rid of the toxic man I'd allowed into my life, and I felt clean again . . . confident. At just twenty-two years old, I was ready to restart my life. And I was ready to find a new man to love.

One night after work, in the middle of a bustling bar full of long-haired, blue-jeaned, hippie types, stood a confident, quiet man dressed like a rugged cowboy out of the old West. For a while, he just stared at me, and then he crossed the bar in my direction.

"Would you like to play darts and can I buy you a beer and, by the way, my name is John."

Direct. I liked that. But he didn't seem pushy, just quietly comfortable with himself. We flirted our way through a couple beers and several games of darts, and I knew I was feeling *that thing* . . . the thing you feel when you've just met someone you know you're going to go at least a few miles with.

I said, "I can't believe I've never seen you around here. I guess I haven't been paying attention."

John said, "Our timing must have been off because I'd never forget such beauty."

Even the cheesy things he said sounded sincere. Because they were. John never seemed to be trying too hard; he simply said what was on his mind. Flirtation led to several dinner dates, movies, parties, and long conversations about our dreams.

Six months later, we moved in together.

John encouraged me to take classes, and my artistic abilities were a great fit for his engineering skills. Together, we designed and produced arts and crafts, like belts and belt buckles, candles, and silver jewelry. We sold mostly everything we made, and what we didn't sell became great Christmas gifts.

John had watched his sister go through three terrible marriages, so he'd vowed to stay away from the altar himself. But his unrivaled belief in me made me believe I'd found my soulmate, which was enough commitment for me at the time.

After John and I had lived together for seven happy years, he was told he'd be needed on a project in West Virginia for approximately two years. The job was in such a rural area in the mountains, I wouldn't have been able to find work there, so we decided to try a long-distance relationship. By then, Trish and Artie had split, and Trish and our friend Judi were planning to move to Atlantic City to become dealers at a new casino. They invited me to come along.

John and I knew long-distance relationships were full of challenges, but as was his style, John calmly laid out a possible plan.

"I won't be able to come home for at least six months, so why don't you go with Trish and Judi? That way, you won't be alone, and you can have a look at how you like casino work. We'll talk as often as possible. And know I love you. You'll always be my pumpkin."

Whenever he called me that, my heart fluttered.

For the next two years, John and I saw each other as often as we could. I had a blast in Atlantic City with my girlfriends, dealing roulette and blackjack. But eventually I just missed John too much to continue long distance. His project had wrapped up, and he'd moved back to West Chester. I wanted to go back to Pennsylvania and start building a life with him.

As much as I wanted to go back to living with John, I needed more of a commitment between us. So on a warm spring evening nine years into our relationship, I dropped down on one knee and said, "I know you've never believed in marriage, but I know you've always believed in me. Will you marry me?"

John got down on his knee and said, "My pumpkin, I love you, and yes, I will marry you."

I threw my arms around him, and we tumbled to the floor and cried with joy. It was the lightest, deepest, fullest happiness I'd ever known. I was going to spend the rest of my life with the first man I'd been able to trust.

When I visited Mom to tell her the news, she opened up about men and marriage in a way she hadn't before. She held a cup of tea with both hands and stared across the room as if she were watching an old film.

"I'm so proud you were smart enough to ditch the dead wood and build your relationship with that handsome John. He's a good man, nothing like your father."

As overdue as such kind of talk was, it was satisfying to hear my mother speak strongly and clearly about the man she'd wasted so much of her life on.

"Thank you, Mom," I said. "That means a lot. It's been a long road, and apparently, I had to kiss a frog, too."

She shook her head and said, "What a dummy I was. How utterly foolish to let my insecurities keep me with a man who never respected me, never loved me."

What could I say? I agreed with her and couldn't think of anything comforting, so I just rubbed her back.

She went on. "I'll always regret how my decisions affected my children. There's so much I'd do differently if I could. But at least now I see you coming out the other side, breaking the chain of pain."

I hugged her and said, "Yes, we're all moving forward. You did your best, and we're all doing fine."

John's mother, Doris, said our wedding day was one of the happiest days of her life because her son had clearly found his soulmate and had finally smartened up enough to marry her. Oh, how I loved that woman. And how grand it was to be married in the presence of a mother-in-law-to-be who wore neither black nor a veil, just a lovely peach dress and a big smile.

Six years later, my mother died of leukemia. During her last week, she apologized for all the times she should have stood up to our father again but didn't out of fear—fear he'd hit her, fear he'd leave, fear he'd retaliate against us kids. She said she loved each one of us, and we were the true pride and joys of her life.

But three days before Mom took her last breath, she said she had something to tell me that was long overdue. I couldn't imagine what secret she'd been holding onto that had anything to do with my life. But when she asked me to come closer, I leaned forward, and she whispered in my ear, "You *were* accepted into the Tyler School of Art. Your father tore up the acceptance letter."

In that moment, my heart seemed to try to blast out my chest wall. Then came the knife. "And you were offered a full scholarship."

A *full* scholarship. I'd been accepted on my merits, and the school *wanted to pay me* to attend. But it had all been stolen from me by a monster. And his weak wife let him do it. Tears burned my eyes.

"It nearly killed me not to tell you," she whispered, her voice now even fainter. "But I knew if I told you against his wishes, you would have confronted him, and then he would have taken it out on all of us."

Now it made sense—my mother's zealous reinforcement of my talents back then.

"You're so talented, Carole!" she'd often said. "You can do anything you want with your talent!" She'd been trying to ease her guilt for being a partner in the slaughter of my dreams.

I started to cry hard but grabbed a tissue and pulled myself together. My mother was dying, and I didn't want to make her feel worse by berating her for not standing up to him, for not standing up for me. I would grieve later, outside this room. I'd share this horrible news with my husband and sisters, and together they'd help me work through it. But there, next to my dying mother, I simply said, "It's okay, Mom, it wasn't your fault. Nobody suffered more than you did."

After a week in the hospital, Mom passed away peacefully, surrounded by her seven children.

Months later, a friend of mine who designed cornices and headboards asked if I wanted to buy her business. I could practically hear my mother's voice whispering, "Do it. Follow your dreams."

Running such a business would call for many skills, including planning, organization, design, sawing, sewing, and building. Between John and me, we had what it took to make a go of it, so we said yes and went into business together.

I'd long been captivated by the transparent beauty of glass, so for years I'd been experimenting with stained glass and eventually began creating my own designs. Because our new business offered so much creative freedom, I was able to incorporate my glass pieces directly into the cornice boards we were building, and the results were unique and beautiful. Finally, my artistic heart was bursting with ideas, *and* I was able to execute them.

I also began creating window designs incorporating elements of my clients' lives. I talked to them about their tastes, researched their décor, got to know their personalities, and then developed glass pieces that complemented their style and told a story. With joy, I dove headfirst into window artistry, combining stained glass with window treatments. One of my favorite creations was a window treatment into which I incorporated eyeglass lenses that changed with the light in the room.

John and I exhibited our work at Vassar Design House, a showcase for local artists to exhibit new design ideas, and my work was featured on HGTV's *Smart Design*. We also wrote and published two glass design pattern books. I now felt completely validated as an artist and businessperson.

But the world was about to change, and sadly not for the better.

The terrorist attacks of September 11, 2001, rewrote the story of my professional partnership with my husband. The tragedy of that day left our country in social turmoil, and not many people made room in their lives or budgets for extravagances like stained glass, cornices, and window treatments. John and I closed our business.

It wasn't long before I began daydreaming possibilities for a new venture, and as clear as a vodka martini, straight up, it came to me: It was time to call my two, spirited sisters, Sue and Kathy. I reached for the phone . . .

CHAPTER EIGHT

Sue, the Matriarch

Sue here again. In this chapter, I'll focus on me. When I was about four years old, my only two siblings, Michael and Carole, pretended to call the police department to have me apprehended and sent away. I didn't think there was anything make believe about it. I thought I was minutes from being grabbed by big, scary men who would throw me into their big, scary car and drive me far away.

Michael picked up the phone and said in a very serious voice, "Hello? Police? May I speak to the department of terrible children who should be sent away?"

I screamed and tried to grab the phone from his hand. "Don't do it! Please don't send me away! I'll be a good girl!"

Mike continued into the phone, "*What's* that? This is my lucky day, because you have *three* open spots for rotten kids who disobey and need to be left in the back woods after midnight?"

What the heck did *that* mean? It sounded dark and terrifying.

"Uh huh, uh huh," Mike said, "I understand. Yes, one pair of shoes. You're sure she shouldn't be allowed to wear anything else when you put her in the police car? *Just* the shoes? Okay! See you in an hour!"

I hid behind the couch and cried for what seemed like hours, but it was probably no more than a few minutes. Mike and Carole grew bored and went outside to play. When I felt sure it was safe out there, I crept from behind the couch, found my mother, and told her everything.

Her response was, "Don't be such a baby. The police don't take children away. Your brother and sister are just teasing you." No hug, no calming words, no admonishing the offending siblings.

There was really no comfort to be found anywhere in those days, so by night I clutched my teddy bear, and by day I tried to be good—barely seen and not heard.

"Got over that pretty nicely, wouldn't you say? The 'trying to be good' thing? Seen and not heard?" Carole says.

I laugh but then say, "You two really traumatized me. You were supposed to look out for me. Good God, with two parents missing in action and two older siblings threatening to send me away, can you imagine what the world looked like through my little eyes? Where was I supposed to find any sense of security in the world?"

"Yeah, Carole. Scary babysitter sister," Kathy adds, sprinkling some levity on the moment.

We all sit in silence, and I know we're having one of those moments—one of those quiet pauses during which we try to grasp the enormity of it all, what happened to us, what we did do to survive it.

For me, memories like that stream by in a kind of fast-moving montage, as if I'm winding the wheel on an old-school microfiche machine looking for the news article I want to focus on. When I land on it, I look up and away, pulling the memory in and then alternating between letting myself remember every bit of it, down to the worst of it, and trying to make myself better by rationalizing that at least some good came of it, like fierce independence.

"I'm sorry about that, Sue," Carole says, looking deeply into my eyes. "That must have been awful for you. Mike and I should have been better to you."

Her apology makes me a bit teary. I don't know that any of us has spent much time apologizing for how we stuck it to each other in childhood, how we turned on each other during our daily struggle to survive. It feels good to hear Carole say this, but at the same time, I think we know apologies aren't necessary. We were all kids, all of us put upon, unguided, and unprotected. We found our way to each other in time and built it all up into something solid.

"Whatcha thinking about over there?" Kathy asks me.

I look away from the microfiche in my field of vision. "About how far we've come. About how we grew up pretty much without parents, but now it's as if I have two mothers. Two sister/mothers. It's as if the universe caught up and paid me back for what I'd been denied for so long."

Carole says, "I was thinking something like that, about how great that we bound together during the hotel years. I don't know if we would have survived it without joining forces like we did."

Kathy holds up both hands and studies them. "I was thinking it's weird my left thumb looks so different than my right. It's like I have the thumbs of two different people."

Carole lifts her phone to her face. "Hello, police? May I speak to the department of rotten kids?"

When I was young, I believed Aunt Diggie was the only person in the world who understood my fears, and as a result, she became my favorite human being. She was a caring, strong-willed woman who became an entrepreneur, and a female entrepreneur at that, way before it was cool. Her husband, Uncle Dixie, had been in a car accident that left him unable to work, so to support their family, Aunt Diggie made boxed lunches and drove around to construction sites, where she sold the food to hungry construction workers. This was in the late '50s, so I like to say my Aunt Diggie invented the food truck.

Aunt Diggie and Uncle Dixie owned a carpet store, which gave me my first look at running a business. I can still smell the carpets that filled their showroom, many of them massive, rolled up, and standing at attention along the walls like huge trees in a magical forest.

After teaching me how to greet customers, Aunt Diggie told me to follow her into the back office, where she said she was going to "show me a few things about bookkeeping."

As seriously as if she were talking to a forty-year-old, she said, "Now Susie, you always have to know how much money you have, so you must keep your books in order."

I had no idea what that meant, but I listened to everything she said and took in as much as I could.

She taught me how to keep the checkbook up to date, deposit money, and make sure it all balanced. All through the day, she said things like, "You're a smart girl with a great understanding of numbers, so you're going to be great at this. You'll be the first person I've ever trusted to be my bookkeeper." It was the first time in my life I'd heard anyone say I had anything to offer.

My aunt and uncle picked me up every other weekend, and I worked on their books as they kept me enthralled with stories of big sales and the joys of offering good customer service. In that setting, I felt grown up and extremely special for being the chosen one. I treasured those weekends.

But I was insecure about my feelings for Aunt Diggie. I was afraid my mother resented all the time I spent with my aunt and uncle, and I even secretly wished Aunt Diggie was my mother, an idea that made me feel both the joy of possibility and the shame of disloyalty.

Oh, what a cocktail of confusion those years were. When I was in my twenties, I was able to share with Mom how my time with Aunt Diggie had made me feel empowered, how it had helped build my confidence. Even when I explained to her I'd been saddled with the guilt of wishing to be away from my family home more than I was in it, Mom listened calmly and said, "You have nothing to feel guilty about. I'm grateful to Diggie because she saw that you're special, she saw your heart. There was something unique between you two, and I wish I could have been that for you."

Mom admitted that because she'd had to run in circles all day trying to keep up with the needs and demands of a bunch of kids and a high-maintenance husband, at the end of the day she had nothing left, no energy for sweet, quiet, one-on-one moments with her kids and no time to even think about how she was leaving them emotionally deprived.

That admission from my mother was a gift. In just a few

minutes of revelation, she relieved the angst I'd carried with me for years.

As I moved into my teenage years, I continued to spend time with Aunt Diggie, but my big sister Carole emerged as my most influential role model. Now several years beyond call-the-police stunts, I could see Carole had become beautiful, mature, intelligent, artistic, and very popular—everything I wanted to be.

As a teenager, I understood that being in a family with seven kids meant there wasn't much money for extras. So at the age of thirteen, I secured a job as an aide at a nursing home, and it suited me. I loved working with the older folks—bringing them treats and spending time just talking to them because they were lonely and had lots of great stories and wisdom to pass on to a wide-eyed country girl. They helped me understand that only I could make myself happy . . . it was nobody else's job.

By the time I was fifteen, Michael had moved out, and Carole followed soon after, so I was left to navigate the social waters of high school by myself. I had a great group of friends, and for a couple years, we did all the typical high school things: dances, parties, sleepovers, and falling in love.

My first love was kind, red-haired Denny, the type of boy who held a door open. It was a sweet love, and I was so starved for affection that every time we kissed and hugged, I felt I'd landed on a cloud in heaven. I wanted to marry him. I could barely wait to marry Denny. By the time I was a high school junior, I was counting the days to graduation after which I hoped to take off and start a life with my wonderful boyfriend, who was already out of high school.

Denny was great with the insides and outsides of cars, and one autumn afternoon he said he wanted to keep my Corvair overnight so he could paint it for me. That day he drove me home in the Corvair, and when we reached my house, we sat in the car for a moment as the car's engine idled.

"You're so pretty," Denny said, reaching to brush a lock of hair from the front of my face.

I said, "You don't have to say that. I'm just okay."

"You're more than pretty, Susie, you're very special, don't forget that, and you have a way of making others feel special. People look up to you."

I barely knew what to do with such kindness, so I just sat there with tears in my eyes.

He leaned forward and kissed me. "I'll see you tomorrow after school when I pick you up in your gorgeous car."

I opened the passenger door and got out. Denny started to drive away, but after several yards he stopped and called out, "You're going to make this world a better place, Susie. Take my word for it." Then he headed down the road, and I stood there watching until he was completely out of sight.

Those were the last words he ever said to me.

After school ended the next day, I waited for Denny in front of the building. But he didn't show up.

I had no way to contact him, so I ran home angry and asked my mother to lend me her car so I could find Denny and let him have it for stranding me at school. On my way to his house, I saw my car parked in front of a gas station, its front end completely smashed in. I slammed the brakes, jumped out of the car, and shouted at the gas station attendant, "That's my car! Where's the guy who was driving that car?"

The guy answered calmly, "I don't know where they took him, but I know he's dead."

Dead? This was Denny. There was nobody in the world more alive.

In that moment, I experienced what I think people refer to when they say, "Time stood still." I exploded in tears as disbelief and grief seared every inch of my body. I couldn't drive, couldn't think. I stood crying until the gas station attendant told me to sit down and suggested I call my mother.

While I waited for her to arrive, the attendant said, "It appeared the driver had an epileptic seizure and crashed into a telephone pole. He was killed instantly. I am very sorry."

My first thought was, I didn't know Denny had epilepsy. Then I tried to process that Denny was gone. I couldn't grasp it. It was too unreal. This had to be some horrible movie I was watching.

Then a cold emptiness washed over me as I realized my dreams had been destroyed. There would be no beautiful future for Denny and me. There was no more Denny.

In the days that followed, I existed in what felt like a heavily drugged state. The sympathy calls, the wake, the funeral—they're still a blank.

My family home remained an emotional wasteland, so I found no sympathy or understanding there and no one to help me navigate the bleak waters my life had become. When I tried to talk to Mom about my feelings, she brushed me off because there was always too much on her plate. So from my own mother, I received no solace or advice on how to move through the pain.

Eventually, my father told me it was time to focus on my future. In the middle of my senior year, he said, "I'm not paying for you to go to college, so you'd better look into becoming a secretary."

In those years, females were almost never directed toward management or entrepreneurship, so even though I'd taken a lot of business courses in high school, I always assumed that what I'd learned in those classes would benefit me as a secretary. I waited out the final months of high school, fully expecting to become some successful male's girl Friday.

But as my senior year was coming to an end, a representative from Eastern Airlines visited my high school to recruit new flight attendants. The job he described was social, called for someone quick on her feet, and would actually pay me to be out of Pennsylvania and far away from my father! This sounded promising!

The process of becoming an airline stewardess took several months of testing and interviews, which I aced, and I was accepted into the Eastern Airlines stewardess training program. My father agreed to pay the tuition of $350. Woohoo! I was on my way!

Then two men put their heads together to crush my dream.

I'd been dating a local guy named Ralph, whom my father-approved of because Ralph was a welder—"a real man's man" Dad had said. Ralph lived with and supported his mother, which to me proved he had a good heart. He was a quiet, intelligent guy with great mechanical and engineering skills he'd developed in technical school. His engineering aptitude made him even more appealing to my self-serving father, who was hatching another of his half-assed business ideas, in this case one that called for engineering skills. Ralph was enamored with my Dad and believed his ideas would make us all rich.

As Ralph and I spent more time together, I began to wake up to our incompatibility. The biggest point of difference was he had no interest in leaving Collegeville—ever. But I wanted out. Now. So one autumn evening before Ralph and I headed to the local drive-in theater, I decided to be bluntly honest with him.

"Ralph, I know you're hoping for more, but I'm going to Boston to train to be a stewardess, and after that, I'll be traveling all the time. I'm so sorry, but I don't think this is going to work between us. I leave in January."

At first, he was quiet and looked kind of sad. I thought he might be trying to figure out the most graceful way to wish me well. But he dropped down on one knee and said, "I don't want you to leave, Sue. I love you. Will you marry me?"

For the first time in my life—and probably the last—I was speechless. It broke my heart to break his heart, but after I could gather my thoughts, I blurted, "I am in *no way* ready to be a wife. There's so much I want to do before I marry, Ralph. I'm about to fly away."

What I didn't know was that the "men" in my life had already put their heads together behind my back. Ralph had already asked my father for my hand in marriage, and I'm pretty sure my dad's response was something like, "One more out of the house? She's all yours!" For him, Ralph's plan hit two targets: Dad would have one less dependent *and* he wouldn't have to pay for my tuition. But by refusing Ralph's proposal, I'd botched Dad's plan for a rosy next chapter, so he retaliated by refusing to pay my tuition and by rescinding his approval for my enrollment to stewardess training.

I was a naïve, eighteen-year-old girl who thought she had no choice, so in 1972, just eight months out of high school, I became a wife.

We were married in March, and then I moved into the ramshackle house Ralph shared with his widowed mother. As a wedding gift, my father helped Ralph install indoor plumbing, and I think it's fitting that for a very long time I thought of my father every time I flushed a toilet.

After my dad's latest business scheme failed (surprise!), Ralph found a job as a mechanic. I'd been working the front desk at a loan company and was moderately satisfied there because I was learning a lot about finance and the importance of good customer service. But Ralph and I just weren't getting along—we were always arguing about money—and I think we both knew how truly incompatible we were. Then, two years into our marriage, I did what lots of young dummies do when their marriages are mediocre and they're saddled with money problems. I got pregnant.

Despite our financial hardship, Ralph was thrilled he was going to be a father, and I foolishly believed a child could save a marriage.

We named our son Ralph, and when I held my baby in my arms, I saw in his eyes something I'd never seen before: undeniable, untarnished, unconditional love. To me, little Ralph was perfect, but his father saw only his son's imperfections. My boy was born with a cleft palate and cleft lip, a condition that called for many surgeries, the first of which was performed when he was only six weeks old. Because my husband had also been born with a cleft lip, like his mother and grandmother before him, he was wracked with guilt he'd passed the condition onto his son. Years later, genetic testing revealed that I, too, carried the gene for a cleft palate. But the guilt of "handicapping" his son tormented Ralph, and that guilt morphed into anger he directed at me.

One night I arrived home at around 10:30 p.m. to find my husband waiting at the front door.

"Where the hell have you been?" he asked.

"I told you I was going to bingo with Mom," I answered and tried to walk past him into the house.

Smack! He slapped the side of my head and shouted, "Bingo doesn't last until ten at night! You're a liar!"

This kind of encounter made me sick for so many reasons. It was humiliating to be abused by the man I'd married and had a child with. It sent my mind back to childhood, to the god-awful days of listening to my father terrorize my mother. And it forced me to realize I was going to be a divorced woman. I was going to be a single parent.

I'd saved just about enough money for young Ralph and me to make it on our own, but not quite, so I moved in with my parents, despite how clearly my father didn't want me there. He liked Ralph and blamed me for the separation, but in a rare show of strength, my mother told him to leave me alone. Then she added, "And don't you ever belittle her in front of her son."

I felt the pride in my eyes as I beamed at her.

When I tucked my two-year-old son in on that first night back in my childhood home, he said, "I'll take care of you, Mommy. I won't let anybody hit you again."

His sweet, protective words made me feel sick. I'd tried so hard to shelter him from the conflict in my marriage. But my very young child had already experienced the same kind of heartache I'd grown up with. I vowed to never let him experience another day of it.

The only good thing about being back home was both my parents doted on my son. Mom and Ralph spent hours playing games, and Dad took him to basketball games. They were far better grandparents than parents, and as I watched them gently interacting with their grandson, I sensed they were taking advantage of a second chance.

Every other week, I drove Ralph into Philadelphia for medical evaluations. The drive to Children's Hospital took a little over an hour, and the appointments averaged three to four hours long. We met with plastic surgeons, dentists, and speech and hearing specialists who evaluated his growth so they could map the surgeries that would be spread out over the next eighteen years. Ralph's father was usually working during these appointments, so for those I was on my own, but he saw little Ralph every week from Friday night and into Saturday and sometimes spent time with our son during the week.

My son and I spent long days, just the two of us, at the cleft palate clinic in Philadelphia's Children's Hospital, and during that time, we forged a bond deeper than anything I'd ever experienced with another person. I don't believe I'd have known true happiness if I didn't have my son. Aside from my siblings, he's the first person I trusted to love me unconditionally, and the bond he and I formed made me start believing in myself. I began to view myself as a good mother, and that perspective helped me believe I could be good at a lot more. In a sense, my son gave *me* life. But oh, how very tired I was. When I told my parents I was exhausted from all the driving and the emotional weight of it all, my father said, "If you'd been smart enough to stay with your husband, you wouldn't be on your own."

After five relatively difficult months, I'd saved enough money to rent my own place, the first place that ever felt like mine, just mine! It was a beautiful, two-bedroom apartment with a kitchen big enough to accommodate my emerging cooking and baking skills. And now that I was single again, I started going out with my crew of girlfriends on the Fridays when Ralph was with his father. I dated now and then, but I'd been so disillusioned by marriage, walking the aisle again sounded about as appealing as a chocolate martini. Then one night on a softball field, things changed.

Softball had always been a part of my life, whether I was playing, watching, or coaching. And I was excited to dive back into the softball culture, so I formed a softball team with my sisters and friends. When a field is full of twenty-something females wearing short shorts and bending over to pick up balls, the bleachers quickly fill with men. Lots of guys from the tavern were happy to hang around and cheer, and I ended up casually dating a few of them, but I rarely introduced young Ralph to my dates because I couldn't bear the idea of my boy attaching to someone I wasn't sure about.

There was one spectator who cheered louder than the rest when I made a good play. Who is this guy, I wondered. Then, with the push of a friend, on an August evening in 1979, I put on my dancing shoes and went on my first date with John.

When John picked me up, I introduced him to my mother who had come over to babysit Ralph, now four years old. Ralph, who sat in the middle of the living room playing with Legos, looked up at John and said, "I know you. You yell at my mom's baseball games!"

John laughed and said, "Yes, your mom is a very good ball player, don't you think?"

"Yes, she's the best," said Ralph. "Have fun." Then he turned his attention back to his toys.

John and I went to a movie, followed by dinner and dancing at a local Mexican restaurant. It was a long night that allowed us time to get to know each other. He was relatively quiet but not shy; he didn't talk a lot, but when he did, he always said something worth hearing. What resonated with me most that night was how he spoke of fatherhood.

He said, "I have two children, but I don't see them very often because my divorce wasn't very civil. My kids are all I think about day and night. It's really hard to be away from them."

I found his honesty refreshing and his love for his children very appealing. After dating John regularly for two months, I felt comfortable telling my son about the relationship. I took Ralph to McDonalds and explained the man who had picked me up that night, the one he'd seen cheering for me at the softball games, was a nice man and that we'd become friends. "I'm going to spend time with him, so you'll be seeing more of him. Is that okay with you?" I asked.

Ralph said, "Is he your boyfriend? Do you kiss him?"

I laughed. "Yes, sometimes we kiss, but we're just getting to know each other. I want to know how you feel about the idea."

He looked up from his hamburger and said, "I'm good. Can I get a dessert?"

John and Ralph became friends quickly. They spent hours together tossing the football around and fishing on the Schuylkill River. John introduced Ralph to all his favorite cowboy movies, and I thought my heart might melt one afternoon when I overheard the two of them playing cowboy games in the next room. I heard Ralph say, "Put 'em up! This is your last chance! I have my trusty pistol!"

I peeked through the doorway and saw John with his

hands up. He said, "Hey, partner, why do you want to shoot me?"

Ralph had one hand on his fake holster and the other pointed at John. "You're a bad cowboy because you robbed the bank!"

John said, "Not me partner." Then he pretended to grab his gun. "You put *your* hands up!"

I continued to watch in silent delight from the kitchen.

"You can't say that!" shouted Ralph. He tapped his head and shouted, "I'm the good guy because I'm the guy wearing the white hat!"

Then the two laughed and ran around the room having a fake shootout.

Ralph and John became much more than play buddies. John became a crucial source of support during Ralph's doctor visits, and he was always the first to visit us after one of Ralph's many facial reconstruction surgeries.

Around Christmastime, John and I had been seeing each other for five months. Just before Christmas, Ralph was scheduled to have another major reconstructive facial surgery, and he opened up to John about some of his fears. Ralph never complained about having surgery, but as he grew older, he became self-conscious about looking different from other kids.

One afternoon, the three of us sat in my living room, and Ralph said to John, "I don't like going to the hospital all the time, but I guess it's the only way I'll ever get to look like other kids."

John responded, "You do look like other kids. You just happen to be more handsome. Do they tease you?"

Ralph said, "Some kids say my mouth looks funny and ask why I have these marks over my mouth, but I tell them I go to the hospital to get them fixed."

John said, "You're lucky because you have great doctors and

a whole lot of people who love you." Then he leaned closer to Ralph and said quietly, "It's important you don't compare yourself to other kids because they might feel bad they aren't as special as you. Do you know what I mean?"

Ralph's eyes brightened. "Yes," he said. "I don't want other kids to feel sad. I'll never tease anybody."

That's when I knew I could really love this man.

Philadelphia Children's Hospital is an extraordinary place where I was able to stay in my son's room after every operation. The pre-Christmas operation was his sixth in four years. This time surgeons would work to connect his top gum, which was currently divided into three sections, and close the gap beneath his nose. Everything went well, and John was the first person to visit Ralph and me after the surgery.

John showed up at the hospital with a little stuffed replica of the green Philadelphia Phanatic, the mascot for the Philadelphia Phillies, and walked into Ralph's room wearing a big smile. But he wasn't ready for the sight of my little boy lying there with a bruised, swollen face. Ralph wasn't bandaged, but he was black and blue, barely recognizable, and the sight of him seemed to take John's breath away. John walked closer to the edge of Ralph's bed.

Ralph greeted John brightly and asked, "Can you give me a mirror so I can see how the doctor did?"

Ralph's innocence nearly knocked the air out of a grown man. John asked if we could step into the hallway where he took deep breaths and asked me what to do. I told him to change the subject and ask Ralph what he wanted for Christmas.

Back in the room, John asked Ralph, "What do you want Santa to bring you this year?"

Ralph took a moment, then replied, "Could you marry my mom so you can live with us? Mom said only married people can live together."

There it was, the most perfect marriage proposal—set up by my four-year-old son. With tears in his eyes, John agreed we should marry. As the three of us hugged and John and I cried, Ralph added, "It would also be great if Santa would bring me a bike."

That's my boy!

On Christmas Eve, 1979, John and I were married by a justice of the peace. That Christmas, Ralph got a stepdad *and* a new bike, and to this day he still claims credit for our happiness.

The day Ralph was born was the happiest day of my life. The day my son orchestrated a proposal from a hospital bed was the second.

A new marriage brought with it a whole new family. Ralph and I were welcomed by his new grandparents, aunts, uncles, and cousins, and I drank in the healthy family energy. John's previous marriage had ended in a difficult divorce that prevented his children from immediately joining our new family. Ralph and I moved into John's home, which was directly across the street from his parents'. The proximity allowed Ralph to spend time with his new grandparents after school. And every day that passed, I felt happier and more secure as life with John exceeded all my dreams of what it meant to be a family.

The years passed, and we continued to be happy. On our tenth anniversary, John and I fulfilled the promise we'd made to each other five years earlier to renew our vows when

John's children (who we rarely saw) could be a part of our celebration. As planned, my fourteen-year-old son walked me down the aisle and gave me away to John. As I walked, I said a prayer of gratitude for every choice I'd made in my life that had led me to the man waiting for me at the end of the aisle on this glorious day of remarriage.

That fall, I was laid off after fourteen years of working for Fleming Foods as an administrative assistant, but I found a new job as an operations manager with a small computer company. Our little family once again settled into the blissful security of routine.

Unfortunately, the next few years were very painful. My sister-in-law, Nancy, passed away after battling cancer; then shortly afterward, we lost my mother-in-law, Pearl, the woman who had warmed my life by genuinely welcoming my son and me into her family. John's father was now elderly and suffering from several health issues, so although John was still about six years from retirement age, he ended his career early to take care of his father.

While the death of a sibling and a parent forever changes a family dynamic and sometimes even a person's perspective on life, for most people even those kinds of losses don't compare to the death of a child. Later that same year, we mourned the untimely death of John's son, Johnny. And when John and I thought we could handle no more grief, John's father passed away.

It was the year 2000, and Ralph had found the person he wanted to spend the rest of his life with . . . a smart, funny woman named Susan (nice work, kid). John and I did our best to heal from all the recent losses by both focusing on the joy of the wedding ahead and acknowledging our gratitude for all the other blessings we had, including our rock-solid marriage.

Ralph helped enormously by moving into his grandfather's house so he could be there to help with the clearing out and cleaning up. He also helped at the funeral as a pallbearer and as a strong shoulder for John, offering the kind of emotional support John had always given him.

A few weeks later, Ralph and Susan were married in an utterly joyful event in New York, and that lovefest enveloped our family in exactly the kind of hopeful happiness we needed.

John and I both retired, and as we were trying to figure out what we wanted to do next, Carole asked if we'd like to help her and her John with their design business. We happily accepted, but a year later came the terrorist attacks of September 11, 2001, when life in the United States permanently changed, and Carole's business collapsed.

She dismantled her business as we and the rest of America tried to figure out how to function in a country that had once seemed invulnerable. John and I spent about two years huddling close at home and considering our professional options.

Then I got a phone call from Carole.

CHAPTER NINE

Kathy, the Delegator

Kathy here. I find it interesting how birth order can shape a person's viewpoint. In my family's totem pole, my older sisters count from the top to down, while I count from the bottom up. (I wonder if my older siblings actually view themselves as "up there" somewhere.) Studies show that younger siblings are more likely to report being funnier than their older siblings—would their siblings agree?—and younger children are said to be more cooperative than older children. But *please*—anybody who grew up with older brothers and sisters knows this brand of "cooperation" is usually exacted by threats, hazing, and generally terrorizing the littler ones into submission.

Given my spot in the lineup, I guess I'm supposed to be a funny cooperator? That's really funny—the idea of anybody labeling me "cooperative." I'm actually pretty good at getting *other* people to cooperate. When you're a natural delegator, that's your role, am I right? *Somebody* has to pilot the ship.

Living in a tiny house with seven children was difficult, especially for someone in the number five spot. If you don't happen to come from a veritable football team of a family, imagine if you will the madness likely to ensue in a household with too many bodies and not enough money, not enough space, not enough parental energy, very few boundaries, and not much sanity. It's a circus and often not the fun kind. Sure, *sometimes* it's the circus of cotton candy, high wire dazzle, and poodles in tutus prancing on hind legs. But more often it's the circus that rolls into town on a dark, creepy, gray, tornado-watch-looking night; the circus that makes newspaper headlines because the elephant has had enough of the ringmaster's bullshit prodding and whipping, so he crashes through the barriers and tramples the audience.

As number five in our circus, two of my primary goals were to get more attention and avoid having to wear the god-awful hand-me-down clothes my older siblings had already worn down to thin sheets of fabric sadness. What helped me immensely in the pursuit of these goals was being Daddy's little sweetheart. Not quite sure how I landed that gig, but who looks a Daddy-sized gift horse in the mouth? Carole and Sue figure my scoring a little tiara had something to do with their being ahead of me and therefore old enough to recognize and sometimes even call attention to what a slime bucket he was. Apparently, I was too young for such disdain (Not to worry; I caught up.), so I reaped the benefits of my ignorance.

Of course, being a father's favorite (especially when that father is a horrible person) doesn't endear a girl to her siblings.

But rather than try to work my way into their hearts, I thought, screw it—let's have some fun. One version of that fun involved singing at dinnertime.

As dinner wound down and we waited for dessert, I often raised my hand and said, "Daddy, I have a song to sing, and after I'm done, I think everybody else should sing for you, too."

I then stood behind Dad and sang my favorite song of the day, which was usually something patriotic, booming, and obnoxious, like, "The Star-Spangled Banner." Once I finished, I'd smile and bow and say how much I was looking forward to hearing the next verses from my siblings. Dad was all in! He directed each of them to learn the next verse of whatever song I'd sung that night, and the following evening they had to stand up and belt out a verse.

I found this spectacle utterly entertaining (although, the Von Trapp family we were not), and having been a serviceman, my father was delighted by the whole nationalistic she-bang. Safe to say, my siblings detested me for it.

My dad wasn't the only adult to fall victim to my charms. Our elderly neighbors, Mr. and Mrs. Croner, had two grown children who'd moved away, and I suspect they liked having my kid energy around.

One Saturday typical of many others, I wandered over to the Croner's backyard when Mrs. Croner was hanging her wash. I said, "It's a beautiful day, and you shouldn't have to do all that yourself. Let me help."

While handing her clothespins, I told her stories about how I was treated at home. "Mrs. Croner, you just can't believe how mean they are to me, and I think it's because they're jealous of the time I spend with you and Mr. Croner. It's not my fault you're so nice to me."

I explained how much I loved singing and that my sisters and brothers picked on me because I wanted to sing "America the Beautiful" after dinner. Mr. Croner was an army veteran, so both the Croners highly approved of my patriotic efforts and viewed my siblings as little brats.

The Croners regularly invited me over for dinner and made special meals for me, usually pork chops and mashed potatoes, which are my favorites to this day. Many times they took me on their shopping trips and bought *me* new clothes! Of course, I loved all the other gifts they gave me as well—the dolls, a basket for my bike, the new boots, and all the other little special things that were just for me and not for any of the circus freaks who lived in my house. Sometimes, on sunny Sunday afternoons, Mr. and Mrs. Croner even took me for a ride in their shiny, red Cadillac convertible. It never mattered to me where we went because the best part of the trip—by far—was waving to my siblings as we rode away so slowly they could surely read my lips, "No Cadillac for you."

Of all my siblings, I looked up to Sue the most. She's three years older than I and was always getting in trouble with Dad, which I thought was hilarious. I was often with her when it happened, so I witnessed the crimes and the punishments in real time. Usually, she'd be grounded either for talking back or for slamming a door. It probably didn't help that I tattled on her.

I know, not cool.

But she launched some revenge my way—don't you worry.

One summer evening, Sue and I were out for a ride when she said, "Something is wrong, I think we've run out of gas. I can't leave the car, of course, so you're going to have to walk to the gas station. Come back with at least a gallon."

As I walked down the road, I heard the honking of a horn as a familiar car zoomed by me with Sue waving at me, mouthing something. Did she just say, "No Corvair for you?"

Sue pulled plenty of stunts like that, but I never really minded because I would have done just about anything to spend time with my big sister. When she turned eighteen, she left home to get married, and I suspect I was the one who missed her most.

By the time I was fifteen, I'd grown up enough to realize I should stop putting energy into terrorizing my siblings and instead start making money. My first job was with the Collegeville Costume Factory, where I packed the finished Halloween costumes into boxes. I was paid based on how many boxes I completed. Before long, I started packing twice as many boxes per hour as I'd done in my first week, but that meant I was making too much money for the costume factory's liking, so they moved me to a different position and paid me by the hour. I learned an important business lesson on that job—I'd be successful in any job I held because I was committed to finding the most efficient way to complete tasks. I knew, even at fifteen, that I wasn't going to be held back by companies that wouldn't compensate my greatness.

The summer after high school, I traveled to Ocean City, NJ, for Senior Week with three of my closest friends. One day during the trip, a cute guy came down to the water and started talking to me as we rode the waves together. I don't know if it was the salt air, the smell of the coconut sunblock, or the boy himself, but I was smitten. As we chatted, I was so busy imagining our future together I didn't see the enormous wave about to hit me. The wave crashed into me, and as I regained my composure, I realized the force of the water had yanked my bikini top off. I was mortified when this sweet guy I'd just met grabbed my bikini top and carried it back to me like a knight in bathing trunks. I'm pretty sure it was the moment he decided I was the girl for him. Lucky for me, he wasn't a leg man.

Later that day, Jack said, "How about we take a walk on the beach and stop for a burger?"

"Why not?" I said.

During that walk, I learned Jack was my best friend's cousin, was headed into his senior year at Glassboro College in New Jersey, and was spending his summer working at a liquor store close to home. I loved his silly sense of humor, and as we chatted about our families and dreams for the future, we both realized something special was happening.

I had already secured a part-time job at a map company as an apprentice draftsperson. I'd also enrolled in business classes at Montgomery County Community College, so I was going to be busy once I got home from my beach vacation.

Jack and I stayed in touch, and our summer thing grew into a serious romance. I knew the two-hour drive Jack made each way so we could be together was tiring, so I was always ready to serve him delicious meals, like lasagna, beef stroganoff, and veal parmesan. Good food was definitely the way to Jack's heart, but he didn't know Sue was the one who'd been cooking those meals. She thought Jack was a good catch and wanted to help me lure him with food, so she prepared the meals at her house and delivered them before Jack's arrival. I realized this was a hell of a bait-and-switch because I had no idea how to cook anything, but all's fair in love.

For the next two years, our relationship grew stronger and stronger as we spent our weekends hiking and camping in Canada and riding bikes through Valley Forge Park. Every day we spent together ended with a sweet kiss.

During one Friday visit, Jack and I were about to pick my brother David up from football practice, and I could tell there was something on his mind. Thinking he might be ready to tell me the traveling back and forth was too much, I asked him, "Are you okay? You seem preoccupied."

Jack grinned, reached behind the driver's seat, and presented me with a beautiful diamond ring.

"Happy Birthday!" he said.

A diamond ring for a birthday present? Well, Jack wasn't a conventional guy, so I took it as his version of a marriage proposal. Two years and countless meals later, Jack and I were married.

We tied the knot on a beautiful Saturday in late June. My sister bridesmaids were dressed in sexy peach gowns with matching floppy hats, and my best friend, Jack's cousin Patty, was my maid of honor in blue. It was a glorious day that led to a festive evening of friends and family dancing and drinking at a local firehouse. Dad had offered to pay for the reception, so near the end of the evening, the caterer handed my father the bill.

Dad reviewed the invoice and turned to me.

"Sorry," he said. "I don't have any money to pay for this."

I was stunned and mortified in front of my new husband. What had happened to my being his favorite?

Thankfully Jack said, "No worries, K, we'll take care of it. Let's enjoy the rest of our special day."

Neither Jack nor I had money with us, but the caterer was kind enough to let us pay in four installments.

For what was left of the evening, I pretended my father didn't exist. When I passed him by the bar or was anywhere near him on the dance floor, he was a ghost to me. I was done with him.

While my love life made me blissfully happy, my job at the map-making office did not. I wasn't getting paid much, and there seemed no room for growth. I saw it was time to move on to something more challenging and lucrative. Carole worked at Weston Solutions, a company that worked on projects to help the environment, and she said she could get me a job there. Even though Carole was my sister, I didn't know her well because she was six years older than I and had married when I was only twelve.

When she told me she'd gotten me an interview, I said, "Thank you so much, I can't believe you trust me to do the job."

Carole said, "You're my sister. I know you can do anything you set your mind to."

The interview went well, and I was offered a position as an apprentice in the draft room. I had no experience in drafting—I didn't even know how to properly read a ruler—but was young and fearless. I was also married to a drafting teacher, so I accepted.

Jack gave me a couple of quick lessons before I started the job. The company put piping into the walls of new constructions, and Jack taught me how to use a scale to understand the different elements of a mechanical drawing, plus enough drafting terms that I didn't walk into the office the next day sounding like a dummy. I knew how lucky I was: Jack was a fabulous teacher, electrician, and carpenter. As long as I've known him, he's been able to design, fix, invent—he really is a Jack of all trades, master of all.

Carole had warned me that the guys in the drafting room were a bunch of characters who constantly played jokes on each other and said I'd have to show them they couldn't mess with me. On my first day, I was introduced to all fourteen of the draftsmen, and a guy named Bobby pulled a squirt gun out of his desk drawer and blasted me with it as he said, "Welcome to the jungle."

The other guys giggled.

I dried my face with my sleeve, grinned, and said, "Just so

you know, I don't get mad, I get even." The room went silent. Not so much as a giggle from any of them.

On Bobby the Prankster's birthday, I made him a cake with a special design feature.

"Here you go, Buddy!" I said, presenting him with a beautiful chocolate cake with chocolate frosting. Then I handed him a knife and said, "Dig in!"

He held up the cake, sniffed it, tilted it, and examined it from every possible angle.

"Trust issues?" I giggled.

One of the other guys said, "Cut it, you wimp! I want a bite of that thing."

After another minute of cake inspection, Bobby seemed satisfied his birthday surprise hadn't been poisoned and wasn't hiding anything sharp, so he began to carve a slice. When the knife made it to the center of the cake, it hit the spring I'd embedded, launched the cake up, and—*Splat!*—right into Bobby's face.

For a second, the guys in the office were stunned. Then all at once, the room exploded in laughter. From what they'd all told me, nobody had ever gotten even with Bobby, but I was committed to becoming a legend.

A guy like Bobby wasn't one to let a cake in the face go unanswered, so on my twenty-first birthday, as I worked at my desk, a handsome stranger dressed in a nice suit and carrying a briefcase approached me and asked, "Are you Kathy?"

"Yes," I said, although I had a feeling I'd regret it.

He opened the briefcase, pressed an enormous pie into my face, and walked out of the office. Again, the office erupted in laughter.

And on it went for three years, prank after prank.

All their silliness aside, those guys made great effort to help me learn. But I wasn't long for the drafting room; I had no plans to attend college to study drafting, so it was time to move on.

The wife of one of my drafting coworkers was a sales rep for a microfiche company and

wanted to go out on her own. She asked if I wanted to be her partner in a microfiche business.

"I'll manage sales, and you can handle operations," she said.

I agreed.

Our company, Micro Mobile, filmed a company's files, then stored them on 3 x 5 microfiche cards. Within a year we had six people working for us and were doing extremely well, but something new was about to change my life again.

Because everything was going well for Jack and me, both financially and personally, we decided it was time to build our own home. Jack was born to build and build he did. Just six months after he'd started the project, we moved into the house that Jack built. Then two months later, I had some news for my husband.

After confirming my suspicion with a drugstore test, I walked into our living room and said, "Jack, I'm pregnant."

He broke down in tears.

Baffled and bit nervous, I said, "J, are you angry? Are you sad? Do you think we aren't ready?"

He said, "I didn't know if *you* were ready. This is a dream come true. Yes, I'm ready. We're ready."

Eight months later our unborn child very adamantly announced a desire to enter the world. Jack and I lived twenty miles from the hospital I was most comfortable with, so I knew we had to be ready to go the moment I felt a twinge of labor pains. We'd gone through six weeks of birthing classes, but nobody had prepared us for how fast we needed to get to the hospital in time to avoid a passenger-seat birth. It was my first time going into labor, but something told me this show was going to be a very fast one. I felt the first pains and screamed, "Jack! It's time! And I mean, *now!*"

Thankfully, it was a clear morning, and weather wasn't an issue. For the next forty minutes, with hands clenched in the ten and two positions and eyes locked on the road ahead, Jack darted around slow drivers and zipped through yellow lights. About every five minutes, I had the urge to push, but I forced myself to hold on until we made it to the hospital.

The baby was moving but not really kicking. It was like having really bad gas pain I couldn't do anything with. Nearly breathless himself, Jack kept telling me to breathe and do my "hoots and houts." As he directed me to hoot, I shouted, "Just get me there, or you're going to deliver this baby on the side of the road!"

My pains were coming only two minutes apart as Jack screeched us up to the front of the hospital. I got out of the car and lumbered my way toward the front door as Jack took off to park. Back then, we didn't have cell phones, and all I could think about was how stupid we'd been not to call the doctor before we left the house.

As I approached the front door, my water broke and I yelled to no one in particular, "My water just broke! I need some help!"

My mom had told me that since it was my first pregnancy, after the contractions started, I'd probably still have a long way to go, but the way I felt, I thought I'd almost have the little one in the parking lot.

I waddled my way through the packed hospital lobby and straight to the head of the line. It was a very busy morning, the lobby filled with lots of visitors coming and going, but there wasn't a nurse in sight, nobody at the counter, either. Now I was starting to panic and wondering where the hell Jack was. It was all beginning to feel a bit surreal. Where was everybody?

Contractions and fear cranked up my adrenaline, and I shouted, again, to no one and everyone, "Can somebody help me? I'm having a baby right now!"

Bizarre as it sounds, this desperate plea still didn't score me any attention from medical professionals. Okay assholes, I thought. Let's see you ignore this! In the middle of the hospital lobby, I yelled, "Fuck you all!" and started stripping off my clothes.

First, I kicked off my shoes, then pulled off my pants and underwear, and just before I'd wrestled my top over my head, a nurse walked—didn't run, *walked*—out from behind double doors pushing a wheelchair.

She positioned the chair under my bare butt and said, "Lady, because this is your first child, I'm sure we have plenty of time."

How the hell did she know that? I was the one having the baby, and I knew it was happening immediately, so I screeched, "This kid is coming out right now so move it!"

With only moderate enthusiasm, she wheeled me into the prep room, where the nurse who helped me onto an exam table gasped, "The baby is crowning!"

Now that I had somebody's attention, I was whisked to a delivery room where the lights hadn't even been turned on yet. By some miracle, my obstetrician arrived and caught the baby approximately seven minutes after I was settled onto a delivery table.

To make that medical comedy of errors even more frenetic, Jack missed the entire delivery because he was held up filling out paperwork and then he pushed the wrong elevator button and ended up on the wrong floor. The poor guy was running in panic from room to room until he finally found his way to the maternity ward, and he stepped into the delivery room just as the doctor handed our new baby to the nurse, who placed him on my chest and said, "Mr. and Mrs. Lanyon, you have a beautiful baby boy."

The expression on Jack's face when he saw his son for the first time was one of the most wonderful things I've ever seen. It was like a combination of joy and some kind of beautiful heartbreak. Jack had been adopted in infancy, and he was now gazing at the first blood relation he'd ever known. The significance of it all made me weep. It was a glorious day.

Sue was the first person I called with the news. She picked up the phone and I said, "I had the baby! We have a boy!"

Sentimental Sue said, "You son-of-a-bitch. We're having your shower today!"

Once everyone realized I couldn't attend my meticulously planned surprise baby shower, we volunteered Jack to dash to Debbie's apartment in my place. Jack didn't want to leave us at the hospital but knew he had to step up to gather all the baby gifts our friends and relatives had so generously chosen for us.

Later, Sue and Debbie told me Jack had been so slow opening the gifts his mother finally said, "Jackie, get away from there or this roomful of women is going to kill you—opening gifts one piece of tape at a time." She grabbed the back of his chair and said, "Out. I'm taking over. Go see your son and wife."

Happy to be released from unwrapping duty, Jack headed

back to the hospital and fulfilled his promise to bring me a piece of the cake from the shower and a little jug of martinis. Oh, how I'd missed being able to drink a martini!

My sisters, family, and friends supplied everything we needed to fill the beautiful nursery Jack had built so perfectly, and even before we took the baby home, they went to our house and set everything up for us. Then, three days after I'd almost deposited a newborn on the floor of a hospital lobby, we were on our way home with our beautiful baby boy, Beau. I think Jack and I sat and stared at him for the first four or five hours until he woke up and we started the job of being parents.

After four weeks of new motherhood, I went back to the office. My return was met with the news that the company was low on funds, which our finance guy discovered when my partner was out sick. He found she'd been writing checks to a bogus account, then directing the funds to her personal account. When I confronted her, she didn't deny it. Even her husband had no idea the sleazy crap she'd been up to, and I agreed not to tell him if she bought me out of my interest in the company. She agreed, and I got the hell out of there.

Three months later, I heard they closed the business. But my faith in the idea of justice was renewed when I heard her husband had found out about her deceit and divorced her.

Two years later, Jack and I welcomed a daughter into our lives with a near repeat of the delivery experience I'd had with Beau. Danielle arrived two weeks early and after a mere thirty minutes of labor. This time Jack was present for the delivery, and once again, his eyes filled with tears at the sight of his new child. Now with two small children to take care of, I chose to stay home and put my professional life on hold.

But some of us aren't built to be full-time, stay-at-home moms. Six months after leaving the work force, I jumped back into it when I secured a job as a word processor operator for Alco Standard Corporation.

As Jack and I were happily rolling along in our careers, our kids were growing up and becoming interested in sports. Attending their games and helping them develop as athletes became a significant part of our lives because it gave us a great way to spend time with our kids.

By the time Danielle turned five, Beau was already playing baseball, and I decided it was time to enlist my daughter in a local softball league. The team needed a coach, so I volunteered, but the league was small and needed a lot more girls involved if it was going to become successful. I also volunteered to become the Girls Softball Commissioner so I could crusade for more young girls to become involved in sports. In my first year as commissioner, we recruited enough girls to fill four teams, and the second year we doubled to eight teams. In our third year, we had twelve teams.

Ever a delegator, I enlisted Debbie and Sue to be my assistant coaches for Danielle's team. I was the head coach who dealt with the parents, Debbie taught the girls the basics of the game, and Sue coddled the girls, so, of course, she was the one they all loved. Even though ours was a young team full of novice players, our team ended up winning the league that year.

As my children grew, so did our commitment to their sports. Beau played football, basketball, and baseball. Danielle played basketball and softball and was a cheerleader. Jack and I attended all their games, which was really important to me. Those were very busy years, but despite our busy schedules, Jack and I made sure every night all four of us sat down to dinner and talked about what was going on in our lives. Our family life was divine.

"Wait," says Carole. "You're saying you don't plunk your kids down on an indoor picnic table in assigned order and make them sing patriotic songs?"

We're all sitting around the memoir table drinking tea. Sue slides the laptop a few inches away from her and says, "You don't make them wait until ten at night to eat? Jack doesn't need to be dragged out of the bar for dinner?"

"Not out of bars," I say. "Only up from the basement workshop. That man could spend a day and a half building a train engine and at no point think about food."

"You did well, kid," says Carole. "You picked a good one."

"I did," I tell her. Then I pause for a moment and stare into my teacup, as if there's an answer to be found there. "I wonder why I got so lucky. You both ended up with good guys, but I wonder why I didn't have to go through a painful first marriage."

Sue says, "Are you forgetting something? You were the golden child. You had a lot of good luck in childhood, and you probably taught yourself to expect good things. Maybe you manifest it, like a self-fulfilling prophecy."

"Do you hear that, Jack?" I say into the air. "Sue is saying I manifested you."

Sue smiles. "Something like that. And the critical part is that you believed you deserved a Jack."

Within the arena of our outrageous childhood, I realize I was a lucky one, and I reaped the benefits. Dad did favor me, despicable parent that he was. And how extraordinary that my wonderful sisters have never resented me for it.

For thirty-three years, I continued to work at Veritiv, which was the company Unisource Worldwide eventually morphed into. I loved my career, and at the height of my responsibilities there, I managed the technical support team and the IT assets at all the company's facilities. When I was ready, I retired with full benefits. But it wasn't long before I was drumming the table trying to decide what to do next. Fortunate for me, Carole had already thought of that.

CHAPTER TEN

To understand how our relationship as sisters and friends *and* our dreams of being entrepreneurs evolved into a business, we should first revisit how we've become so close. A big part of the equation is food. Food always has and always will play an extremely important role in our lives. We love to cook, we love to entertain, we love to innovate, and we love to eat. Cooking for people and serving them food makes them happy, and it makes us happy. What could be better than building a business around that?

Because we've spent season after holiday after year after year planning and executing all the details, tiny and enormous, that go with putting together themed parties, holiday spreads, summer cookouts, and birthday soirees, we finally realized we were practicing teamwork, delegation, and compromise—massively important elements of a solid business team. Without being conscious of it, we were pouring the concrete for the skyscrapers that would line our future.

It certainly hasn't hurt that we have the support of our three husbands—John, John, and Jack (the "J Team"). Years ago, those three not only saw the value in bonding as the husbands of us three dynamos—a united front, if you will—they became friends, so you can imagine how much fun that adds to our adventures. As a group we even pioneered our own "Gourmet Club," which always includes the six of us, of course, and on occasion, some other lucky couple or two. Once a month we put together a special dinner consisting of a main meal prepared by the hosting woman, an appetizer or wine brought by the guests, and a dessert made and served by the hosting man. Carole and Kathy have presented fabulous entrees, including rack of lamb, pork tenderloin, shrimp scampi, and clambakes. Carole's John and Jack have treated us to some fabulous desserts, including chocolate mousse pie, baked Alaska, apple torte, and crème brûlée. When John and I host, we swap tasks: John creates the entrée, perhaps his fabulous shrimp crepes or a veal piccata. Baking is my passion, so I create the dessert, maybe a cheesecake, eclairs, or some type of custardy tart.

The club gives me reason to experiment with more recipes—to branch out creatively—and this outward branching led to my adding liqueurs to baked goods. When I baked my first amaretto cake, I realized how much fun it is to bake with booze, and to this day I love the way people react when I tell them their dessert is laced with amaretto, rum, or limoncello. They get this, "Oooh! I'm about to get away with something *naughty!*" look that amuses me.

I've experimented with rum in chocolate cake, but I couldn't get the booze to behave. It was too strong. I made liqueur éclairs, but those were a flop because no amount of booze is going to make an éclair better than it is boozeless. I tried infusing cookies with different types of liqueurs but wasn't able to get the alcohol flavor strong enough to warrant adding the alcohol. Then hallelujah and praise the goddesses of all-purpose flour! I found my way to the promised land—the infused cake. A lot more on that very soon.

Another of our collaborations that has always called attention to our great love of creating and sharing food is "the family work weekend," which involves getting together to help one of the family members complete a home project, like adding a new roof, porch, or deck. The guys, under Jack's direction, do most of the construction work, sometimes joined by friends who want to be involved.

We sisters prepare lots of great food for the weekend—breakfast, lunch, *and* dinner, as well as snacks and desserts. These are *feasts.* (We certainly aren't going to be outdone by a bunch of dudes wearing tool belts.) Most menus include ribs, steaks, sausage, pasta, potato salad, and veggie sides and always end with cakes, ice cream, cookies, pies, and candies.

Even the kids are involved. They're assigned clean-up jobs and are constantly called to, "Run to the truck and get the big shovel" or "Go get me three more of those red thingies." We females serve the guys cool drinks all day and run errands when they need more materials. The whole shebang is our version of a barn raising, and in the evening we camp at the house—indoors and in the backyard—so the project can be finished in a weekend. At the end of a weekend like that, we fall asleep with a thud and a full heart.

"Okay," I say to Kathy and Carole, as I patter my hands on the table in some version of a drumroll. "All this talk about shared work reminds me there's some information we still need to add. Who's up for an exercise that will be annoying, maybe even frustrating and excruciating?"

"Who could refuse such a temptress?" asks Kathy.

Carole says, "You had me at annoying."

How could anyone not love these two? "Okay, as you fellow creative writers probably know, it's not good writing to draw any character as being all good or all bad."

"Of *course*," says Kathy. She mouths to Carole, "What's she talking about?"

Carole shrugs.

"It means we have to try to say something positive about our father."

Crickets.

"Something that shows we don't view him entirely negatively."

There's silence for several minutes. "Carole, who exactly are you pointing those middle fingers at?" She makes a snarly face.

I say, "Okay, I'll start. In the father lottery, we drew a self-serving, unkind, negligent, abusive, deceitful, and undeniably sleazy human being."

"You're crushing it. What do you need us for?" says Carole.

"But he taught us some invaluable things about business and work ethic, right?"

"Taught?" Carole asks.

"Okay, I'll try," says Kathy. "He took us on a super-fun family vacation to Atlantic City."

"Which we all paid for," I say. "We did all the work. We earned all the money."

"Yep, we did," says Carole. "He did jack."

Kathy says, "You know, Carole, I read that when someone is awful, it's because he himself experienced awfulness, probably in childhood. So are we maybe supposed to cut him some slack because his parents sucked, too?"

"No."

I say, "Maybe? But how much slack? He didn't know he was making us cry when we stood in front of him crying? He didn't know we were hungry when we hadn't eaten dinner until ten at night? He didn't know he was betraying every one of us by *having another family*?"

"This is hard," Kathy says. "Maybe we should go back to talking about barn raisings."

Carole clears her throat and as she speaks, looks intently back and forth between Kathy and me. "The man emotionally slaughtered our mother, did everything he could to destroy our individual dreams, sold our family home, and let them take or demolish everything in it. His shitty parents didn't *make* him do any of that. Let's move on."

She makes a compelling argument. None of us is going to make it to the land of sunny forgiveness quite yet. So I guess we'll just have to say that for losing a lot of our childhoods to child labor, we did indeed learn and hone skills that have paid off tremendously in our work lives, and I guess that was because of the ticket we drew in the father lottery.

Kathy slaps the table. "Wait. I thought of something."

Carole and I lean in.

"He taught us who not to marry and how not to parent . . . and pretty much how not to be, in any category."

Well, that's something!

In addition to the Gourmet Club and barn raisings, we three cater family and friends' engagement parties, weddings, birthday parties, and any kind of event that could be made better with great food. We don't charge for any of it, only ask guests to bring a side dish, bottle of wine, or their favorite libation. We do it all for the fun and the love (same reason we drink vodka from triangle-shaped glasses).

Summer picnics are always a big deal, and every year we try to outdo ourselves and each other with recipes. Carole hosts the Memorial Day picnic, and her offerings usually include delicious spareribs with green bean salad and the best coleslaw this side of the Rockies.

I host the Independence Day party, and my standard dishes are sausage and peppers, lasagna, and my specialty, macaroni and cheese. I also love to make cheesecakes and cookies for dessert. Kathy finishes the season with a Labor Day picnic with grilled delights—her specialties—like steaks, burgers, dogs, clams, and corn on the cob along with her signature potato salad, which, as Kathy describes it, is "all about the Hellmann's . . . none of the Miracle Whip crap."

Our picnics are always attended by seventy-five to one hundred guests (sometimes more), each of whom bring a dish. Can you imagine the table space we need? Somebody, anybody—raid your corporate conference rooms! But we provide around 80 percent of the food and drinks. No matter which one of us hosts, each event is always organized by the three of us. Although we'd love to include raging stories of hair-pulling, backstabbing, head-slapping, and snipey arguments that ended in tears before we finally figured out how to work like a well-oiled machine, we've always enjoyed working together. Sometimes it seems the universe is paying us back for having dropped us down the wrong chimney.

Kathy is the strongest delegator in our group, which is a damned fine skill to have; if you play it right, delegating might be the only job you end up with. Eventually, we decided to hold all of our ever-expanding parties at Kathy's house because she has the biggest home and yard. The family-wide Christmas at her place is no small endeavor, and as always, we all dive in to make the event a festive and culinary delight. Picture seven siblings, plus spouses, plus offspring, then throw in about four to six lifelong friends who are like family (minus the heinous childhood), and you end up with a party of about fifty. Each year, we celebrate this holiday on December 23, which ensures that together we'll share a Christmas experience while also freeing this unruly band of marauders to spill out around town and city and state to spend time with in-laws and others on the actual holiday.

For years it had been clear to all three of us that we had great fun together, whether we cooked, entertained, watched a movie, or scrubbed a floor. And one day, Carole gathered us together, shook some martinis, and started a serious conversation about the future.

"Ladies," she said, handing each of us a frosty cold one with three perfect, skewered olives, "it's time to rethink what we're doing. As much as I love working with my husband, it's time for a big change, and I've decided my change is going to involve you two."

You have to love that kind of surety, don't you? Great leaders point to the rushing river and say, "The raft is leaving. Get on it."

Kathy and I sipped from our glasses of distilled perfection as

Carole continued. "We love working together, right? We work well together, yes? What if we start a business that involves food? We certainly know our way around the kitchen, and even though I'm not a baker, I have a recipe for specialty breads and butters that could be our first product line."

If I didn't have so much respect for vodka, my sip of martini might have shot right out of my laughing mouth and onto her lap. "Did you just imply we should start a business based on something *you* bake?" I gasped.

Kathy was now near hysterics herself. Carole, maintaining what composure she could despite a decent bit of vodka in her bloodstream, smiled and said, "We can talk recipes later. But think about it! We all have business experience; we could succeed at anything we do as long as we do it together."

That shut Kathy and me up. The togetherness card, well played, sister. We sipped in silence and let the idea wash over us.

Forming a three-sister team and plunging into a business together would call for our hopping over some logistical hurdles. Kathy hadn't retired yet, Carole and John were trying to recover from financial fallout from their business closing, and I was doing at least thirty hours a week of computer work from home. But despite how many potential obstacles we might have all envisioned in those quiet sipping moments, we knew what was about to happen: we were about to turn a big, fat page in the book of our lives and go into business *with siblings!*

Even though the idea made us giddy as schoolgirls, we were women in our fifties who'd already clocked enough life experience between us to fill a twenty-volume encyclopedia set. So we started talking through our preferences and deal-breakers. Kathy blurted hers first. After working in corporate technology, she wanted to do something simple because she'd fully burned out on red tape, tedious meetings, and bureaucratic "blahdy blah." She said, "I'm so fried right now, I don't want to do anything more complicated than ask people, 'You want decaf or regular?'"

I spoke up next. "I'm done with sitting in offices and pushing paper. I want to interact with people. I want to offer the public something that will make them smile."

Okay, so that ruled out my singing lead in a jazz band or working the stripper pole. But I figured there were still plenty of make-people-happy options left.

Carole had the most experience working for herself, and she said we'd need to come up with a lot of solid ideas to get this thing moving. We put our addled brains together and came up with the idea of opening a small breakfast joint, a place where "everybody knows your name." We thought we'd serve specialty breakfasts as well as the old standards: eggs, bacon, and pancakes. But we came to the relatively fast conclusion we simply didn't want to take on the financial burden of leasing and outfitting a restaurant.

Next, we decided to do some research, so Carole and I attended a workshop on how to market a food product. The class was taught by a couple who had created their own business based on a family mustard recipe, and the big message we took from the seminar was that selling a single product and making it profitable was an expensive, complex mission.

They basically told us, "Don't try it unless you have lots of money to spend on research, marketing, distribution, and manufacturing on a very large scale."

You might think we walked out of the workshop and straight into the nearest martini bar to drown our newly dashed hopes. But no! Don't think you can stop *us* with valid information and fact-based warnings. After these very experienced entrepreneurs gave us countless solid reasons to turn and run, we decided to make and sell specialty butter.

Over the years, Carole had experimented in the kitchen with an array of compound butters featuring fresh herbs and unique flavors, all of which included some type of alcohol. What the hell, we thought, that idea is as good as any. We decided our first product should be Carole's house butter, a compound butter with cranberries, toasted pecans, amaretto, and brown sugar that tastes delicious when spread on bread and can be used as a sauce for fish, poultry, beef, and even pasta. But, as we learned quickly, it's an expensive product to make and market in mass quantities. (Gee, if only someone had told us that in a workshop.). So we thought we could build some capital by selling the butters *with* Carole's rustic bread.

The quick-bread recipe doesn't require yeast, so it was easy for Carole to make. She used a recipe from an old friend and tweaked it to make it her own.

As delicious as the bread is when handmade, it doesn't scale well. But we didn't know that yet. We were still looking at beautiful batches of bread and butter through the rose-colored window of the bakery that housed our impulsive fantasies.

We made three flavors of the rustic bread—apple, blueberry, and cranberry—and the plan was to tap some of Carole's contacts to get us in at a local, upscale farmers market, and then we'd move on to some local breakfast spots.

Of course, we still needed a business name. Having grown up together, gone on to pursue other careers, and then found ourselves working on a business together, we realized we'd come "full circle." And so we became Full Circle Flavors.

Carole pursued several local restaurants until a local breakfast chain owner agreed to talk and taste. As Carole sat with him, buttered a piece of bread, and explained the possibilities for the butter's uses, the owner asked his chef to try the bread sautéed, which gave them the idea to use it as a specialty French toast item. He immediately ordered six hundred loaves, two hundred of each flavor, to be delivered in two weeks for his Mother's Day specials.

Woohoo! We were in business! And being small town girls, we closed the deal with a handshake.

The first step was to find a commercial kitchen to bake all the bread, because all products sold to the public are required to be produced in certified kitchens. We found a firehouse with a certified kitchen that we could afford to rent. Then, after hauling the ingredients and equipment the fifteen miles to the firehouse, we spent the next four days in a living hell of our own making.

None of us had ever used convection ovens, so we ran to our computers, learned a few things, and went on to make two hundred loaves of cranberry bread, two hundred loaves of blueberry, and two hundred loaves of apple. Our inexperience with the convection ovens ended up producing several loaves were overcooked and dry, so one by one, we shot them like basketballs toward the trash can, and then got back to the business of making more bread.

Before long, we looked like three *I Love Lucy*s being overrun by the machines, staring at each other with bug eyes, each looking crazy with white flour dusted throughout our out-of-control hair. Then we had an electrifying three-way epiphany: We neither enjoyed this process nor were we any good at it! Every day of that slog, we woke up moaning our version of the Dunkin Donut slogan—"Time to make the *f#%!ing* bread!"—and with each passing hour, we'd ask ourselves, "What are we doing here? We don't make bread."

But we survived the process and triumphantly pulled into the parking lot of that café to deliver two hundred loaves of each flavor of bread to our new customer. But the guy we'd shaken hands with wouldn't even taste them. He refused *every flipping loaf.* "They don't look as I expected."

Carole said, "They look *just* like the bread you sampled that made you order six hundred loaves. What's the issue?"

"I don't want them," he said and walked away.

We rolled all our bread back to the parking lot and drove back to Carole's house, where Kathy said, "Why didn't we even try to negotiate? We might have gotten him to take them."

"Rookie mistake," Carole said. "And we could have offered the loaves that appeared smaller at a discount, which would have been a fine idea because he was planning to use them for French toast anyway."

We shook our heads. Instead of trying to strike a deal, we'd just picked up our football-type loaves of bread and gone home. We all agreed we didn't have the experience to be fast on our feet, and lacking that experience, we lacked confidence.

Carole said, "How about we throw out the small loaves and donate the rest to the local VA?"

Kathy and I happily agreed. The staff at the VA raved about the bread for months, and we received handwritten thank-you letters from several VA patients deeply grateful because they hadn't eaten anything homemade in ages. So Breadgate didn't end up feeling like a total bust. We chose to view the experience not as a failure but as an excellent lesson learned—several lessons, in fact:

1. Know who you're doing business with.

2. Do your research. (Does the fun little item you make at home translate to large batches?)

3. Sign contracts.

4. Don't bake bread.

As we three like to say, "When one door closes, you might have a ghost." Then we laugh silently as the listener pinches her forehead and tips her head to the side.

We quickly decided that, in the future, we'd make breads only in small batches—six loaves to a batch. (So bread the lesson mentioned above? Not learned *quite* yet.) The next step was to find a venue where we could offer samples of our butters and breads, which presented a whole new problem.

Standing and offering samples for hours at a time is exhausting, physically and mentally. And, with that kind of work, you're not really making any money for your time. We were paying for all the ingredients ourselves, so we knew we'd need a business loan, but we weren't ready to take that leap.

We considered hosting home parties to get the word out about the breads and butters, but that wasn't the business model we were looking for. Carole went through her list of clients to see who might have a connection to get us into a retail environment. Debbie, one of Carole's loyal glass clients, convinced us to pursue a local, high-end farmers market bakery to propose sampling and selling our butters and breads at his stand on weekends.

The market was located in the Main Line area of Wayne, PA, and catered to an affluent clientele. It featured about thirty vendors selling all kinds of fresh delights, including meat and cheeses, vegetables and fruits, baked goods and coffee. It was a well-established spot and was always packed. Throughout the site, there were just a few tables and chairs where people might sit for a coffee and donut. For the most part, people kept strolling.

Pete, the owner of the bakery/bread stand Debbie had pointed us to, sampled our bread and butter, and said he'd sell our bread only if we sampled it with the butters and only on consignment, which we later learned wasn't a standard in selling food products. We agreed to his terms and gave samples to his regular customers, who stopped by for their weekly orders of rolls, cupcakes, cookies, and pies.

The breads didn't go over well.

Fruited breads can't compete with classic rolls and breads for weekly orders. Fruit makes for more of a specialty bread, so we decided we'd give up on the bread part of our three-sisters business dreams. But the butters were a hit because, let's be honest, nothing is as good as real butter on bread—any kind of bread.

After that first day, we continued to sample the butters at Pete's farmers market stand—using his breads. We were a great attraction thanks to our love of meeting people, and we let almost nobody pass by without one of us pulling them into a friendly chat. Pete wanted to keep us around because of the energy we brought to the market's atmosphere, so after a couple weeks of selling our butters, he asked if we had anything else he could sell. Right away, Carole suggested my amaretto cake, and he said, "Bring me one, and I'll let you know what I think."

I dashed home and pulled my baking pans from my baking cabinet. For a while, I daydreamed about how thrilling it would be to finally debut my beloved cake for the public and find out what *the people out there* thought of my creation.

The recipe is relatively simple but still quite special, greatly because of the alcohol and the process I use to get the amaretto into the cake. The result is just delicious. Humming and smiling my way through the rest of the day, I baked three perfect amaretto cakes and delivered one of them to Pete at the farmers market. He took the cake to a dinner party the same evening.

For the rest of the night, I pictured his guests taking bites and imagined them raving about the flavor, texture, color . . . the everything. Then I slipped into a dark cloud of self-doubt. Maybe this was all in my head. Maybe there was nothing special about this cake. Maybe I should get a job waiting tables.

The next morning, I took my time driving to the market. I wasn't in any hurry to have my dreams officially throttled, not so soon after the bread debacle. As I approached the stand, I saw Pete talking to a customer. When he saw, me, he kept talking and didn't really acknowledge me. Oh God, I thought. Avoidance—that's the sign. He didn't know how to tell me the cake was a flop.

Buck up, I told myself. You're an adult. Act like a professional. I walked over to our little corner of the table and started handing out samples of our butter on Pete's bread. After several minutes, Pete wandered over and said, "Good morning, how are you today?"

Not a word about the cake. What kind of torturer was this guy? I thought he'd jump right into the news, good or bad, but he busied himself giving direction to his staff, telling them where to place the cookies and donuts. Then he stepped toward me and said, "We need to talk."

Oh, Lord, here it is, I thought. Not once in the history of the world has any good news started with, "We need to talk."

I took a big breath. "Okay," I said, "here I am."

A bright smile spread across his face. He said, "The cake was out of this world! It made me the star of the party. There wasn't a crumb left, and people were asking for more." Still smiling, Pete said, "How many can you bring to the market every week?"

Oh my God! We were in! He really wanted to sell our cake! I told him, "I'd like to bring a couple more cakes and just sample for a week or two to get a feel for how much interest there is."

Pete said, "Perfect. That will make them come back when you're ready to sell. You'll sell them for twenty-five dollars, and I'll take five for each. Does that work for you?"

I called Carole and Kathy, and we all agreed to his terms. We would be officially "on the table" for the following Saturday—in fourteen days. That night Carole, Kathy, and I shook ourselves a round of martinis and toasted to showing the amaretto cake to the world.

Kathy breaks in. "That was a bust. Another rookie mistake, agreeing to terms before figuring out the costs that went into making those cakes. Oy."

She was right, of course. We were overzealous, but as we toasted to our latest success, we felt nothing but joy. We didn't know how the cake would be received by the public, but the three cakes we'd be sending to the farmers market for sampling would be the very best we could offer. All we could do was do our best work, try to believe in ourselves, and clink our glasses together.

CHAPTER ELEVEN

"Come *onnnn* amaretto cake! No pressure, little buddy, but our future might rest on your . . . um . . . on your every crumb. You can't know this because you're a cake, but if you win over the good people at Lancaster Farmers Market, you'll pretty much be responsible for our professional futures, our financial freedom, and our happiness in general. If they reject you, we'll be left with nothing to do but churn butter."

Again, no pressure.

Given that this little confection is so important to our story, it probably makes sense to explain a little bit about the cake soldier we deemed worthy of leading the charge. More than forty years before this potentially game-changing launch, which we're now calling Amaretto Day, I took my first run at the cake's recipe.

Ralph was just six months old, and while I was lucky enough to be a stay-at-home parent at the time, I needed an artistic outlet. Don't get me wrong, I'm no Carole; I can barely stay inside the lines in a toddler's coloring book, but I believed I could create something special with my somewhat self-taught baking skills. When it's a matter of flour, sugar, salt, eggs, and butter, how bad can it be? I wasn't just going to bake, I decided to start experimenting.

Some people warn against being too experimental when baking, claiming "cooking is art, while baking is science," so I'm not sure what gave me the confidence to experiment with recipes for baked goods. I just know I wanted to create something uniquely mine. I'd recently tasted a rum cake at a party and marveled at how moist it was, but I thought the rum flavor was overwhelming. I decided to take a run at an amaretto treat for my first booze-soaked creation.

"Wait a second." It's the voice of Kathy. I look up to focus on her face. She looks very confused. "The alcohol was overwhelming?" she says. "Who are you, and what have you done with Sue?"

"Is actual Sue trapped under something heavy?" asks Carole. "Is she locked in a basement?"

"It was *too* boozy," I say. "The alcohol flavor overwhelmed the cake."

"You're not making any cocktails for me," says Carole.

"Or me," adds the other one.

"When did I offer to make either of you a cocktail?"

They stare at me silent, unblinking.

Let's move on.

As I gathered the ingredients to create my first liqueur-infused cake, I was reminded of the days when I spent countless hours in Aunt Diggie's kitchen learning the difference between baking soda and baking powder (and finding out the hard way cocoa powder *isn't* delicious by the spoonful). Whenever Aunt Diggie and I baked a cake, pie, or batch of cookies—and they were always delicious—I always daydreamed about what I might do to make the confection a little better.

In the years that followed, I baked countless cakes, cupcakes, tarts, and muffins. Usually starting from recipes I ripped from magazines in a doctor's waiting room, I then added as much of my own flair as I could by adding fruits or flavorings, like nuts and vanilla. I read countless books about baking to understand the effects of different ingredients so I could create my own recipes. Still very much an amateur, I created several flops in the form of dry cakes, chewy pastries, and flavorless cookies, but each failure brought me closer to competency and confidence. I baked and baked and baked—for birthday parties, anniversaries, retirement parties, graduation parties, bake sales, and other big-deal events—and I found immense joy in it. But now it was time to take a step up.

Amaretto was my drink of choice at the time, so I prepared a standard yellow cake batter and added a heaping cup of amaretto and chocolate chips. Then I topped the mixture with toasted almonds. As the cake baked, the aroma that wafted through the kitchen was heavenly. My kitchen smelled like butter, sugar, chocolate, and amaretto.

The timer chimed, I pulled the cake from the oven, used a toothpick to check that it was fully baked, and set it on a rack to cool. Then I looked at it, fighting the urge to cut off and nibble a piece.

Now what? I didn't want to frost the cake because I wasn't a fan of booze in buttercream, so I created a glaze by adapting a recipe I'd found in a magazine. I cooked amaretto, sugar, butter, and water until it boiled and bubbled. It wasn't a bad idea, but I had to trash the first four batches because, once again, too much alcohol. Then on batch five, I got the balance right. The glaze had a buttery flavor with a subtle amaretto background—not too rich, not too sweet. I poured the glaze over the top of the cooling cake, but it didn't soak in, so I ended up with a pool of brown sugary ooze that spilled over the edge of the pan. Okay, *now* what? I remembered making a "poke cake," which involved stabbing little holes in the cake as it cooled and dripping liquid Jell-O into each hole.

Using a skewer, I poked about twenty holes into the top of the cake, poured the hot glaze into the holes, brushed it on top and down the sides, and voila! The glaze seeped into the cake beautifully.

Then it was time to let the others weigh in.

"I'm not a fan of amaretto, but I'll try it," said Carole.

"Great," I said. "Love the enthusiasm."

"Gimme a piece. *Chop, chop,*" said Kathy.

"That's more like it," I said, placing a piece of cake in front of each of them. They lifted their forks and took a bite.

Kathy spoke first. "Oh wow. It smells great and tastes great. Really moist—love it."

"Yes, the alcohol keeps the cake really moist," I said.

"Really moist," said Kathy.

"Stop saying 'moist.' I hate that word," said Carole.

"Why do you hate the word 'moist'?" mumbled Kathy through a mouthful of cake.

"Yeah," I said, "What do you have against 'moist'? What did 'moist' ever do to you?"

Kathy said, "Not good to hate the word 'moist' if you're talking cake. People like moist cake."

"Stop it!" screamed Carole.

I made a mental note to say "moist" as much as possible in the presence of Carole.

Carole said, "Amaretto is much better in a cake than in a glass. This is delicious."

I considered that tasting a great success and made more and more amaretto cakes for various events. Soon, it became the cake everybody asked for. Even though for years I'd been creating truckloads of cheesecakes, pies, eclairs, and countless other custardy desserts, the amaretto cake became the king that relegated all the other contenders to a kind of honorary court, highly regarded companions who are often invited to the best events but never wear the crown. I even suspect—no, I'm sure—that I've been invited to many a party only so I'll bring an amaretto cake. It may sound paranoid, but you tell me what it means when a friend writes, *Pool party starts at 1:00. If you don't think you can make it, just leave the cake on the front porch. Wiinnk.*

Moving forward, on each of the next two Thursdays, I baked three amaretto cakes to be sampled at the farmers market two days later. We still hawked our specialty butters, so on cake inauguration day, we had our multitasking work cut out for us. Still tucked at the corner of Pete's bakery stand, we had just enough room to add business cards and cake samples. The butters were next to us in a refrigerated case, and as always, we explained how they could be used in many delicious ways. But right away, it became clear the cake was going to be the center of attention.

Carole launched into the first of what soon appeared to be an endless reserve of intrusive greetings and salesy quips. Kathy was right there with her, the two of them filling the air with cheery spiel, like seasoned carnival barkers.

"Step up to the bar," said Carole. "We have butter. We have amaretto cake. That's right—I said butter *and* I said cake. A delightful duo—come on over!"

"Amaretto cake samples, free for you!" said Kathy. "A treat for your tongue. Stop here for a delicious freebie you won't forget!"

"No-guilt booze on a Saturday morning! Hidden in a delectable piece of cake!"

"Grab 'em while you can—they won't last long!"

Who *were* these two women? I knew they were quick thinkers, but you'd have thought they were barking from a script. The carnival calls just kept coming.

"Getcha some cake, ladies! Best breakfast around!"

"Hey there, fellas, don't be shy."

"One little sample won't hurt that girlish figure!"

Sure enough, the people stopped. And they tried samples.

Even though the samples were just a bit bigger than bite-sized, we went through all three cakes each weekend, and during those two weekends, we took nine orders for amaretto cakes. Time to get baking. I spent the following Wednesday and Thursday baking sixteen amaretto cakes, nine that had been ordered, six that we hoped to sell, and one we'd cut up for samples. All six sold quickly, and the following weekend was Easter, so we knew we'd have a lot of traffic by our table. This was exciting! What to do first? I'll tell you what we did first, we put the cake before the horse by dashing out to buy a big old shmear of three hundred adorable pink cake boxes. We're like the girl who buys her prom dress months before she has a date. We're the first-time mothers-to-be who haven't a spare minute to read parenting books but find plenty of time to buy twelve colors of striped onesies. Ah well, we say it's better to be overzealous than unexcitable.

Now that we were all set with pink boxes, the question was, without a commercial bakery ready to go, how were we going to knock out enough cakes to make a big splash at the farmers market and beyond? We'd decided fifty would be the magic number for the upcoming Easter weekend. Our cakes had been made only one or three at a time, at home and with very special attention paid to each (by me, someone who bakes).

It's like having an only child—you can give him all the attention in the world. But once you're producing for mass consumption and therefore need to crank them out in bulk, how are you supposed to give them all the attention they deserve? To paraphrase Mary Steenburgen in *Parenthood*, with your first kid, you freak out if they get even a scratch; by kid three you let them juggle knives.

Now that we needed to produce an enormous family of cakes, the three of us decided to bake as a team. That meant I was going to have to train Thing One and Thing Two to follow my instructions and not go rogue. Lord, give me strength.

I'd always baked each cake in a ceramic bowl because the ceramic made it easy to pull the cake ever-so-slightly from the walls of the bowl, which allowed me to brush the cake's sides with the liqueur glaze. Then the cake would soak up all that infusion goodness until it was ready to be served naked; that's "old world style," no frosting. And trust me, frosting would only be overkill. It would be like powdering farm fresh strawberries in a layer of sugar. (If this is your idea of improvement, get out of my kitchen.)

I owned only three of these bowls, so I needed to find at

least a dozen more. After searching several kitchen shops and combing the Internet, I hit pay dirt when I walked into a gourmet store near my house that actually had twenty-five bowls. Hallelujah! I had no idea how I would have navigated the glaze issue without the right baking vessels. Cross a biggie off the list.

In the meantime, I directed Kathy and Carole to buy forty pounds of flour, thirty pounds of butter, and forty pounds of sugar and said I'd be dashing around town picking up the other ingredients, including three cases of amaretto.

"Why do I have to pick up the baking stuff? Why can't I pick up the booze?" Kathy whined.

"I have the most experience buying booze, of course," added Carole. "We should do what we're good at."

I had to shut down this mutiny fast. I clapped my hands like a cranky high school orchestra leader. "*Ladies*! Focus! If we were free to do what we're good at, I'd be baking, and you two would be promoting, pricing, managing, haggling, designing, ordering, and all the other goodies that go along with business. But right now we need to crank out the product! And for the record, being the one to get the amaretto is no prize—that stuff is heavy as hell. Also, make no mistake, until the right time, it's going to remain *unopened*."

"Well, when you put it that way," said Kathy.

We hustled into town and were soon back with all the ingredients. We dragged it all into Kathy's house because she has a double oven (of course she does). Both sisters stood at attention as my assistant pâtissiers, while I communicated kitchen terms.

"Okay, girls, first I want to emphasize that this is baking, so we *must* be careful with the measuring."

"Measuring what?" asked Carole. She headed to the liquor cabinet. Or maybe that was me.

Kathy said to Carole, "You usually just cook, so maybe you don't know much about measuring. *Baking* calls for precision, which is why I don't do it—unless you count ripping open a box, spilling the powder into a bowl, then dropping in two eggs and a quarter cup of oil. I have a quarter-cup measuring device thingie, so that really helps."

"Focus," I said. "First lesson: Measure carefully, level off, then drop the ingredients into the mixer. Measure, measure, measure. No winging, no flinging. No 'more or less is fine.' Measurement is king."

They stared as if I'd just recited the *Magna Carta* in Latin.

Kathy spoke. "Is baking really this complicated? Betty Crocker swears it's no big deal."

Preempting any annoyance on my part, Carole said, "It's clearly more complicated than we non-bakers think. Let's just zip it and be good foot soldiers."

I tapped Carole on the shoulder and said, "That's an extra piece of cake for you later, little girl."

Kathy snarled something about fairness, but she's the youngest, so we ignored it and got back to work.

The rest of the baking session consisted of lots of gaping looks as I barked instructions like, "Boil the glaze!" "Poke the holes!" "Brush the tops!" I felt like Captain Queeg on the deck of the USS *Sugar Cane.*

One critical step was teaching my sisters to boil the glaze long enough for it to achieve a foam state, which allows the sugar and alcohol to meld. The process involves stirring the mixture just enough to combine the ingredients without removing all the air, then simmering the glaze for about six minutes and timing it to be ready right around when the cake comes out of the oven. Kathy got pretty good at it, so she became the official glaze mixer.

Our system was going as well as I could have hoped. My baking assistants were efficient and almost mastered taking direction without complaint. But there were issues.

I looked up from the cake I was working on. "Carole, take the beater out of your mouth."

Carole removed the beater from her mouth.

"Maybe wash it, too?"

"Can I poke the holes in the cakes? I want to poke the holes," whimpered one of them.

"I want to poke holes, too," chirped the other one.

"Okay, you toddlers," I said with grace and patience and sophistication and elegance and maturity and charisma and class and more patience and—

"Omigod, get on with it. 'You toddlers' what?" one of the sisters demanded.

"Yes, you two can poke holes and brush the tops." I took a long, deep breath as I flashed back to why I once ran screaming from a camp counselor gig.

Now that I think a little harder, this scene above might not have played out *exactly* as I've described it here. But as I've mentioned before, when you're the one typing, you're the boss. Together we made the cakes. *Fifty-one* of them. Working together, we measured and mixed, poured and poked fifty-one moist, delicious, amaretto-infused rounds of confectionary delightfulness, all baked *without* the help of a commercial facility. Using Kathy's two ovens, we baked eight cakes at a time. The mixing, baking, infusing, wrapping in plastic, and packing in pretty pink boxes, took us just over two hours per batch of eight.

It's difficult to describe how tired we were at the end of that day. We were covered in flour, some of us more than others (Carole). Our knees creaked. Two of our backs ached so much we couldn't straighten for hours. But we'd pulled it off in time for our big day, and now it was time to find out if the good people of Wayne, PA, were willing to give their money for our cakes.

Early that Saturday morning, one day after the baking marathon, we packed fifty-one boxed cakes into the big shopping bags we'd bought from Sam's Club and loaded them into Carole's little hatchback. We packed one more bag with napkins, knives, toothpicks, and hand wipes.

The farmers market was a twenty-minute drive from Kathy's house, and we arrived about two hours before the opening bell. Before we unloaded the car, we walked around the market to do some recon. Because we didn't know how big our table would be or whether we'd be expected to dress it up, our resident artist/designer had packed an extra bag with a polka-dot tablecloth, an Easter basket, and some little holiday decorations. That's our Carole.

Lucky for us, Pete had put together two four-foot tables, draped a white tablecloth over them, and topped them with little Easter decorations, so all we needed to do was we set up our display, which consisted of forty-nine cakes boxed in pink, the other two to be cut for samples, a pile of business cards, and a stack of napkins.

Our table was near the entrance to the market, so we were in a great spot; we'd be able to nab shoppers when they were fresh and their wallets were still full. As we unloaded the car, we giggled like a trio of elementary school girls whose crushes had just asked them to dance. Still sore from the day before, we were pumped with adrenaline and the hope that the day was going to be the first day of the rest of our joyful business lives.

We arranged our cakes in a pyramid that provided a kind of security wall behind which we could cut cake samples without anyone touching or spitting on the goods. And we looked very food-service professional wearing our plastic gloves and black aprons. With everything set up and ready to go, we had about forty-five minutes until the customers would start arriving. I sat down and was hit with a wave of emotion. It was all so much—the work, the fatigue, the anticipation, the hope. I'd put so much of myself into this endeavor, and today we'd find out how the public felt about a creation that represented me in countless ways. Would I be a disappointment to my sisters? Tears burned my eyes.

Kathy and Carole quietly sat down on either side of me. For a second, we sat together in silence, then Carole wrapped her arm tightly around my shoulder and said, "What's your problem, crybaby?"

I shielded my eyes with one hand and shook my head.

Kathy said, "I'll give you something to cry about."

"Yeah," said Carole, "how 'bout I grab a TV and find us a beer commercial with some Clydesdales and a missing puppy?"

I said, "I hate you," and we all laughed.

As I dabbed my teary eyes, Carole kept her arm around my shoulder, and I asked, "What if they don't like it enough to buy?"

Carole said, "We have proof, dum-dum. The two weeks of sampling told the story. They love them, they ordered them, they're still asking for them. Today is going to be a breeze."

"But wait," said Kathy, "what if they rip through all the samples but don't buy anything? Does anybody know where the office of sibling disownment is?"

Carole swatted her on the forehead. "Shut your cake hole."

"If nobody buys, will you guys still want to come over and bake together?" I whimpered.

"Not likely," Kathy said.

Carole swatted her again.

I was starting to feel a little lighter, but I was still haunted by doubts. At twenty-five dollars per cake, how many would we sell? If we didn't sell very many, what would we do with the rest? Did we even have the acumen to pull off running a business about baking and selling cake? So many questions.

We knew this event wasn't only about what we'd baked; today was about us. We and the cakes went hand in hand. Not only did we need people to love the product, we needed them to like us. For us, this whole thing was about connection, getting to know people, and making them happy. We were to be the faces of this extravaganza, the three-headed spokesmodel, the triple-brained Vanna White—or whoever the current-day Vanna White is. For us, this day might decide whether we should make a go of this cake thing at all.

We'd already dropped over $600 for ingredients, $50 for the pink boxes, and who knows how much in gas as we ran cake-related errands. Unfortunately, we didn't keep track of the time we spent shopping and baking, but who would we send the bill to anyway?

It was time to lift the curtain.

The people began strolling by our table, and right away

Carole called out to no one in particular, "May we offer you a taste of our amaretto-infused cake?"

A red-haired woman stopped to look up and down the length of the table. Her pinned-up hair and floral dress were so tidy, she looked like someone dirt and dust knew better than to mess with. "Isn't it a bit early for liquor?" she asked.

"Is it?" Carole replied.

"It's eleven o'clock somewhere!" said Kathy.

"You mean five o'clock?" asked Mrs. Tidy.

"Do I?" answered Kathy.

I said, "It's the new breakfast of champions!"

"Ha!" laughed a muscular, gray-haired man who'd just sidled up next to the tidy lady. "Which champions would those be?"

"Well, we're not supposed to reveal this," said Carole, leaning forward, half-whispering, "but we just baked eight of these for the US Olympic swim team."

"Do *you* want to swim like an Olympian?" I asked.

Both potential customers laughed as they gave in. "Okay," said Muscles, "I need to try this cake."

With gloved hands, Kathy handed each of them cake on a toothpick. Muscles popped it into his mouth and said, "This tastes like *more*. Can I have another sample?"

Mrs. Tidy nibbled her sample as delicately as I would have expected and then said, "I didn't expect *that*. This is very special. Do they have to be refrigerated? Do they freeze? How long do they last, and how much do they cost?"

Speaking to them both at once, I said, "The cakes are good for up to two months, no refrigeration needed, they freeze well, and they're twenty-five dollars each. How many can I bag for you?"

Muscles and Mrs. Tidy bought two cakes each and said they'd be back next week.

As they walked away, Kathy uttered something between a whisper and a scream. "We *did* it! It's *on!*" Then she and Carole slapped an awkwardly off-center high-five. A drive-thru car wash couldn't have wiped the smile off my face as I watched my sisters celebrate after selling just four cakes.

The rest of the day swam by as we busied ourselves accosting strangers, talking dessert and trash, laughing, and answering countless questions about cake.

"Do I need to refrigerate it?"

"No, just keep it wrapped in the saran."

"Can I get drunk?"

"You certainly have my permission to get drunk, but you won't get there by eating this cake."

"How long will one of these cakes stay fresh?"

"For at least two months, but we're having them tested to confirm the shelf life. And sir—yes, you in the Jimmy Buffet shirt—you asked the booze question? We're also testing to confirm alcohol level in case you ever see reason to share this cake with a kid."

On and on it went. We sold those forty-nine cakes in three hours, long before the market closed for the day. We cleaned up the table, stuffed our bags in the car, and left to have lunch and celebrate.

Pete took $5 per cake, so we grossed $980, so clearly we were on our way to becoming millionaires! Then we did a little math. After spending $650 for ingredients and packaging, we ended up earning $330, which didn't include our time and labor. We earned a big goose egg—financially, that is. Because that day we were rewarded with something much bigger: We now had public confirmation of what we already knew—we had something special on our hands.

CHAPTER TWELVE

The three of us took turns being the Saturday sample lady. During those Saturdays, with delight, we each witnessed what we named the "wait for it" moment.

It happens when a reluctant-looking shopper agrees to sample the cake as if she's doing us a favor. She takes a bite, smiles, says thank you, and walks away without a word. Then, about six or seven steps away, she stops, turns back, and says, "Oh my God!" and she heads back our way to buy a cake. We've lost count of how many "wait for it" moments we've watched with glee at farmers markets and other events, but they make us giggle every time.

"Wait for it" is almost as delightful as the reaction we get from countless men who seem to think outwardly gushing over our cakes will get them in trouble with the women in their lives. They'll wait for the girlfriend or wife to wander off to another part of the market and then sneak back to our booth to buy a cake for themselves; a cake they then have to stash somewhere in the car and, we presume, eat in secret later. We laugh as we watched them slink off to slip the cake into the trunks of their cars and then scuttle back to the market, dutifully searching for their significant others.

Those husband hijinks are a big part of what prompted us to eventually produce a smaller version of the cakes. We wanted to name the small versions Sneak-Aways but didn't want to give away our treasured customers' secret. (How's that for thoughtful?). We named them juniors.

But at the beginning, we hadn't started making juniors yet. It was all about the full-sized amaretto cake.

Carole and I spent a lot of time in Kathy's kitchen, cranking out butters and cakes to be sold every Wednesday and Saturday. We kept selling the cakes for $25 each, and Pete kept taking $5 off the top. We sold the six-ounce butters for $8 each, and Pete took $2 of that. We figured out it was costing us almost $11 to make each cake and $4 per butter for ingredients. So we realized that on a day when we'd sold fifteen cakes and five butters, we'd taken in only $330 or $110 each. But that didn't factor our labor or gas, and we'd already dropped another $400 on ingredients and materials. This wasn't really turning out to be a profitable enterprise.

Despite not having figured out how to actually make money, we were pleased with the popularity of our cakes. And while we were patting ourselves on the back, Pete made another request.

"Girls," he said, "the cakes are fabulous, but I need you to bring something else in here to sell, another baked delight. Also, we aren't selling more than one or two butters a week, so maybe it's time to let those go."

After a brief team meeting, we agreed to kill the butter arm of our business and decided Kathy should make her "Smoke and Mirrors" brownies, aptly named because although we advertised them as homemade—and, indeed, they were made in a home—they started with a mix.

For their debut alongside the amaretto cakes, Kathy prepared a tray of eighteen of these box-brownie delights, cut them into four-by-four-inch squares, added her special touch—a sprinkle of powdered sugar—and packaged them in clear clamshells. Every one of them sold for $4.50 each, and Pete kept $1 per brownie. Pete asked if we could bag all the crunchy edges Kathy had cut off to make the brownies beautiful, uniform squares. He wanted to sell those too, but no go—Kathy usually munched her way through those as she trimmed.

The brownie arm of our business ended up earning us $63 per batch, less the 30 cents per brownie to make, and we always sold out of those delights right away. Sometimes we sold entire trays at a time, and people started asking about the recipe. Dammit if we were going to rat ourselves out, and we soon reasoned we might diminish our growing brand if somebody discovered that an item we called our own could be whipped up by anybody with two bucks, an egg, and some vegetable oil. We retired the brownie line.

After those first two successful farmers market experiences, we knew we needed to figure out how and where to make multiple cakes at a time. The Kathy kitchen had served us well, but it was time to get serious. While we could have gone back to renting bakery space in the firehouse where we'd made the bread, that place cost us $150 per day, and getting there meant an eighteen-mile commute each way. So even though a return to the firehouse might have included regular sightings of deliriously good-looking fire guys, we took the big-girl road and decided to keep our costs (and hassle) as low as possible.

We found a local manufacturing bakery with an excellent reputation and made an appointment to discuss renting their kitchen, part-time. Chad, their head baker, agreed to meet with us, but he assumed we wanted *him* to make our cakes, not that we intended to use their space to do our own baking. Renting to us wasn't an option for Chad's bakery because their insurance wouldn't cover us. If we burned the place down, they'd have been screwed.

This wasn't long after the horrific events of 9/11, which led to a shrinking economy, so a lot of manufacturing bakeries were losing their large customers, like airlines and casinos. Chad's bakery really needed extra income, so they were determined to convince us they should make our cakes. We were concerned about the logistics because the process to make our cakes requires extensive labor, and we feared it might be impossible to keep the costs low enough to sell the cakes at a profit.

Chad was a very handsome, sweet, exceptionally talented baker in his late twenties, who had already built a terrific reputation for making beautiful wedding cakes and pastries. We chatted at the little table in the front of the bakery, and Chad offered suggestions for how to make the cakes at a reasonable cost.

"What if you replaced real butter with margarine?" he suggested.

I looked at him through narrowed eyes. "I'd rather ram hot knitting needles deep into my ear canal."

Chad shifted in his chair and cleared his throat. "Um, okay, what about instead of actual liqueurs, you used flavorings?"

"After which I guess I'll ice the cakes with Vick's VapoRub."

Chad looked at Kathy and Carole with fear in his eyes.

"What Sue is trying to say," said Carole, leaping in like a

White House aide in the midst of a standoff with Iran, "is that we've perfected the recipe. Let's see where else we might be able to cut costs."

Chad downed the contents of an enormous glass of water. "What about in the infusion process? Maybe we can add some efficiency there," he said.

"I'm listening," I said.

Chad sat up in his chair. "What if you could find a machine to infuse the cakes? Wouldn't that cut the labor cost?"

Kathy, Carole, and I looked at each other. Maybe young Chad had something there. Even though our infusion process led to all kinds of childlike glee from a couple of women I know, hand-poking cake holes took too much time, and the process lacked the consistency we'd need if we were going big. In order for us to be able to sell to the public, the amount of glaze we used and the weights of the finished cakes had to be the same(ish) every time, so we needed a system that would deliver that consistency.

Right away I thought my son and his father—the two Ralphs—might be just the guys to help us. This part of the story is where we point out the value of not burning bridges between you and an ex (unless the guy is an unredeemable asshole, in which case hurl him off the bridge—then burn the boat and then burn the bridge). I had remained friendly with my ex-husband Ralph, a skilled industrial engineer, who at the time was building unique equipment at a food processing plant where my son, Ralph, runs the production. If I knew anyone with the skill to create the kind of infusion system we needed, it was Ralph and my son Ralph would help him.

I told Chad what I was thinking, and he said, "They'll have

to use needles to infuse the glaze and some kind of system to keep the glaze hot for the infusion."

I assumed there would be plenty of engineer-y details involved in making a machine like that; all I could do was ask. If the two Ralphs were willing to give it a try and if they could pull it off, we'd be able to keep the costs low enough to hire Chad as our baker.

Meanwhile, for our partnership to begin, I was going to have to give Chad the cake's secret recipe. This wasn't easy for me. It's kind of like the terror a mother feels the first time she leaves her newborn in the care of her husband.

Wait, that's not what I meant. I meant *in the care of a stranger*. Yeah, *stranger* is what I meant to write. Not *husband.*

I pulled out the NDA I'd tucked into my bag before going to the bakery (because I'm an optimist), and Chad was happy to sign it. Then we all shook hands and hugged.

Chad offered to bake samples to our specifications until we felt he'd gotten it just right. And he never charged us for all the samples he created, which was another reason we knew we were working with our kind of guy.

Getting the recipe just right was bound to be no small feat because it had been created by a novice—me—who knew bupkes about how a recipe developed for one wee cake at a time translates to volume production. But Chad was a seasoned bakery chef with considerable experience developing seamless processes for difficult recipes.

The bakery was very near Kathy's office, so at around 4:30 every Wednesday afternoon for the next three weeks, we sisters headed to the bakery to try Chad's latest. Each week, he presented us with at least six different cake samples to taste, each time having tweaked the ingredients and ratios per my direction. I could taste the difference if he used margarine (which I think he sneaked in once just to see if I'd notice) instead of butter or would add an ingredient not called for in the recipe. None of his early iterations were better than my original—in my opinion. And Carole's opinion. And Kathy's opinion.

To Chad's credit, he never once became snarky or snippy or snotty as I surely would have if three newbie cake broads kept telling me, "Gee, this is delicious, but I don't know . . . *it's just not quite there yet*." Each time we sent him back for another round, he was perfectly happy to get back to it, always reaching for perfection.

Six weeks into the samples and tasting, he presented us with a sample that was clearly the one.

"This is it," I said. "This is the one."

Chad smiled.

"And thank you for sticking with butter," I said.

"You're welcome, your highness," he said, before genuflecting and kissing my hand.

"Good grief," Carole interrupts. "*Your highness*? Really?"

"Tell the story right!" snaps Kathy.

Fine.

"You're welcome," said Chad. "No question—gotta be real butter."

"And I really like the quality of chocolate you're using, way better than the no-name bits."

"Absolutely," he said.

"This is fabulous," said Kathy, reaching for another sample. "The recipe is just right with a big wet kiss of the amaretto flavor."

"Dare I say it, this tastes just like Sue makes it?" added Carole.

"You may dare," I said.

Chad had done it. He'd replicated my recipe. And it was difficult to tell who was more relieved.

Chad was so impressed with the version of the cake we settled on, he took one of our amaretto cakes with him when he visited his elderly Italian grandmother. Then that sneaky grandson shared a piece with Grandma Italiana without telling her the cake's recipe wasn't his.After one bite, she exclaimed, "*Mio caro ragazzo! Alla fine, hai preparato qualcosa di delizioso invece che solo carino!*"

Who says I grabbed that text off Google? *Who* says I don't speak Italian?

For the less-cosmopolitan readers, Chad's grandmother was proclaiming, "My dear boy! Finally you made something delicious instead of just pretty!"

We considered this extremely high praise because Chad is an extraordinary baking talent, known for creating both delicious and beautiful delights.

Now, about getting that all-important booze into the cakes. Most people probably think making a cake deliciously boozy is as simple as splashing a half cup (or two or four) of rum or amaretto into the batter before baking. Well, it ain't. And as you know from reading about the dedicated efforts of the cake-poking sisters—for subtle, alcohol-soaked perfection, you need to first add liqueur before you bake the cake *as well as* slipping that magical fluid into the already baked cake. And how does one do the latter? Not by dumping the hooch on the cake's head or sitting the cake in a pool of the happy sauce or even mixing the booze of choice into frosting. No, no, no. If it were that easy, every Martha, Julia, Gordon, and Emeril would be making world-class cocktail cakes.

Beyond having some of the liqueur dropped into the mix, these babies need the alcohol to be more or less shot right into their skin, like a flu vaccine (*Ew.* Forget I said that.)

After researching several bakeries and infusion systems, I couldn't find any options small enough that the air pressure needed to infuse the glaze wouldn't blow up our cake. Very fortunate for us, the two Ralphs agreed to design a cake infusion system tailor-made for our cakes. Ralph senior had a private shop with the necessary components to build a model, and the assignment intrigued him. Necessity for spirited cakes turned out to be the mother and ex-wife of invention. My son Ralph actually just managed procuring whatever parts his Dad needed to build the infuser.

Ralph senior met with Chad to talk specs and then designed a handheld piece of equipment made with needles that could infuse the glaze consistently throughout, one cake at a time. Only two weeks later, we were presented with a one-of-a-kind infusion system. Ralph senior had designed the needles to exact specs, so the holes lined up as needed and perfectly saturated the cakes with glaze. He then built a head to connect the twenty-four needles and created a hooking device that allowed hot glaze to pipe up into them. The cake-infusion process remained somewhat labor-intensive, but it worked. We were ready to give it a try.

Nutty as it sounds, we still hadn't thought much about packaging. Our cakes had no wardrobe. If we didn't step on it, we'd be handing naked cakes to people on the street. This, we knew, wasn't the path to greatness, nor was it the best way to keep the health department out of our hair.

It was time to make use of Carole's artistic talent. At

Kathy's kitchen table, we talked design and logo. Kathy, a master delegator, said, "Sue, you came up with the recipe, and clearly, I'm doing a great job at taste-testing. I say the design responsibilities should be Carole's."

Carole was already ahead of us. "How do you guys feel about polka dots? I think they'd add great personality to the boxes. They say 'fun' to me."

"Yes!" Kathy replied.

I nodded and said, "Mmm" because my mouth was full.

"Great. I'll draw some samples of what I'm thinking, and we can discuss them next week."

Well that was simple, but we still needed product names and a logo.

We batted some words around and soon found ourselves back in time to when teenaged Carole worked at the bakery that sold *prosperity buns*. We wanted to give our line of cakes a name that conveyed a message beyond which flavor was which, and the word "prosperity" resonated with all of us because it linked to our wish for our business. We named our line Prosperity Cake. Now we needed to make sure the packaging tied into that message. We needed a logo!

For decades, Carole had been doodling an image of a tree that looked like the archetypal tree of life. She grabbed a pen and started jotting.

"What about this?" she said, turning her art pad around to show Kathy and me her simple drawing of a lovely tree with a symmetrical dome of branches and wide-reaching roots. "It conveys a certain—"

"Optimism?" Kathy said.

"Yes, I think so," said Carole.

And there we were again, in simple agreement. We would go forward with polka dots and our version of the tree of life to represent our cake line.

Assisted by Tanya, a talented, box-manufacturing salesperson who we contacted about box pricing, Carole designed a black box with white polka dots and a prosperity tree on top. On the tree's branches we added the words, *prosperity*, *success*, *hope*, *health*, *believe*, *imagine*, and *dreams*, all things we wished for our customers and ourselves. We felt it splashed our brand with a look of levity and the spirit of hope. Then, typical of the spaz sisters, we were so excited—and optimistic—about the future of the biz, we ordered ten thousand boxes on the spot. How's that for looking down the road?

"Oh, good God," Carole says. "Something just occurred to me—"

"Congratulations," says Kathy.

"I mean it! The way we used to dive in and order business cards and boxes, not waiting first and seeing, not pausing before leaping. Getting all fired up about an idea and just diving in. Does that remind you of anybody?"

"Wash your mouth out," I tell her.

"What am I missing?" says Kathy.

I smile at my younger sister. "She's referring to the name that must no longer be spoken."

"Not all that different than the corn dive and the catering dive and the hotel dive, right?" Carole says, shaking her head. "Maybe we inherited a bit of impulsiveness? Excitability?"

Kathy looks from Carole to me to Carole again. "Excitability's good, right? Everybody likes someone with a pulse, someone who gets fired up for an idea, right?"

"Yeah, but it's the 'leap before you look' thing Carole's referring to."

Now Kathy looks resigned. "Well, hell. I was kind of hoping we weren't actually his kids. I'd be perfectly happy to call you two *half-sisters* if it meant being free of *that* bloodline."

I tell her, "Sharing one quality with Voldemort doesn't prove paternity, but I don't think Mom was dabbling in other dudes, do you?"

"A girl can dream," says Carole.

Tanya suggested we create the boxes using heavy corrugated material so we could package and ship the cakes in one box, but following that advice ended up costing us. After we'd shipped a few cakes, customers called to complain.

"I intended this cake as a gift, but the box is dirty and dented from shipping. I need you to send me a clean box."

Welp. Chalk another up to the learning process. And as much as we enjoyed looking down the road, it took us some time before we learned to also keep our eyes open for *bends* in the road. We hadn't considered we might expand to add other cake flavors, for which we'd want different color boxes. *Whoops,* again.

As a result, we still have a couple hundred of those original boxes lying around.

It's taken us years to go through them all because as we've created new flavors, we've had the boxes made in colors that we think complement the flavors beautifully.

"New flavors?" you shriek.

Why, yes. There are more. Would you like to hear about the flavors we added to the line? Would you like to hear about those in mouthwatering detail? Okay. But first we need to take you on a little trip through New York.

CHAPTER THIRTEEN

One Saturday morning about four months into our weekly farmers market routine, Carole stood at our table, stopping customers in her usual folksy way—asking people where they're from, telling our cake story, enticing them to try a piece of "zero calorie cake that won't add even a millimeter to your waistline." (Ah, the freedom of the farmers market.) At around 11:00 a.m., two women, one in her sixties and the other in her forties, Carole guessed, introduced themselves as mother and daughter.

"Don't you ladies look lovely," said Carole. "You're so nicely dressed for a farmers market. Are you going somewhere special?"

The daughter said, "Yes, we're here for a wedding, but there's a break between the church and the luncheon, so we thought we might find something here to munch on later."

Her mother said, "We're having a girls' weekend, which we don't get to do often because of my daughter's job."

The daughter smiled and said, "The ceremony just ended, and we have to wait until one o'clock for the lunch."

The mother said, "And we can't check into our hotel until after three."

"Sample of amaretto cake?" Carole offered.

They both tried samples, and the daughter said, "Delicious! How much is it?"

Carole said, "Twenty-five dollars. And hey, I have an idea for you—why don't you buy the cake then pick up a bottle of wine at the liquor store next door, so tonight you can relax in your hotel room enjoying cake and wine and your time together."

The daughter said, "That's a great plan. And I'll share what's left of the cake with people in my office."

"Thank you," said the mother. "Now I get to spend more time alone with my girl!"

Then off the happy twosome went, polka-dot box in hand.

The following Saturday, it was my turn to sample at the farmers market, and just as I arrived, the market manager ran over to my table and handed me a piece of paper.

"I just got a call from a woman who said she's a producer for a food show in New York!" she said. "She wants to talk to you or one of your sisters. She left this phone number!"

"Is this a joke?" I said. "Are you guys pranking me?"

"Not a joke," she said. "Go, go! Make the call!"

I ran to the bathroom for privacy and called the number. After one ring, a woman said, "Martha Stewart Show, how can I direct your call?"

The Martha Stewart Show? When I could find my voice, I said, "I'm Sue Katein from Full Circle Flavors and was given this number to return a call to the producer, but I don't have her name, just this number."

The operator said, "Hold, please. I'll connect you."

At this point I was sweating and shaking. I tried to calm down by taking deep, slow breaths. A few minutes later, I heard a woman's voice say, "You must be Carole's sister, Sue. I'm Kate, the producer here. I met Carole last Saturday when my mother and I stopped at the farmers market. She offered us a taste of your fabulous amaretto cake, then gave us a great idea for how to spend the evening, which we did. Just us with wine and cake in our hotel room."

I answered, "That sounds like Carole. She can always put together a great time, even if she's not invited."

The woman laughed and said, "Unfortunately, Mom and I ate all the cake! Some for dinner, more for breakfast the next day—we couldn't stop ourselves—so I wasn't able to follow through with my plan to let some of my colleagues try it."

By now I could hear my heart thundering.

She continued, "I wonder if you can bring a cake to New York for our host to try. Carole's dynamic personality, the cake, and the fact that you're three sisterly entrepreneurs makes yours a great story. If our host agrees, you could share your recipe and your story with our audience."

What? Did she just suggest I share my cake recipe on national television? The very recipe I was currently protecting with an NDA?

I didn't want to sound ungrateful, so I said a round or two of, "What an opportunity!" and "I can't wait to tell my sisters!" But then I asked, "Is that a deal breaker, whether or not I'll share the recipe?"

"Yes," she said. "That's part of the point for us—introducing our audience to new dishes they can make."

I wanted to say, "I think I'd rather stick a hot glaze injector in my eye," but I told her we'd discuss it and in the meantime, of course we'd be happy to deliver cake to her offices.

She said, "Great! Just leave it with the receptionist anytime during the week, and I'll be in touch." Then she gave me the address and hung up.

I walked out of that farmers market bathroom shaking my head. What the heck had just happened? This was big . . . very big!

I called both sisters, and the essence of their replies was the same.

"ROAD TRIP!"

We got together the next day to plan our strategy. After hugging, then jumping up and down like three teens who had just met The Beatles, we calmed down and plotted.

Right away Carole said, "If we're going to be in the city anyway, why don't we stop by the *Rachael Ray Show* to see if we can submit our cake in a smaller size to be a snack of the day? I've been emailing the producer of that show for weeks but haven't heard anything. We could just show up!"

Kathy said, "Great idea. And let's think about where else we might just drop in while we're there."

For several months, we'd been talking about producing a smaller size cake to offer people who didn't have use for full-size cake (like those guys who slinked off to their cars to hide a big cake from their women) but we hadn't yet taken a run at it. This New York trip seemed like a great reason to get to it.

I said, "Yikes. If I need to crank out a bunch of little cakes, I'd better step on it. Let me bake a test run of a few twelve-ounce versions. If they're any good, we can figure out how to package and promote them."

Carole said, "We can wrap the little cake in a clear cello bag tied with a black-and-white polka-dot bow and slap our label on the front."

Well, that was quick. As our minds raced around everything we'd need to accomplish before we trucked up to the Big Apple, I jotted a list of things that had to happen:

1. Decide if we're willing to reveal our recipe and process on TV.

2. Name the new twelve-ounce cakes, order their packaging, and get the bakery onboard to produce a batch.

3. Discuss building a website. If we got ourselves on a TV show, how were people supposed to find us afterward? We'd need to step on it!

4. Have shirts or aprons made with our name and logo.

5. Plot our day in New York. We'd already decided that in addition to swinging by the offices of Martha Stewart and Rachael Ray, we needed to give Oprah a visit! Maybe we could entice *O Magazine* to introduce us as a new product.

A couple days later, we picked up the one hundred juniors Chad had made and took them to Carole's to place in those cello bags tied with black-and-white, polka-dot bows and slapped our label on the front. We were ready for that road trip!

We'd pulled it off. Only ten days after the producer had invited us to deliver cake samples to Martha Stewart's show, we were locked and loaded. It was a bright, cool October day—perfect for a road trip adventure. Kathy had emptied her trunk, so we had room for the five big boxes, each packed with twenty juniors. I'd had our prosperity tree logo and our names printed on the left breast of black polo shirts, and now we looked like were part of a real business.

As soon as we'd piled into Kathy's car, the yattering started.

"We're going to be famous!" said Carole. "I wonder what I'll wear to the Academy Awards."

"Do tell how an appearance on a cooking show lands you at the Oscars," I said.

"This is how things happen!" she said. "One day, it's television, the next the big screen!"

"Uh huh," added Kathy. "What's your screenplay about, again? Or are you taking acting classes in your free time?"

"Full Circle Flavors, the movie!" said Carole, as she opened her laptop to shop for full-length gowns.

Ah, the world loves a dreamer.

The ride to New York wasn't going to take more than two hours, so right away I wanted to spread the big question across the dashboard. "Okay, girls, what do you think about sharing the recipe with the public?"

Kathy chimed in first. "I wonder what they'd think if they knew we'd have to bring the infuser and the air compressor to run it. How excited are their viewers going to be about a recipe that requires *those* machines? Or are we supposed to tell them about the cake poking?"

Carole said, "I'm not keen on the idea of giving away our recipe so early in our business. Sue, what do you think?"

I said, "I wish they'd feature the cake without asking us to give up the secrets. I guess I don't see the payoff for us if we're just going to pull back the curtain."

As usual, our three minds were aligned. We decided we'd drop off the cake, but if they insisted on getting the recipe, we'd say no.

As we drove, our stomachs leapt with dreams of mass exposure and huge sales, and we tried to calm ourselves by sharing the advice our husbands had offered before hugging us goodbye.

Carole said, "John told me we should stay calm and not let

them see how nervous we are. He said to try to come off like 'well-seasoned' entrepreneurs."

"Jack said we're not the greatest actresses, so we should probably just be ourselves," said Kathy.

I added, "My John said, 'Don't get lost, and let the cake speak for itself. It's good shit.' That's my guy. Maybe he should write our marketing materials."

We talked about how lucky we were to have our husbands' unflinching support, which they'd demonstrated in a hundred ways. They accepted that our diving fully into the cake endeavor meant for some time we'd be working day and night without any income. They'd already packaged, picked up, loaded, unloaded, and delivered countless cakes, and they promoted us to anyone who'd listen.

We also talked about how grateful we were for the help of our bakers, the farmers market associates, our circle of friends, and our circle of hooligans (come to think of it, that's only one circle)—everybody who contributed to our success. Our friends were so loyal and invested, several of them were on the sidewalk to yell and clap as we drove off for New York City.

Although we'd all been to New York to see shows, none of us had ever *driven* there. Who the hell drives to Manhattan? Who drives *in* Manhattan? Anyone with half a brain takes a train, cab, Uber, or limo. Or, if you must, maybe a bus. But here we were, headed into the big, bad Holland Tunnel and about to come out the other side into an angry sea of street vendors, ruthless pedestrians, and taxi warfare. Although New York City might be considered a scary place for country mice, we never felt scared, just a bit intimidated by the grandeur. Musicians and beggars roaming the sidewalks, businesspeople walking fast enough to break bones if they collided, blaring car horns, flashing store signs, the smoke from a corner sausage vendor's grill. All of it made us feel small but at the same time revved up.

Maneuvering through the heavy traffic, one-way streets, and rushing rivers of pedestrians was no small feat, but Kathy is gutsy. She obeyed her GPS, and somehow, we ended up at the back door of Martha Stewart's TV studio. Of course, we had no idea where to park, so the plan was Kathy would idle as Carole and I dashed to the front to drop off the requested cakes.

We hustled toward the front desk receptionist. "Good morning," I said, mustering my best, I-know-exactly-what-I'm-doing voice. "We're here to deliver cake samples to Kate, the producer, as requested."

The receptionist was dark-haired and very pretty—I thought she looked like a young Carole. She welcomed us and asked us to wait.

"Thank you," I said. "And we're looking forward to seeing her in person. We need to talk through a few issues she mentioned on the phone."

As the receptionist spoke quietly into the phone, we stood in the lobby trying to look patient. It was a small office, and the walls were plastered with pictures of Martha Stewart and tasty-looking desserts.

The receptionist hung up the phone and, in a kind voice that seemed crafted to let the little people down gently, said, "I'm so sorry but Kate isn't available to talk to you now. Her assistant is tied up as well."

That was disappointing but not entirely unexpected. As we

handed her the three cakes, she said, "I'll make absolutely sure these get into her hands. I expect she'll be in touch as soon as the host has tried them."

We thanked her and headed for the door, as deflated as two girls who'd shown up five minutes too late to meet Santa. But we'd crossed our first goal off the list, so onward.

We dashed back around the building only to discover our getaway car was nowhere in sight. As it turned out, Kathy had been involved in a game of chicken with a cop who had told her to move it along and "don't let me find you back here, illegally parked." So what did Kathy do? She drove around the block and then planted herself in the very same spot.

We saw her coming around the corner to park illegally again, and as we made our way to the escape vehicle, we saw the cop speeding her way with lights flashing and siren blaring. We sprinted to the car. Kathy had opened the front and back windows on the passenger's side, so Carole and I dove into the open windows just in time for Kathy to take off at high speeds with our torsos hanging half out as we swerved and spun through the streets of Manhattan.

"*Why* are you lying to these good people?" Kathy interrupts. "What's with the sirens and the flashing lights? You're full of it, and really quite obviously."

"You don't know," I tell her. "You were busy driving. Ask Carole if it happened."

"You kind of blew it with the bit about diving into windows," says Carole. "You should try to be a better liar."

Buzz killers.

Okay, so while a mildly curious police officer may or may not have been headed toward our car to hand Kathy an angry ticket, Carole and I yanked the doors open and jumped in the car, and we took off for our next stop.

"Happy?"

"Just keeping it real, sister," says Kathy.

The next stop was to the studio of the *Rachael Ray Show*. It was now 10:00 a.m., and this was a warm October day. Since we were already ladies of a certain age, we were sweating like monkeys in the Atlanta Zoo in August. It didn't help that we were laughing like at the absurdity we faced at just about every intersection, where we either came *this* close to running down jaywalkers who seemed to think some invisible force field protected them from oncoming traffic or turned the wrong way down *yet another* one-way street. If the situation were a math equation, it would be chaos plus construction multiplied by unfamiliarity over adrenaline equals a giant case of crazy in our near future.

That's not to say we country girls weren't entirely delighted by the strange sights and smells that sprawled across the city. With our heads jerking right and left, we pointed out sidewalk hot dog and falafel vendors covered in sweat as steam rose from their carts; six-foot, twenty-something girls in tiny skirts who appeared to be on their way to a *Vogue* shoot; a man and woman with matching royal blue hair and arms covered in even bluer tattoos; salt-and-pepper-haired men who looked completely comfortable and cool (bastards) and put together in crisp shirts with ties (and sometimes jackets!); and countless young women wearing business suits and sneakers and carrying enormous tote bags as they dashed down sidewalks and then disappeared into subway entrances. It was a feast for our small-town eyes. As much as we were enjoying the parade, we had to focus and find our way to the studio.

Kathy continued to navigate the city like a pro and eventually stopped in front of a cement building with a tiny side door with no name on it. Trusting GPS, Carole and I tumbled out of the car, opened the trunk, grabbed twenty juniors, and stormed through that little door into a very tiny lobby, which we trusted was the receiving area for the *Rachael Ray Show*.

Shortly after our graceful entrance, we were met by a very tall, stern-faced guard. We tried to play it cool and stroll past him as if we knew exactly where we were going. But as we moved, he moved. Figuring we weren't going to outrun him and given we had no idea where we would have gone even if we'd made it past him, we stopped.

"Ladies," he said, "you can't go past this point without a pass."

Carole replied, "Oh, hello there," as if she'd just now noticed him. It was all I could do not to bust out laughing. She continued, "We'd just like to know which floor the *Rachael Ray Show* is on because her producer asked us to drop off a sample of our buttery-delicious, moist-beyond-belief, liqueur-infused amaretto cake. And we'd be delighted to leave one with you for being nice enough to let us upstairs."

The guard's eyes were now very wide. He said, "I'd *love* one of those cakes, but I'm sorry—it would be a security violation for me to tell you the show is on the fourth floor."

Again, I had to stifle a belly laugh. This was our kind of guy! We slid a junior amaretto cake across the glass countertop and into his enormous hands, then speed-shuffle-walked to the elevator like a couple of ten-year-olds trying to rush to the diving board after their mother yelled, "Don't run at the pool!"

Despite having no invitation, no idea where we were going, and no assurance we weren't about two minutes from being hauled off for trespassing, we pushed elevator button number four.

As the door opened, we hopped in, but the ride up to the fourth floor gave me a moment to realize what we were doing, and I started to fall apart. I was sweating and shaking, now nearly in tears from fear of being arrested as soon as we stepped out of the elevator. I whined, "Carole, we don't have an appointment. We're trespassing. Please, please, please let's go back out. We can ship them some cake."

Carole looked at me with the warm gentleness of a nurturing big sister and said, "Stop being such a big baby and fake a smile!"

When the elevator door opened, we were greeted by a young man with perfectly groomed, black, wavy hair, piercing blue eyes, and a jawline that could cut through a two-by-four. We've since referred to him as Eye Candy (or EC depending on who else is present). EC asked if we had an appointment, and Carole said, "We're scheduled for eleven thirty. I'm sorry, we're a bit early."

In that moment I was so impressed by her, I forgot about being sick to my stomach with fear.

To my amazement, EC called back to the producer, and a few minutes later a lovely young woman dashed into the reception area gushing with apologies that she hadn't replied to Carole's emails.

"I'm *so* sorry," she gasped. "I didn't realize we had an appointment." She explained she was new to the job and hadn't been told her predecessor had scheduled time with us.

How's *that* for dumb luck!

She said she'd be happy to taste our cake, and I thought I'd fall over with gratitude—for this woman, for the hungry first-floor guard, and most of all for Carole, fearless Carole.

We presented the flustered young woman with nineteen of our junior amaretto cakes and lots of our business cards. She said, "The packaging is fabulous. If they taste as good as they look, we'll be in touch."

Buzzing from what felt like a genuine victory, we made our way downstairs and past our favorite guard, who wore a big smile and a shirt covered in crumbs. We headed out to the door just as Kathy was pulling down the street with not a sign of the Heat on her tail. But there was no place for her to pull over, so she just slowed down and we ran alongside the car laughing until she could stop and let us jump in.

I know what you're thinking, but this one is *true*.

Our next step was to drop off cake to *O Magazine*, and *O* were we feeling confident. Once again, we hadn't been invited by so much as the guy who pulls the dead leaves off the lobby plants, but we'd decided invitations and permission were overrated. As we saw it, the idea of three crazy broads pumping booze into cake for money was an excellent subject for an article, and they'd be lucky to hear about us.

We found the building—a tall, modern-looking skyscraper that covered most of the city corner—and we did our now standard routine—Kathy dumps and runs while Carole and I improvise the schmooze. We had to walk around most of the block to find the front door, and once inside, we found ourselves in a kind of futuristic office world inhabited by at least fifteen people at desks, all of them separated from us by what appeared to be bullet-proof glass. The whole scene was kind of creepy. Just standing in front of it gave us the feeling you get when you're at Immigration Control, and they're looking from your passport to your face to your passport to your face. Then they ask, "Do you have anything to declare?" and even though while in Guadalajara you bought nothing more than a cheap piñata and a gallon of tequila (long since passed through your plumbing), for some reason you feel sure that this is it—you're about to be dumped into a Mexican jail with only a cockroach to keep you company for the next twelve years.

But we're not the types to be intimidated by the implication of a potential shoot-out, so we stood up straight, led with a smile, and tossed around the phrase, "liqueur-infused cake." Right away, two receptionists agreed to take our cakes and hand them over to a decision-maker."You and your business might be a *great* subject for a piece in our magazine," one of them said with a syrupy smile. We left six junior amaretto cakes behind, and as we exited the building, we wondered how long it would be before they ate the cake and forgot our names. My bet was that the cake was gone before we hit the street. Still, it felt like a bit of a victory because we'd just gotten ourselves within a step or two from a decision-maker. Maybe.

Once out on the sidewalk, sure enough, we spotted our sister arguing with yet another police officer. We hustled to the car and got out of there, now committed to finding a good martini and a burger. Rachael Ray's EC had recommended a place, which we found with very little struggle (we were becoming quite the citified women, now having been on the island for all of three hours), and behold there was an open parking space right out front! And even better—it had no parking meter, which only further convinced us we were traveling under a lucky star.

Inside, the little café was decorated like an outdoor garden. There was a lovely ivy-covered trellis along one wall and beautiful assorted flowers on each table. It was just after 1:00 p.m., and the lunch crowd had thinned, so we had the place practically to ourselves. As fast as we could wrangle a waitress, one of us ordered an icy Grey Goose martini with orange slices and a bacon cheeseburger with fries. Then the other two said, "I'll have what she's having."

I don't know if it had anything to do with the long drive to the city or the nutty escapades we'd just endured, but being able to sit quietly in this darling restaurant sipping our favorite drink made us blissful. The burgers practically made us weep: enormous patties of fresh Kobe beef under crispy bacon, fresh lettuce, ripe tomatoes, and thick cheddar cheese, all topped and bottomed with a fabulous brioche roll. And those fries! They were beer-battered and perfectly crispy.

We sat there for about an hour soaking in the day, plus another round of martinis—for just Carole and me because Kathy still had to drive. We raised our glasses to what felt like a massively successful trip, our hearts very happy. Then the bill arrived: $145 for three burgers and five martinis! This was 2009, and we were used to small-town Pennsylvania prices, so the number caused a bit of a jolt, but we'd never had such a fabulous lunch outside of our little town. We split the check, then sauntered out to the sidewalk, feeling smug that we had only a few feet to walk, thanks to scoring princess parking.

Crap! Shit! Dammit, dammit, and triple crap!

There was a white piece of paper lodged under the windshield wiper, and no, we weren't fortunate enough to discover it was a flier for Scuzzie Bob's Daytime Dance Emporium. It was a big, fat, stinking parking ticket. So much for our dumb luck; in this case, it was just a matter of dumb. What kind of country ninnies pull up in front of a restaurant in New York and don't know that somewhere around there is a machine waiting for their parking money? Answer that and no cake for you.

We've since referred to that lunch as "the $300 burger." It was $145 for lunch and $155 for the ticket. But we decided not to let the $155 slap dim our spirits as we climbed into the Kathy mobile and headed back through the maze of nutty, bustling Manhattan streets to find our way off the island and back down to Pennsylvania.

As we were heading down I-95 toward Philly, we received a call from Michael, our lawyer who had been working on trademarking Full Circle Flavors, LLC. He was calling to tell us another food company had already snagged the name. *Blarg!* We'd have to come up with another one we loved just as much. Well, we were buzzing from a day well spent on our business (and an afternoon priming a buzz), so it was a perfectly good time to brainstorm. Soon, the air in the car was filled with bad ideas and maybe even a couple good ones.

"Drunken Cakes, Inc!"

"Liquor Cake Specialties!"

"CooKin Sisters!"

"Three Drunk Girls!"

"Sister Slickers!"

"Boozy Bakers!"

"Tipsy Treats!"

After several miles, we stumbled on the realization that we're three spirited sisters, and dammit if we don't do everything fully, so we chose Full Spirited Flavours. We loved the double meaning attached to *spirited*, and we thought the European spelling of *flavours* might help us stand out in a cool, cosmopolitan way. Then again, more than a few people have asked, "Do you *not* know how to spell 'flavors'"?

Satisfied with the product of our highway brainstorm, we made it home safely, flopped into our beds, and slept the sleep of the genuinely happy.

CHAPTER FOURTEEN

Still high from our invigorating trip to the Big Apple, we knew we had to be prepared in case we actually got a shot at being a snack of the day on the *Rachael Ray Show*. Lawyer Jim put together a contract, and within a couple of weeks, we all signed our partnership agreement.

I don't want to reveal the specifics, but I'm proud to say it's now recorded in a legal document that I'm to be called the High Priestess of Pastry.

"Stop it," says Carole.

"Are you trying to give us credibility problems?" asks Kathy.

"Doctor of Dessert? Cake Crusader?" I offer.

"Okay, I'll play," says Carole. "Custard Crackpot."

"How about Tart Tart?" says Kathy.

She and Carole awkwardly high-five.

I say, "You guys are doing it wrong. I'm going back to the story."

Now we needed a website. And Kathy, being the most computer savvy of the three of us, was unanimously voted chief website officer. But designing and building a site was beyond her expertise, so she called our friend Leslee, a skilled photographer and computer whiz who had web design experience. Together they handled the site's design and hosting, photography, company information, contact information, and every other detail necessary to give us a professional online presence. We launched our shiny, new Full Spirited Flavours website and sat back to wait for the cash to roll in. We waited and we waited and we waited.

What a shocker when we realized people don't just show up after you hang an e-shingle. What happened to, "If you build it, they will come?"

Okay, we were going to have to do some more outreach. It didn't take us long to realize that, at the moment, we were only a full-spirited flavour. It was time to create those other flavors we'd been talking about.

Carole, who's really good at keeping her finger on the pulse of non-tech-related contemporary culture, told me limoncello was becoming popular and advised me to create a cake with that delicious lemony liqueur in it. I wasn't crazy about lemon cake—I've always been more of a chocolate gal—but I did as she said. Sometimes she's still the boss of me. Kathy also liked the idea of a lemon option, so I tried my base cake recipe using limoncello liqueur. I mixed a batch of the batter and added white chocolate bits for another layer of flavor, poured it into the cake pan, topped the batter with a buttery crumb mixture soaked with limoncello liqueur, then baked that little beauty.

We three tried it and agreed we'd found our new flavor, so I delivered a case of limoncello to Chad and asked that he make limoncello cake samples in both large and juniors sizes. The three of us gathered to taste Chad's samples and were delighted with the results. It wasn't too tart, wasn't too sweet. It was a winner.

Of course, well before the Optimism Sisters had any idea how successful that flavor would be, we went ahead and ordered five thousand yellow boxes with white polka dots for the full-size cakes and five thousand yellow bows with white polka dots for the juniors. Of course we did!

Next, we needed to find some delicious but reasonably priced limoncello, which meant it was time for a liqueur tasting! I bought three bottles of limoncello recommended by a liquor store manager and told the girls to come over to taste. We all agreed on a brand, and the following day I bought three cases and delivered them to the bakery. So now we had two cakes in the line.

Right away, the limoncello cake was a smash hit. We went through those first five thousand yellow polka-dot boxes in about six months. Limoncello quickly became our biggest seller, and to this day retains its crown. I was thrilled to see how versatile my recipe was, and I went to work on the next flavor. While I was pondering, we heard from the *Martha Stewart Show.*

Our unwillingness to share the secret recipe was indeed a deal breaker. Not letting viewers try to make the cake at home wasn't going to work for their show's format. Alas. But we felt good about our decision.

We never heard from *O Magazine* (cake thieves!). But our junior amaretto cake did end up being featured as a *Rachael Ray Show* snack of the day! We got the call about two weeks after our big New York adventure, and the opportunity was particularly satisfying because we'd stormed the Bastille to get it. We weren't invited to be on the show—just our cakes—but we were okay with that. We were excited and ready with a fully functioning website, the address for which would be plainly visible on the label affixed to every junior cake's packaging. Now it was time to get the bakery baking!

Chad baked us two hundred amaretto juniors, which we bagged and bowed before we dashed to New York (in and out without incident) to deliver the day before the show was to air. We also delivered a full-size amaretto cake for Rachael to serve at her personal Thanksgiving day dinner. We weren't invited to be part of the audience (*sheesh!*), so we watched the cake give-away on TV. The highlight for us was when the show's guest, Harry Connick, Jr., the gorgeous piano-playing crooner with the yummy southern drawl, held up one of our amaretto cakes (which at the time we still called prosperity cakes) and said, "I feel prosperous already."

We jumped up and down like preteens as Carole yelled, "He's soooo good looking, and he's touching our cake!"

After the show aired, we processed website orders for over three hundred cakes, and we received a lovely thank-you note from Rachael herself for the cake we gave her. In addition to lots of accolades and comments gushing customer satisfaction, we heard from countless people asking whether we offered other flavors.

Uh oh. We had momentum, and we weren't about to let it lag. We needed to move fast. The limoncello cake was ready to launch, and we agreed we needed two more flavors. Time for another meeting.

Carole said, "I think we should consider a chocolate option. We have to have a chocolate cake, right?"

"Gotta have a chocolate cake," said Kathy.

"Nobody has to convince me," I said. "We just need the right liqueur with it. Not sure what it should be."

"Give it some thought," said Carole. "You'll come up with a great combination—you always do. And for one more cake flavor, what about another citrus version? Look how well the limoncello turned out."

She had a point. Given the success of the limoncello cake, why not dabble in other citrus options?

As I wandered through a liquor store, I saw an ad for orangecello, made by the same company that produced the limoncello we were already using. I thought, why not? Maybe people loved all kinds of citrusy cakes. I placed a bottle of orangecello in my cart. Now what about the chocolate cake? What would be the best liqueur flavor to infuse it with?

Over the years I'd baked with other liqueurs, including Kahlua and Irish cream, but I quickly learned that some liqueurs, delicious as they may be in your morning coffee or poured right down your gullet, don't behave well in a cake. They call too much attention to themselves, and we were committed to creating cakes that included liqueurs whose personalities didn't stomp over everything else. I'd recently seen recipes online that added raspberry to chocolate, so I decided to try Chambord with my devil's food cake recipe. Armed with two new bottles of liqueur, I headed back to my kitchen.

I started with the orangecello. My thought was if I mimicked the limoncello recipe, the white chocolate chips might deliver a tasty creamsicle-flavored cake. I baked some demos, and I thought the cake turned out quite well—moist and flavorful. And it would look so pretty nesting in an orange box with white polka dots! But of course, I needed my partners to taste and approve before I could dive into ordering crazy numbers of boxes. Right? I called the girls and told them to head over. They walked in and sat down, and I placed a slice of the orangecello cake in front of each of them.

Before they dug in, Carole asked, "What made you try orangecello?"

"I saw a sign for it in the liquor store and figured it might deliver a kind of creamsicle thing."

"I love creamsicles," said Kathy. "What a great idea. I hope it reminds me of the ice cream truck."

They picked up their forks, and I waited, nervous because we really needed two new flavors, and I just wasn't sure about this orange cake. It tasted good, that was true, but to my palette it seemed *really* sweet, considerably sweeter than the other two flavors we were now producing. But I decided to zip it. Maybe some people like really sweet cake.

I watched my sisters slowly take a few bites and savor the flavor.

Carole said, "It does taste like a creamsicle. I think the hint of vanilla is great, and it works well with the white chocolate chips."

I sat quietly, forcing myself not to comment.

She continued, "The texture is the same as the amaretto and limoncello, but the taste is unique. Kind of sweet but let me try a couple more bites before I say more."

Uh oh. She needed more time.

Kathy said, "Yep, creamsicle. Definitely tastes like creamsicle. I don't think I've ever heard of a creamsicle cake. Ever."

Oh great. Maybe there's a good reason nobody makes creamsicle cake.

Then she added, "I'm really liking this! It's a little sweet, but sweet is good, right? Cake is supposed to be sweet."

Well, yes, cake is usually sweet. But when people eating a

piece of cake keep saying the word *sweet*, it sends nervous waves through the insides of a baker.

"I say it's a go," said Carole. "I can already picture pretty orange with white polka-dot boxes and matching bows!"

Ah, great minds.

Kathy said, "I agree with Carole. It's a yes."

The three of us don't waste time when it comes to making decisions. We don't need meeting after meeting to help us figure out if we like something. So what did we do next? We ordered five thousand orange-and-white polka-dot boxes and five thousand matching bows.

Then we set up a small tasting with several trusted friends and watched as they took bite after bite.

Taster number one said, "It's good but too sweet for me. Can I have a piece of amaretto cake?"

Taster number two agreed. "Yep, way too sweet. I wouldn't buy it. But how about some limoncello?"

Taster number three said, "You'd better hope the price of sugar doesn't go up." Then he took a big swig of coffee.

Crap. I knew it. I'd missed the mark. That was a blow. But we learned another good lesson: Bring in the beta eaters before buying another huge shmear of boxes!

What about those five thousand orange boxes and bows? Don't panic, Sue. Just wrangle the team a way out of this. I'd have to think fast and create a flavor that belonged in an orange box.

What other kind of cake could I make that had an orange personality? Maybe something using Grand Marnier? Nah. I'd baked with it before. It was another one that stood up too proudly in a cake. Next I considered rum, but that was another liquor that could be too overpowering, and there was nothing *orange* about it. I didn't want to start putting fruit in our cakes, but then I thought, what about baking in a touch of dehydrated mango and then infusing the cake with a coconut rum because that's a liqueur, not a liquor. I'd recently been to a party where I'd tried a Bahama Mama, a fruity cocktail made with coconut booze, and I loved the coconut flavor.

I picked up a bottle of coconut rum and headed back to the kitchen. I dropped some dehydrated mango and coconut rum into our yellow cake batter, topped it with toasted coconut, baked it, and then infused the cake with a coconut rum liqueur glaze. As the cake cooled, I took three deep breaths, twirled in a circle, and rapped the counter four times with a mixing spoon. After the orangecello incident, one couldn't be too careful.

About twenty minutes later, I sliced a piece and laid it on a dessert plate, grabbed a fork, and tried my first bite. I closed my eyes and thought, this tastes like an island vacation, so dammit if we don't have another winner.

Now it was time to bring in the beta eaters. I baked three full-size and six junior-size cakes and then invited ten taste-testers—eight pals and two sisters—to meet the following day at Kathy's house. As usual, everyone I invited replied with some version of, "I don't care if the cops deliver my kid home in hand-cuffs. I'll be there!" They arrived and hopped into seats around Kathy's dining room table, and I placed ten pieces of cake in front of ten eager test rabbits.

Then I hopped a plane for Vegas.

No, that's not right. I sat there in silence and chewed my thumbnail.

Carole spoke up first. "Wow, I didn't expect that! I'm not a rum girl, but the coconut flavor with the mango background is terrific!"

Okay. Not a bad start.

Kathy said, "I don't like rum, either, and I definitely don't like mango, but the cake manages to hide them *and* complement them!"

Not what I'd call a flaming endorsement, but at least it sounded positive.

Taster number three said, "This is the best rum cake I've ever tasted. And for the record, I'd drink rum if you served it in a rusty soup can."

Also not a bolstering endorsement.

Taster number four said, "Oooh! Makes me want to strip off my clothes and dance to the rhythm of a steel drum."

Um.

Taster number five said, "Deeelicious. My sister's lips blow up like balloons if she eats mango, but I think this cake is worth it. It's her birthday next weekend—put me down for two."

Clearly, our friends are special.

The rest of the taste testers expressed lots of *oohs* and *ahhs* and other declarations of "go for it!" Despite some clunky feedback, the response was positive. The mango coconut rum cake was a go.

Now I needed to get moving on a chocolate option. The next day I baked a chocolate cake flavored with Chambord, but *merde!* The raspberry flavor disappeared into my devil's food recipe. I still wanted to find a way to create a chocolate/raspberry combination, and Chad suggested we try Razzmatazz liqueur. He vouched for the quality of the liqueur, and a bonus was that it cost a lot less than Chambord. I whipped up another batch of chocolate cake batter, dropped in some fudge-like chocolate chips, baked the whole shebang, then infused the cake with Razzmatazz. And oh my, did my kitchen smell delicious as that cake baked. I could practically *feel* the chocolate wafting around the room.

After the cake cooled, I tried a big bite and then pulled a muscle patting myself on the back. This cake was *delicious*, and I hadn't a shred of doubt my sisters and whoever we rounded up for a tasting were going to go crazy for it. I topped the cake with a splat of pink ganache stripes for color, and I was satisfied it was ready to debut.

After squeals of "yes!" all around, we officially had our fourth flavor. Before long, I replaced the ganache strips with tiny pink chips for drama, but in time we ditched the pricey pink business in favor of a sprinkling of chocolate crunchies. Then we ordered five thousand, raspberry-red-and-white, polka-dot boxes and five thousand bows.

Now that we had four flavors to offer in two different sizes, we continued our efforts to boost sales by asking local retailers, like small mom-and-pop delis, little grocery outlets, beer distributors, and liquor stores if they'd sell our cakes. Meanwhile, Carole increased our presence in the community by getting us coverage in magazines and newspapers.

As demand increased, our website was causing us problems because its interface wasn't user-friendly. Online buyers—like me—have no patience; if it isn't easy to use, they go elsewhere. What we needed was beyond Leslee and Kathy's pay grade, and fortunate for us, we had a skilled web expert ready to help.

A friend of Carole's, Tom Kirkpatrick, who was an experienced web designer with extensive programming experience, offered to help us but refused to let us pay him. He's that kind of guy.

As Tom was building our new website, we knew we were overdue to find some office space. We'd been running the business out of my house, where I was set up to manage the accounting, and Carole's shop, where we packed and prepared the cakes for shipping. Things had gone relatively smoothly, but we knew it was time to move operations into a professional space and give our husbands a break. As we (mostly Carole) were reaching out to retailers and searching for other venues to sell our cakes, it became obvious we needed a place to conduct meetings and present ourselves as a serious business. We needed enough space for three desks and a big table we'd use to assemble orders and when necessary, clear off for meetings. Lucky for us, the bakery had no problem housing all the boxes, so we didn't need much additional storage space.

Carole made appointments for us to look at four offices. We turned down the first three easily—too big, too small, too expensive. Then we strolled into option number four, a four-hundred-square-foot former artist's studio nestled behind the main office of an accounting firm. It was located in a serene, wooded area, and the space included a small deck, plus several windows that provided lots of light. The office was small, but we thought it was perfect for us, except for one teeny, tiny detail. There was no indoor plumbing. No sink, no toilet. That we went ahead and signed a lease anyway can't come as a surprise to anyone who's been following our tendency toward flash decisions. (How many boxes did we buy?) We realize this kind of forward-storming energy doesn't always allow for, shall we say, circumspection. But since we weren't going to bake there, we figured what was the big deal? Well, sure, no sink to rinse coffee cups or cake sample dishes. And oh sure, there was that little matter of having to traipse—through sleet, hurricane, or heat wave—a hundred feet to the nearest available ladies' toilette. But what about the pleasure of never having to *clean* the toilet? Did you think of that, Ms. Whisky Glass Is Half Empty?

We signed a two-year lease and then ran to Staples to buy three new desks for a whopping $99 each. Kathy's company was doing some remodeling and planned to throw away all kinds of office furniture and equipment, so she suggested we do some dumpster diving over the weekend. For that kind of search-and-rescue mission, we knew we'd need some muscle, so we called on my son Ralph and Kathy's son Beau to be our collectors and movers.

Oh, what a day that was! We all met up in the back of the office building at 8:00 a.m. and were amazed at the volume of great office stuff that filled those dumpsters. There were computers, filing cabinets, tables, trash cans, and other miscellaneous office supplies. We knew we'd have to do some serious digging and sifting to get to the best of what was in there. I'm talking, "Give me ten fingers, where are my latex gloves, holy shit is that a raccoon?" dumpster diving.

And even though Carole and Kathy kept urging me to just take a table and maybe a filing cabinet, I wasn't having it. I was in free-shit heaven! Maybe none of it was new, but it was all new to us! As our company's accountant, I saw it as my fiduciary responsibility to strap on a hazmat suit and plunge, arse up, into a huge metal box that over the years had probably been home to gobs of toxic repugnancies, bacterial horrors, and other unthinkable disgustingness. But thanks to *some of us* being on the not-so-prissy side, we left with about $1,000 of free start-up office goodies.

With the trucks loaded, we headed to our new office. Thank goodness we had the boys to move the big filing cabinet into place along with seven chairs and an enormous bookcase we'd also saved from dumpster death. The last piece of furniture to go through the door was a very cool wooden table, a large, round piece with a protective glass top, which we placed in the middle of the room. Carole later draped a tablecloth of our now-signature black-and-white, polka-dot design under the glass, and that centerpiece made the room look adorable.

We placed four of the chairs around the table and the other three in front of our desks. We cleaned the miscellaneous office supplies, including trash cans, pen holders, and desktop organizers and placed them around the office. Finally, we decorated the pale-yellow walls with glam shots of our cakes and not-so-glam pictures of us along with a sign that read, "Life Is Short, Eat Cake First" and another that read, "You Had Me at Cake."

We rewarded the guys with sandwiches and beers at a nearby restaurant, and after lunch we sent them on their way. But we three were too wound up to go home yet, so we dashed back to the new headquarters of Full Spirited Flavours and rearranged until we agreed we'd created a highly efficient workspace. After we puttered around making lots of little shifts and tweaks, Carole stood back and directed Kathy and me as we pushed a desk just a little more to the left, tipped a picture frame just a little bit to the right. Then we stood back with our hands on our hips to evaluate the overall setup, the feng shui of it all. It was perfect.

Do you remember the first time you lived in a place you were paying for yourself, those first days in an apartment that was just yours—yours to decorate or mess up—all yours? That's how we felt. It was thrilling.

The next day we showed up for our first exciting day of work in our new digs. As we settled into our chosen desks, I asked Carole and Kathy, "Who do you want to be today? Manager, purchaser, secretary, vice president, treasurer, buyer, king, jester?"

And that little exchange became part of our routine: We show up, we settle in, and then we chose our titles for the day.

Childlike titling aside, we needed to assign the real responsibilities within our new enterprise. Since our first days in business together, we've reached over and overlapped roles like hungry kids at a buffet. And—like those hungry buffet diners—we're happy to try new foods and eat what lands on our plates. But for the sake of organization (and in the interest of playing to our strengths), we divided our responsibilities like this: Carole was to be in charge of research and design; I was in charge of recipes, accounting, operations, and shipping; and Kathy was the boss of tech. Carole and I both also handled purchasing, while Carole and Kathy worked on marketing. We three considered ourselves madly responsible for sales. We worked on sales in our sleep. We thought about sales while we cooked. We thought about sales in the shower. We were always selling. We were a three-headed sales creature with extra arms to wave people down on the street.

Once settled into our office and sure about our cake flavors, it was time to get serious about the booze. We were going to need a lot of it.

CHAPTER FIFTEEN

Buying liqueur by the bottle wasn't cost effective because the bakery had to open the bottles and dispose of them, which meant added labor costs. Bottle breakage in a commercial bakery is also an issue; glass chards flying around isn't great for cake safety.

The hunt began for a better option.

Carole had been sparing us Pennsylvania liquor store prices by zipping over state lines like a bootlegger to bring back carloads of alcohol from Delaware. This wasn't a long-term solution because of the archaic Pennsylvania laws that deemed it illegal to bring into Pennsylvania alcohol purchased out of state, whether one bottle or ten. Every time Carole headed off to Delaware, Kathy and I would wait and sweat as we pictured her being hauled off to the clink. So, bottles weren't the answer anymore. We needed booze by the barrel.

Established in 1884, Jacquin's in Philadelphia is America's oldest producer of cordials. We wanted them to sell us amaretto in fifty-five-gallon barrels, but that wasn't going to be as easy as placing an order. To buy that much booze at a time, we'd need a bulk liquor license from the good old state of Pennsylvania because they own and control all liquor sales in the state.

Requiring a license for large booze purchases is the state's way of tracking all the liquor sold so they can make sure they're getting all the tax money they're owed.

In addition our having to leap that hurdle, before Jacquin's would accept our order, they wanted us to prove we were for real and that we genuinely needed large volumes of alcohol for cake. For months, Carole badgered one of their VPs to visit our office for proof, and then one rainy September afternoon, a couple of months after we'd moved into our office, a dignified looking, professionally dressed gentleman carrying a case of mixed liqueurs knocked on our office door.

"Hello, my name is Kevin," he said. "I'm vice president of Jacquin's, and I've received many, *many* calls, emails, and letters from a woman named Carole who apparently has the energy of seven teenagers. She's been badgering me for amaretto in large barrels."

That's our girl! Carole had worn him down, so he decided to see if we were a legitimate business or if she was just a party girl trying to stock a frat house.

Carole stood and held out her hand. "Hi, I'm the seven teenagers."

Kathy and I introduced ourselves, offered Kevin a cup of coffee, and sat him down at our little polka-dot-topped table.

He said, "I've never had a request for large-volume amaretto to make cake. Barrels are usually sold to individuals bottling it for specialty stores in other states."

"Well, Kevin, as you can see," said Kathy, gesturing to the posters and photos all over the office, "we're all about the cake."

"And your cake was featured on *The Rachael Ray Show*?"

"Snack of the day!" bellowed three voices, almost in unison.

"Impressive. Why the need for barrels? Just how much liqueur do you use?"

I told him we were selling one hundred cakes per week.

With a twinkle in his eye, Kevin said, "If I'm going to be able to help you, I'll need to gather all the information there is. So, cake?"

I placed a full amaretto cake in the center of the table and served him an enormous slice. We sat quietly as he took his first bite. Both his eyebrows and forehead went up. Then a second bite, then a third. Then he said, "Let's talk."

I explained our infusion system and said, "If the bakery has to open and later dispose of the bottles, that adds to our cost. And it's taking at least four bottles per batch of eighteen cakes."

As Kevin listened, he cut himself another piece and ate it. Then he cut another sliver and nibbled on it. Then he cut just a corner and ate that. Then he pinched a bunch of crumbs on his plate and ate those. Then he cut another slice. And then there was no cake left. In the ninety minutes Kevin had been in our office, hearing about our business model and our need for booze by the barrel, he'd eaten a thirty-six-ounce amaretto cake, a size we suggest offers ten to twelve servings!

For those who like practical conversions, that's two-and-a-quarter pounds of cake. For an even more visual comparison, it's the equivalent of about twenty-six Twinkies.

As he finished the last bite he said, "Okay, I get it."

Carole said, "You know, all that time I was hounding you, I was also trying to score us limoncello, coconut rum, and Razzmatazz by the barrel. But none of the men I left messages for called me back. It has me wondering if there's a boy's club here that won't let us in."

Kevin smiled. "Not really a boy's club, but there aren't as many women in management as there should be." Then he cleared his throat. "That cake is the best thing I've ever tasted. We must help you continue to produce them."

We wrapped up our very successful meeting, but before Kevin left, he set a case of different liqueurs on the table—crazy flavors, like birthday cake vodka, espresso vodka, and peach rum—and said, "Maybe you can make a cake out of one of these flavors?"

I told him I'd give it some thought, but I silently doubted I'd be interested in expanding the line. We now had four cakes we considered perfect, and we'd all agreed to focus on quality over quantity. We smiled as we waved goodbye to Kevin.

But before we could roll out the barrel, we had to secure that bulk liquor license. Chad confirmed the bakery could house a very large barrel of liqueur for us, so we submitted the paperwork and paid the nominal fee for the license, and two weeks later, we had a bulk liquor license. One week after that, we had a barrel of amaretto standing in Chad's bakery, a barrel that saved us over 40 percent off the bottle price.

We'd told Chad our suspicions about the boy's booze club, so he introduced us to a guy in New York who he thought might be able to help us navigate some of the barriers to entry. This guy had been making tequila cakes, and he gave us the name of a contact at a small limoncello distiller in New Hampshire. It was the contact we needed.

Fabrizia Spirits, a small distillery in New Hampshire, run by brothers Phil and Nick was brand-spanking new to the world of alcohol production and distribution. Because we had inexperience in common, we felt an immediate connection to these guys. I called Phil to ask about buying their limoncello in fifty-five-gallon barrels, and he agreed to send us a couple bottles to give his liqueur a test run.

I baked up a few cakes using Fabrizia limoncello and was thrilled with its clean, lemon essence, which was light but sweetly present and genuinely improved the flavor of the limoncello cake. I could tell it was quality stuff—better than what we'd been using—so we ordered a fifty-five-gallon barrel.

All set for amaretto and limoncello, we still had two alcohol issues left. There were plenty of distributors that produced coconut rum, but not all their rums had flavor strong enough to work well in cake. Alas, I accepted there was to be more rum drinking in my future. I also researched options for volume rum purchase and found four contenders, but only two of them—one sold in Florida, one in Texas—delivered flavor that balanced well with the yellow cake and mango. And only one of them was willing to ship fifty-five-gallon barrels to Pennsylvania. It was an easy choice to make.

That left the Razzmatazz. This was trickier. Not a terribly popular liqueur, it wasn't easy to find in big barrels.

Carole and I sent email after email and left countless messages for distributors, but our communications were met with silence.

What the hell? These people don't like money?

To make the issue even more urgent, our chocolate razz cake was getting extremely popular, with about fifty cakes being ordered every week.

Our tenacity (and a lot of free cake delivered to doorsteps) led to zilch. Not even free cake scored us a return phone call, and I consider that one of the world's great unsolved mysteries. We were getting desperate, so Carole called Kevin at Jacquin's and asked if he had any advice or connections that could end our frustrating search. Right away, he reached out to a VP at Beam Suntory, the distributor of Razzmatazz, and set up a meeting. Three weeks later, a delivery guy rolled our first barrel of Razzmatazz into the bakery. *Whew.*

Eight months after our first sampling at the farmers market, we were really in business.

Tom finished our new website, and now all four flavors in both sizes were on full display for the public. He told us we had lots of space on the new site should we want to expand in any way, so we called another meeting of the minds (which meant we got up from our desk chairs, walked to the middle of the room, and sat at the round table) to discuss possible new flavors and products.

Kathy started. "How about a peanut butter liqueur cake? I love peanut butter."

"Eat a peanut butter cup," I said.

"Well *that's* not good brainstorming behavior," said Carole. "Put your open-minded hat on."

"Okay, okay," I said. "I've never heard of peanut butter liqueur, and we can't house anymore barrels anyway. I say we stick with our decision to make only four flavors, but maybe we can create other sizes and shapes? Kathy, can I offer you a peanut butter cup?"

"That's better," said Carole.

"I'll take two," said Kathy. "Three if the chocolate is dark."

"What about a four-ounce-size cake?" Carole asked.

"I like it," said Kathy. "Just a bite or two. Maybe four if you're in mixed company."

"We could make a variety pack with all four flavors," I said. "Let me look into what it would take to do that. I've also been thinking about the possibility of making really teeny cakes and packaging them like a box of chocolates."

"You never know *what you're gonna git*," Kathy drawled.

"I see what you did there," said Carole. "But in this case, we should probably make sure they do know *what they're gonna git*."

The meeting lasted approximately twelve minutes, then we returned to our workstations.

I ordered four-ounce paper cake cups shaped like flowers, baked a dozen little cakes of each flavor in the paper cups, and presented them to the girls. We agreed they worked for a new size. Naming them was the easy part because they were shaped like a flower. We decided to call them *Blossoms.* Now we needed somebody to help us design a new box.

And we were growing. We needed more money. We needed to build our customer base and throw some money into marketing. Gotta spend it to make it, right? Yeah, well we had no problem spending it; we'd just dropped ten grand on alcohol and another four grand on pretty polka-dot boxes, so we were light on cash, and we weren't going to see any incoming unless we got serious about sales.

Sales, sales, the heart of every business is sales. Once again, thank God for Chad.

Chad had already introduced us to Bob, the guy who hooked us up with our limoncello supplier. Bob owned a little company that made tequila-infused cakes, and he needed someone to ship his cakes, so he offered us the job, and we took it. It was a way to make some extra dough (see what I did there) to pay our rent.

One of his marketing strategies was to send a cake as a birthday gift to everybody who agreed to be added to his mailing list. Being in business on his own (poor lad didn't have a gaggle of sisters to lean on), he needed help processing the birthday cake orders, which included packing and shipping them via FedEx once a month. Oh boy, did *that* turn out to be a bigger job than we'd bargained for. Each month, we picked up 300-450 cakes from the bakery, typed up and printed labels, carefully placed the cakes in boxes along with marketing literature, and drove them to the closest FedEx shipping center. Kathy and I did most of this work as Carole was busy finding new venues to sell our cakes. What was supposed to be a simple side gig took up so much of our time, we fell way behind on our own marketing and sales campaigns. So after two years, we politely gave our notice.

Tom had upgraded our website, and after working with our marketing content for quite some time, he had a big suggestion. During a meeting he graciously hosted at his house, he gently said, "Ladies, I think it's time to consider changing your logo."

I heard a whooshing noise. I think it might have been Carole gasping. "Change our w . . . w . . . what?" she managed to say. Kathy ran and grabbed a cold compress and held it to Carole's forehead.

Tom said, "I just don't think the prosperity tree accurately represents the company. You're Full Spirited Flavours. What's the tree doing in there?"

We all sat in silence for a moment. Then Carole's bottom lip quivered. "It's . . . it's . . . about prosperity."

Not her most convincing argument.

Tom continued, "Also, it's kind of old-fashioned and not in a good way."

Wow, this guy was really good at the tough-love thing. Would Carole survive all this love?

Tom said, "I recommend letting Paul take a run at some new logo ideas."

Tom's nephew, Paul, was a talented graphic designer, and we knew we'd be lucky to get him.

"What do you think, Carole?" asked Kathy.

"About what?" she replied, mindlessly sketching trees on the back of a phone bill.

The rest of the conversation is fuzzy in our minds (trauma can do that), but eventually we all agreed the tree-of-life logo didn't represent who we were, so we asked Paul to sketch some ideas to help rebrand us a bit. Agreeing to say goodbye to the old logo made us understand the literary world's "killing your darlings"; damn if we didn't love that tree, its look, its origins, its meaning. But Tom was right: it wasn't serving our brand, so we had to let it go.

After just one week, Paul presented us with a new logo we all loved: within a solid black circle was our company name topped with spirited polka-dot bubbles.

It's bright and lively, and we think it accurately reflects who we are, full-spirited and prancing around in polka-dots.

Around the same time, he also finished the blossoms packaging design, which featured pictures of the cakes surrounded by colored polka dots and spotlighted our new logo. But—*whoops.* Remember that time we bought a metric shit-ton of boxes bearing the old logo? And that other time we did the same? And that other time? Yep, we had about twenty thousand boxes with our old branding. We fixed that issue by slapping a very costly new logo label over the tree on every box.

Meanwhile, I was experimenting with yet another cake size, a bite-sized option that I thought we might call *Petites.* I envisioned we'd offer all four flavors packed sixteen to a box, like assorted candies. They turned out to be too small to infuse, so we had to soak them in the liqueur, but while soaking gave them the liqueur flavor we love, it didn't deliver the long shelf life our cakes were becoming known for. No-go for the Petites, but that didn't mean it was no-go for their boxes! We'd already ordered five thousand (of course we had), and there was no way to re-purpose them, even with a new label. Anybody looking for some old useless boxes?

Around this time, Chad dropped a bomb we hadn't seen coming. He said his bakery was closing its doors.

No! Not the tree of life *and* the Chad gang! For almost four years, we'd proudly been a small part of what kept their bakery afloat after the terrible hit of the post 9/11 loss of their airline clients. But they never fully recovered and were now accepting they had to close up shop. What could we do but thank them for all their exceptional work and wish them all well in their next endeavors?

We needed a new bakery. As we considered what to look for in our next bakery partnership, we reviewed our relationship with Chad's bakery. They gave us the idea to create the glazing infusion system, which proved priceless. They also adapted our recipe for bulk production, which ensured that when someone bought one of our cakes, it looked and tasted like the one bought last week. Adorable as a lopsided, homemade cake topped with sprinkles and trick candles is, we needed to guarantee uniformity. (Damn, that sentence was hard to write. The day I home bake and then serve a shabby looking, lopsided cake is . . . *never*.)

Bakery number two was run by a skilled pastry chef who wasn't a fit for us. After working together for two years, he said making our cakes was too much work for the money. Hearing that this baker wanted to end our relationship didn't break any of our hearts because we'd grown tired of his anger management issues that sometimes led to broken infusion needles.

Our days of managing toddlers were long behind us, so we moved on and found bakery number three, which was in Boston. It might not seem very far from our little town near Philadelphia, but it's a distance that feels greater every time you make a six-hundred-mile round trip to deal with a recipe that's still not coming out right. We never went into full production there.

Bakery number four, a small outfit in New Jersey, had an experienced management team, but their Romanian lead baker spoke very little English, and the language barrier caused a lot of challenge when we tried to communicate that a cake wasn't quite right.

"This one is a bit dense," one of us might say.

"You want cake dents?" we might hear in reply.

We would say, "As you can see, this cake is a bit flat."

"Who call you fat?"

Sigh.

They also had trouble keeping our infusion system clean. The needles that infuse the glaze required cleaning by sterilization after each use. If they weren't properly cleaned, bacteria could build and lead to mold, which meant cakes ended up in the garbage. This is like pouring limoncello down a drain, and what kind of unholy animal would do that?

After six months with that bakery, we once again started looking for another option. We were committed to getting the bakery situation figured out if it meant buying our own bakery and cranking out the cakes ourselves. It was starting to look like that's what we might have to do. While preparing to break up with bakery number four, we discussed it.

"I'm too old and too tired to do all the baking," I said, "and obviously you two aren't bakers. The idea of us being the bakery for this business endeavor is idiotic."

"Agreed," they harmonized.

Conversation over.

That was easy.

Then came bakery number five. Oteri's in Philadelphia. This was a well-established Italian bakery known for producing top-notch baked goods. They were family owned and run, and after we spoke to a few of their happy customers, we felt confident they were the bakery we needed. We'd often thought of approaching them, but we'd heard through some grapevines they weren't taking new cake production clients. I came up with the brainy idea we might slip in the door if we asked them to create a liqueur-infused cookie, then later we could move in for the cake kill.

At the time, Kathy was traveling for work, so Carole and I interviewed Oteri's. They had three retail stores, and we scheduled a meeting with them in their flagship store where their office and main bakery were housed. Even from the sidewalk, we could tell this was a special place. The front window was filled with fabulously decorated wedding cakes, and as we entered the bakery, we were enveloped by the delicious scents of chocolate and cookies. Bernie, one of the counter girls, greeted us with a smile and directed us to an office down the hall where the bakery owners waited for us.

Owners and bakers Jimmy, Lisa, and Walt stood up and greeted us with handshakes. Lisa explained their bakery had been founded in 1904 by her great-grandparents and passed down until she took over in 2006.

"As you can see," she said with a smile, "we're a family business, like you. It's a line of cookies you're looking for?"

Right away, Carole fessed up. "I have to be honest. Because we heard you weren't taking on new cake customers, we thought you might consider a smaller product line to start. We hoped that would get us in the door."

Lisa laughed. "I was *wondering* why you weren't asking us to do your cakes!"

Jimmy asked, "Who makes the cakes for you now?"

Carole said, "We're in a tough spot. We need to leave our present bakery because . . . well, let's say their standards don't match ours. We make four flavors of liqueur-infused cakes, and right now we need between fifty and a hundred of each flavor per week. We're shooting to produce two hundred per week of each as soon as possible. But we heard you aren't taking on any new cake customers. Is that right?"

Jimmy said, "Don't believe everything you hear. Anyway, we were making rum cakes for a client we won't name, and she disappeared without paying her bill. But she left cases of rum and some expensive cake molds. Maybe we should see if anything she left behind could be of use if we make your cakes."

Did he just jump ahead to talking like potential partners? I was so excited by the possibility of working with Oteri's, words weren't able to make their way from my brain to my quivering mouth. One look at me and Carole could see she needed to lead the charge.

She said, "We buy our liqueurs in fifty-five-gallon barrels and house them at the bakery. Would that be a problem?"

Now Jimmy was excited. "You get your liqueur in *fifty-five-*gallon barrels? Wow. What a great way to house all that booze. I've never even heard of a bakery having barrels of booze! Did you bring any cake with you?"

Did we bring any cake? We carry cake around in our purses, glove boxes, and front pants pockets. Within minutes, I was back from the parking lot carrying four cakes, one of each flavor.

"Which would you like to try first?" I asked. "Limoncello, amaretto, mango coconut rum, or chocolate razz?" As Carole and I lifted the cakes from their boxes, Jimmy watched like a kid waiting for Grandma to serve him the biggest piece of warm apple pie. "No need to choose," I said. "Let the slicing begin. Have a couple of spare knives?"

Walt brought us plates, forks, and knives, and I sliced samples of all four cakes. Then Lisa, Jimmy, and Walt tried each one, and let's just say it went very well.

Lisa looked up from her plate and said, "You have something very special here. Let's get your cakes going so you don't lose the customer base you've worked so hard to build."

I tried to hold back the tears welling in my eyes. Something about this encounter was like being wrapped in a giant hug, and I knew why we needed that so badly. For many years, the three of us had worked so much and fought so hard. This cake business meant everything to us. All those years of being raised with no support, no guidance, and complete lack of the comforts of security. As grown up as we were by now, we were still hungry for some sense of surety. In that Philadelphia office of that lovely family business, I knew we were about to become part of the family.

When Carole and I left the building, we were both in tears.

Oteri's hadn't yet made us so much as a cupcake, but we just knew.

The following week, Jimmy sent his team to pick up our liqueurs, infusion machine, boxes, molds, and labels from bakery number four. I had already given the recipes to Jimmy and Walt, so we discussed all our processes, and waited for the first test batch.

After only two runs of each flavor, they got them all just right. Now feeling secure with our new bakery, we turned our attention to restaurant sales.

Limoncello was a family-owned Italian restaurant in West Chester, PA, with a reputation for not offering outside vendor products on their menu, so we knew they'd be a tough sell. But that kind of challenge only gets Carole's blood pumping harder.

Limoncello offered its customers a free shot of limoncello at the end of each meal, and we were determined to convince them to add a piece of our limoncello cake to their end-of-the-meal tradition. Carole got to work. She sent dozens of emails to Frank, one of the restaurant's owners, and he finally agreed to let Carole give a tasting presentation to the family.

Landing this restaurant was so important to us, even Carole was nervous, but on a brisk fall day at 10:00 a.m., she marched into that restaurant like a soldier. The place was very quiet, except for the bustle of chefs and workers in the kitchen preparing for the lunch crowd. The three owners, Maria and her sons, Frank and Paul, sat at a table next to the bar sipping coffee and waiting for her presentation.

After introducing herself, Carole described the features of the cakes she knew would be especially appealing to restaurant owners. "They stay fresh for up to three months without refrigeration, but they also freeze well." All three of them nodded. Then Carole sliced and served samples of both the amaretto and limoncello cakes.

Maria spoke first. "This is very special, especially this limoncello."

Now Carole knew it was time to hit them with the secret weapon. She said, "Before you serve your customers a piece of limoncello cake, we recommend you take sixty seconds to make it irresistible. You simply drop a pat of butter in a sauté pan, and when the butter gets hot and sassy, place a slice of the cake on top of the butter for thirty seconds, and then flip it. Let both sides sauté for about thirty seconds and serve quickly."

Paul sliced a few pieces of the cake, dropped them on a plate, and hustled back to the kitchen. In a few minutes he returned with three warm, sautéed pieces of limoncello cake. After they each took a bite of warm, buttery cake, they stepped away for a private meeting.

Five minutes later, Frank returned and asked, "How many of these do you have in your car—here, right now? We'll take whatever you have, just the limoncello. The amaretto is great, too, but the limoncello is a perfect fit for us."

Prepared as usual, Carole had eight limoncello cakes in her trunk. That same night, the restaurant offered our limoncello cake to their customers.

After a couple of days, Frank called Carole with a resounding, "Signoras, our patrons have spoken. This cake is worthy of our menu."

All three of us were in the office and about to go home for the day when Carole took that call. After she hung up, she looked at Kathy and me and shouted, "We did it! They want our cake!" We jumped out of our chairs, shouted, and danced around the room. Then Kathy shook up a batch of celebratory limoncello martinis, and they tasted like victory.

In our second year working with Limoncello, we learned a big lesson about selling to restaurants. Maria told us that if her restaurant was going to continue serving our cakes, they needed to be bigger. Unwrapping, slicing, and disposing of all the packaging for our thirty-six-ounce round cakes for restaurant use was calling for too much of the staff's time.

As we all know, necessity is the sister of invention.

We worked on a solution. I had a very large pan that could bake a loaf cake big enough to be cut into twenty servings, so within a week, I baked a sample. Maria and her team were very pleased with the result, so as fast as I could, I had forty stainless steel, food-grade loaf pans made at a machine shop so we'd soon be ready to fulfill orders of party loaves. Our relationship with Limoncello was secured.

Now we went full force shooting for more restaurant business. Just two months after working with Oteri's, we added four more restaurants to our lineup. Then we thought, why not offer the five-pound loaves to retail customers? We gambled people would want to buy the five-pound cake for their bigger gatherings, and our gamble paid off. The loaves have been a successful part of our retail sales since 2018.

In addition to web and restaurant sales, we expanded our

reach by working with small local businesses, including Epps Beverages and the seafood market, Capt'n Chucky's Crab Cake Company. The proprietors of both businesses became like family to us, not only by selling our smaller cakes on site but by helping us find new customers. The kinds of relationships we'd been building with people like Carol and Bob of Epps and Nancy, Chuck, and Kim of Capt'n Chucky's, plus our teams at Oteri's and Limoncello made us feel safe and warm. Local, familiar, intimate—that's just our style. But despite how comfortable we were with these local relationships, we knew if we really wanted to grow, it was time to get out of our comfort zone and go to *the show.*

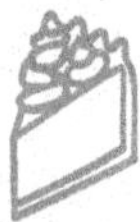

CHAPTER SIXTEEN

Ready for the big time, we signed up to present our wares at booze shows.

"That's not what they're called," says Kathy.

"Nope," adds Carole. "Not *booze shows*."

Fine.

Never let it be said I don't defer to the best interests of the team. (Never let it be said behind my back). Let me start again.

We knew we'd truly plunged into the world of marketing once we started signing up for *food, wine, and beer shows.* We even did well at coffee and tea shows because, of course, a piece of cake with a cup of coffee or tea is a delightful thing. *And* we threw ourselves into festivals. Also, charity benefits. We were putting ourselves out there. Obviously, our product belongs in the booze and food shows. "But what about the beer shows," you ask. "Have you started infusing our cake with *beer?*"

Nah, we belong in all these shows because they all pretty much say "party!" As exhibitors, we agree to provide free samples in return for the ability to sell our products on-site, and of course, on-site means on the site of a bunch of rowdy people who have been drinking, in some cases, all day. Imagine a liquor-themed convention crawling with happy drinkers, and now picture our table in the middle of it and covered in cake. We've all been there: You're neck deep in a night of partying, and when the evening is about to wrap up, you realize you're kind of hungry. Even more significant, you're completely disinhibited by the booze, so when somebody snoops through the host's cupboard and finds a Costco-sized stash of mint Milanos, you all turn into a room full of jackals. Well, the booze shows are kind of like that, except that it's the middle of the day, and we ain't hiding the cake. Step right up and have a slice.

Our first big show was a two-day food and wine event at a casino in Atlantic City, and the event producers had advised us there would be four thousand attendees, "at least, so you'd better show up with a whole lot of inventory." So armed with eight hundred cakes, advertising literature, a few small signs, and a little box to put all that money in, we set out for AC.

The timing wasn't great because Kathy was unavailable that weekend, thanks to a previously planned getaway to Aruba with Hubby Pants. *Have a great time, Princess.* To stand in for her, we hired two of our buddies (yes, it took two to replace Kathy), Trish and Judi, staunch supporters of our new company and lifelong friends. Torrential rains had flooded the loading docks, so dressed in rolled-up sweatpants and flip-flops, Carole and I literally waded our gear and supplies to the dock.

"Good God, I hope there are no snakes in this water," Carole said while sloshing her way from the car to the loading dock carrying a case of cakes over her head.

Right behind her, and with my arms equally loaded, I screeched, "*Snakes!?* What the satanic symbol are you talking about?"

"I can't see to the ground. What if there are snakes down there?"

"What about the Loch Ness monster? Worried about him, too? We're in the middle of a city, you loon." I kept sloshing forward, trying not to look down.

"Haven't you heard of alligators in urban sewer systems?" she said.

"*Why* are you trying to freak me out when my hands are full?"

"Don't you feel anything brushing against your ankles?"

"I'll give you something against your ankles."

From their safe, dry perches on the loading dock, Judi, Trish, and Carole's John laughed at us until we finished navigating the shark-infested waters and handed them the goods, which they loaded onto pushcarts. Then Carole and I hustled to the safety of dry land, and we all hauled the goods up to the convention hall.

We immediately staged our booth with business cards and hundreds of junior cakes in their see-through plastic, tied with bows, and full-size cakes in polka-dot boxes. Then John skedaddled on home, and it was down to the four of us females to carry the weekend. This gig was a huge deal for us, so it was difficult to calm ourselves down. *Four thousand* attendees? We needed to go back to the hotel and relax or we'd never be at our best for game day.

We'd booked two rooms for the four of us, one for Judi and Trish and the other for Carole and me. Judy and Trish came to our room for a little pre-dinner happy hour before enjoying a lovely meal in the hotel restaurant. We were back in our rooms by 8:00 p.m. Good girls—plenty of time for plenty of sleep.

But nope, plenty of sleep was not to be ours. Carole and I were like a couple of sixteen-year-olds the night before attending prom with the hunky loves of our young lives—we were a jangled tangle of nerves marinating in a bucket of adrenaline, so we flipped and tossed all night.

Finally, in the convention hall the next morning, we removed the drapes that had kept the cakes hidden all night and staged our takeaway materials, which we knew weren't going to last more than a couple of hours. We were so inexperienced that, not only did we neglect to print enough company literature for the show, we'd prepared barely any cake samples. What a couple of knuckleheads—all dressed up to face an enormous crowd, but within an hour before the show, we'd managed to cover only one pretty plate with thirty-six cake samples.

We'd brought the cakes in big cases, so I used one of them as a makeshift table and started cutting, cutting, cutting with the pace of a New York butcher on Friday afternoon and keeping the knife clean with an occasional swipe of a paper towel.

When people started arriving, we handed them samples from our hands—no toothpicks, no forks, not even napkins. Yep, we were literally *handing* them pieces of cake. FDA police, anyone? Later that day, I dashed out to a grocery store and bought plastic containers and toothpicks so on day two we could offer samples without looking like amateurs.

As the show ramped up, the four of us were like hawkers running a carnival ring toss. "Step up ladies and gentlemen, and taste something very special—booze in cake!" Since we had a product most of the attendees had never seen or tasted, they didn't know what they'd been missing and appeared happy to pass us by. But as the day went on, word got out that somewhere in the convention hall was a booth serving cake with alcohol in it. By the afternoon, the traffic at our table was heavy. A few convention goers even became party buddies, who hustled around the show and kept coming back to our table with liquor samples. One guy named Bobby, who looked like a young Brad Pitt, brought all four of us shots of tequila, flavored vodka, and a dish of pretzels. Bobby got lots of cake samples.

In two days, we sold about six hundred cakes, which meant two hundred would be heading home with us. But we soon realized that wouldn't be a problem because after the show our website blew up, and within a week we emptied our inventory.

After we recharged from that exhausting weekend (and after Princess K returned from her umbrella-drink drinking, hammock swinging, steel drum dancing island getaway), we regrouped as a trio and talked about how to up our trade show game. We learned a lot from watching how the big kids did it, and we decided our first step toward convention center greatness should be to build a booth people couldn't just walk past, one that might spare us having to accost people. We'd held our own at the Atlantic City show thanks to our general lack of shyness, but why not let a sexy booth do more of the work?

We designed a large back banner featuring five-foot-tall pictures of our cakes. Small and delicious is attractive, but *huge* and delicious is a real attention getter. At future shows, we were amused by people sampling the cake, then pointing to the sign and saying, "I want one *that* size!"

Feeling confident thanks to our new-and-improved booth and processes, we signed up for food and wine shows that featured local and Food Network chefs. It's hard work lugging in precut cake, tables, chairs, signage, literature, linens, cakes, bags, boxes, and the all-important money box. But the work of the show itself—offering the samples, being "on" with customers, and then ringing up and bagging the cakes we sold—is utterly exhausting. These shows aren't for sissies.

Although we tend to refer to these events as *trade shows*, they are not; a trade show is an event where companies show off their newest products and services to other businesses within the industry. But we actually attend the kinds of food, wine, liquor, and beer shows where we can sell our products directly to the public.

We dove into those waters and for nine years, with the help of free labor in the form of two of our husbands, John and John, kept swimming our way through one-, two-, and three-day shows. Each show led to another bump in website sales, and that kept our bakery busy. For a time, everyone was happy to be part of the food show machine.

We also took part in charity-focused shows, including benefits for local breast cancer organizations, homeless shelters for women, the Philadelphia Boys and Girls Clubs, Victorious Women, the Philadelphia Orchestra Fundraisers, and the PA Restaurant and Lodging Association. As a vendor, we always donated 10-20 percent of our proceeds from the show to the featured charity, and we supplied free cakes for door prizes. All the shows we participated in taught us lessons, introduced us to people we'll know forever, and helped keep our growing business afloat. But after almost a decade of being showgirls, we decided it was time to throw more promotional energy in a direction that scared us the most: online sales.

As we all know, people meet their spouses-to-be online, people bank online, and slap each other in the face online. And man, do people shop online! A company needs to understand social media communication and online advertising. Not many years ago, the preceding sentence would have sent all of us into a three-way death stare. It's no secret that we're more of the shake-your-hand-and-then-shake-you-a-martini kind of gals. But we're not resistant to progress; just last week, Carole traded her flip phone for a smartphone, and Kathy got a credit card with a chip in it.

"Isn't your new car the first one you've owned without an eight-track player?" asks Kathy.

Pay no attention to her.

Anyway, we accepted we were going to have to take our shop to the airwaves (or whatever the hell kind of waves can actually send a message from my computer to yours in under a second), which meant somebody was going to have to pilot the online plane. I suggested we rock-paper-scissors for it, but the other two convinced me this wasn't a wise method of decision-making. (Hmph. Name *one* childhood dilemma that couldn't be settled with the sweet efficiency of one-two-*boom!* On a related note, I don't recommend choosing scissors. Took me years to realize that almost nobody ever goes one-two-*paper*.)

Okay, so who was going to handle our social media? About forty-five seconds of listening to one of our kids talk about using Instagram convinced us it was time to enlist the help of a youngin'. We knew, of course, that hiring an experienced marketing specialist would be costly because we'd be paying for their time and knowledge by the hour. All three of us have had enough business experience to know that one of the most important management skills you can have is the ability to hire the right person for the job.

We started by enlisting the help of a so-called marketing guru we'll call Blerp. After sniffing around online and asking just about everyone we knew for a recommendation, we found Blerp through a fellow entrepreneur. Blerp suggested we spend time beefing up our reach by using Facebook and Twitter.

Great idea, Blerp. That's kind of what we found you for.

We tried working with another two "marketing professionals"—we'll call them Yip and Yap—and they proved equally useless. As Blerp had done, Yip and Yap did little more than tell us what we should do rather than what they were going to do for us. They offered lists of people to contact for more exposure and delivered little speeches about all the reasons we should be willing to pay $1,000 to actually learn how to reach those contacts.

Good grief, we thought, is this what modern-day marketing expertise looked like?

Well, we're nothing if not idea people, so we started thinking and ideating between the three of us. Yes, you read that correctly—I wrote ideating. We needed some new ideas, so we sat down to ideate. Apparently, these are words now. I use them here only to mercilessly mock the corporate culture that would hurl such verbal vomit into an already jargon-clogged lexicon.

We bounced other ideas around.

Kathy said, "Do you think there are any ad agencies that would be willing to work for cake?"

"No," answered Carole, "no, I don't."

Undeterred, Kathy said, "What if we bought billboard space and plastered it with a gigantic cake and showed a bottle of limoncello being poured into it?"

"I like that idea," I said, "except the part about buying the billboard space."

Our brainstorms weren't delivering anything we could use, but after several weeks of researching ad agencies and the price of newspaper and radio ads, the light finally came on.

"Maybe we're going about this all wrong," said Kathy. "We're just turning over the same kinds of rocks that got us Blerp, Yip, and Yap."

"Yes," said Carole, "repeating the same behavior and expecting a different kind of marketer. Come on, we're smarter than this!"

"And why are we looking under rocks? Shouldn't we look for social media professionals who make *themselves* findable?" I asked.

"That makes good sense, sister," said Kathy, "except we tried that and ended up with nada. But we're right here in a college town. Why not get ourselves a hungry college intern?"

"Hey!" said Carole. "*There's* an idea. If we find someone hungry for experience, we can certainly offer that. And if the intern is just plain hungry, we can fill its mouth with cake."

Ursinus College was happy for the chance to offer a few of its top seniors an accredited internship. They said we needed only to be a legitimate business (close enough) and willing to pay minimum wage. Perfect. That's our favorite wage (to pay).

Oh, relax. You know we're generous.

The school sent us three names and profiles of ladies who were qualified and asked that we interview all of them to offer them interview practice, so we scheduled all three interviews for the same day.

We'll call candidate number one Kiss. She was a cute little

blonde who pulled into Kathy's driveway ten minutes late for our interview. Peeking from behind curtains, we watched her emerge from her car wearing gray sweatpants and a T-shirt with a big pair of lips on it. I answered the door, then introduced Kathy, Carole, and myself. Then we waited for Kiss to introduce herself.

Silence. Kiss glanced around the walls of the foyer as if she was in the market for a new painting.

"And what's your name?" asked Carole.

She said her name and then blurted, "How much would this internship pay?"

Say what?

Carole asked, "Would you like to hear about the job first?"

Kiss looked at her blankly and said, "If the pay is too low, I won't need to know."

As Kathy headed toward this glittering beacon of the future, I feared for Kiss's safety. But Kathy simply opened the front door and said, "I'm pretty sure this isn't a fit. Have a nice day." A confused-looking Kiss turned and walked back to her car.

"Did that just happen?" I asked.

"I weep for the future," said Carole.

We'll call candidate number two Mary, because her name was Mary. Mary showed up five minutes early dressed in a cute plaid dress. This was promising.

"Hello, I'm Mary," she said, extending her hand after we greeted her at the door. "I'm here to meet Kathy and her sisters for an interview."

It was a great start, but after we described our business and explained we were looking for marketing help to build our website, she stopped us.

"This sounds like lots of fun," she said, "but I plan to be an accountant, so I'm looking for an accounting-heavy internship. Thank you, ladies, for your time."

We wished her luck, and Kathy escorted her to the door.

"Why are they sending us candidates who want accounting-heavy internships?" I asked Kathy.

"Have we done something to piss off Ursinus?" asked Carole.

"I don't know, and I can't imagine how," Kathy answered.

At 3:00 p.m., we opened the door to a tall, dark-haired girl dressed in a dark-blue, tailored suit. She extended her hand to Kathy and said, "Hi, my name is Sydney. I'm here from Ursinus College to interview for a marketing internship."

After introductions and a few stealth glances of hope among us sisters, we showed Sydney to a seat at Kathy's dining table.

"Here are some copies of my resume," she said, handing each of us a piece of paper. "Thank you so much for this opportunity. I must apologize because I really don't know anything about your company. The college only gives us the address and name of the person we're going to meet. If I'd had the chance, I would have researched your business and been better prepared."

Calm down, I told my pulse.

Carole said, "We never get tired of talking about our business, but first tell us a bit about you."

Sydney told us about her background, then said she was in her senior year, soon to be graduating with a degree in English and a minor in marketing. Carole, Kathy, and I then tripped all over each other as the facts about our company and our current business needs tumbled out of our mouths, the gist of which was that we sold liqueur-infused cakes and needed help building a customer base for our online and other retail sales.

Sydney flashed a smile that could light up a room. "Did you say *liqueur* cakes?"

Carole said, "Yes, we put liqueur in cakes, and we buy the alcohol in fifty-five-gallon barrels."

Sydney said, "This sounds like a cake for me! I mean, this sounds like a great product."

Carole asked, "What can you tell us about your plans after you graduate?"

"I'm still up in the air, but I like the idea that marketing will make use of my English skills. I think this internship opportunity might give me a look at how that could work."

I asked, "Do you have a lot of social media experience?"

"Yeah," said Kathy, "this is a very big question because these two can barely spell *social media*."

"Oh really, Miss Multimedia," I sneered, "tell us all about *your* social media expertise."

"At least I know what a hashtag is. Do you?"

"In fact, I do. Hashtag snotty sibling, hashtag know-it-all, hashtag *boom*."

Sydney raised her eyebrows. I could see I'd impressed her.

"Don't let her fool you, Sydney," Carole said. "Sue loves Jimmy Fallon, and as I'm sure you know, he does a whole hashtag thing."

I glared at her. "Judas."

Sydney laughed and spared us further sniping. "I haven't majored in it, but I've had classes in it, and I use it for research and play."

"How do you play with it?" asked Carole.

Kathy snickered. "She's not talking about using her iPhone as a snowboard, Grandma. She's talking about playing games online."

Carole stuck out her tongue, and Sydney almost spat some of her drink.

"Let's get to the important stuff," I said. "Want to try some cake?" And before Sydney could say, "Hell, yeah!" I presented her with a sample of each of our four flavors.

In between bites, she said, "Mmmm! How can I? Yum. That is, what is it you . . . oh wow. . . yum!"

Fairly quickly, we figured out she was trying to ask us about our goals, so one—or maybe all—of us answered. "We work food and beverage shows, but we need a lot of help building an online presence."

Sydney asked, "What do you do at food and beverage shows?"

Carole said, "We offer samples, we network, and we sell cakes."

"Sounds like you ladies are already doing a lot of networking and advertising, but I do have ideas for how to increase your online presence. It can't be too difficult when you're selling something this good."

Kathy asked, "What else can we tell you to help you decide if you'd like to take this on?"

"I already have some ideas," Sydney replied. "Can you give me samples of whatever marketing materials you have, and I'll take a few days to propose a plan? Also, more cake, please."

We took that to mean we were hired. I mean, *she* was hired. Er, that day, somebody was hired. Well, almost. We scheduled a meeting for the following week at a local pizza shop close to the college to discuss Sydney's ideas and to see if we all felt this would be a good fit. In truth, we planned to meet at the pizza joint to see if *Sydney* thought it would be a good fit. We were already in love; we'd found our Sydney. We wish a Sydney for everyone. For your next birthday, ask for a Sydney.

The next Friday afternoon, we walked into the pizza shop to find Sydney seated at a table with three folders placed around the table. She'd put together a little presentation that offered several ideas on how to use Facebook and some other social media platforms to increase our online presence. She also offered ideas for how to get local retail shops to sell our cakes. It seemed she had an endless stream of ideas, all good, and most of them involved her doing the work! All that and she still hadn't asked what the job paid.

My sisters gave me the nod. "Sydney, before we go any further," I said, "we'd like to offer you the position as our intern. We can only offer you minimum wage to start, but there will be plenty of cake and free meals in it for you. What do you think?"

Sydney said, "Yes, yes, yes! I really look forward to working with you ladies, and minimum wage is fine. Let's get started right away."

We'd made it official! Then we ordered lunch and spent the next two hours reminiscing about our youth. The pizza shop had been one of our high school hangouts, a place we escaped our hotel-life nightmare for a couple of hours here and there, a place where we could just be kids and not have to feel like somebody's free labor. So as Sydney listened, the three of us took a stroll down Memory Lane.

I pointed to a booth in the corner and said, "I remember the first time Carole and I sat in that booth and sneak-smoked by holding our cigarettes low and blowing the smoke under the table."

Sydney gasped, "You were allowed to smoke in restaurants?"

"I wouldn't say *allowed*, exactly. I was fifteen. But yes, back then adults were allowed to smoke in restaurants."

"Back then, Sue and I weren't, shall we say, often dissuaded by laws," said Carole.

"I preferred to think of them as guidelines," I said.

Carole reminisced that she'd sat low in another corner booth smooching with a boyfriend or two. Kathy could only add that she'd tattled on us about all of it.

This went on for several minutes, and as much fun as it was to laugh about our teen years, we didn't go too deep into our youth, for Sydney's sake.

I look up from the computer. "How do you suppose Sydney might have reacted if we'd told her about the cesspool?"

"Like everybody else does. Laughed her butt off," Carole says, not laughing her butt off.

I look back down at the computer screen and try not to smile.

Each week, we met Sydney and ate pizza as we talked through our latest marketing strategies. One of her many successful ideas was to set up recurring ads on our Facebook page, offering cake specials just before holidays. Offering Buy One, Get One was a great incentive. Those ads led to at least a 20 percent sales boost with each holiday special, so they paid for themselves fifty times over. This was a great building block that increased our followers and our ever-growing email list.

Sydney kept her promise to draft a letter directed to bloggers. Then, armed with names and addresses of eighteen bloggers, we printed the letters, shipped a blossom variety pack to each of them, and asked each of them for a review. The response was fantastic. For every blogger we sent a cake to, we received a glowing online review, and saw a 20 percent increase in sales. Sydney also produced delightfully creative videos that featured the three of us as cartoon characters, and she posted them online. Our business grew, we were all having fun, and Sydney never once complained about being paid only minimum wage.

She was going to graduate soon, so we knew it was time to offer her a full-time position and a raise. But before we could make an offer, we got the news we'd dreaded since the start of the glorious era of Sydney. After seven months of being an enormous help to us, Sydney was offered a position in the marketing department of a major advertising agency in Philadelphia. As sad as we were to see her go, we were delighted that working for us had helped prepare her for bigger things. We still stay in touch with our Sydney, and she even tosses us free advice now and then when we find ourselves stuck in a marketing conundrum.

With Sydney off into the business world, we needed to brainstorm some new ideas to maintain our growing buzz. That's right, I wrote another trendy term. I used *buzz* without irony. Never let it be said we're not willing to evolve. That said, I refuse to say or write and might not even acknowledge *ideate, put a pin in it, circle back,* or *bandwidth.* Go ahead and run that up the flagpole.

CHAPTER SEVENTEEN

Now that we were back to navigating the marketing waters without Sydney at the helm, Carole suggested reaching out to Linda, one of her former glass customers who also happened to be a broker for QVC. Linda agreed to taste our cakes because she was always looking for new products to introduce to the show. We hosted Linda for a lovely lunch featuring Carole's Caesar salad with grilled chicken, and for dessert, amaretto cake sautéed in butter.

With a mouthful of cake and a smile, Linda said, "I'll do everything I can."

We finished lunch, said goodbye to Linda, and waited. We expected to hear from her within a day or two, but several days went by without a word. While we waited, our childhood insecurities resurfaced. All these years later, we're still haunted by what it meant to come from *that* family. We were the kids who didn't get invited to many holiday parties because "there are just so many of you." Ours was the father who openly cheated on our mother. We were the mess of kids fathered by the town drunk. And now here we were, happily married, settled, educated, and with miles of business experience already behind us, but every day we had to wait for an answer rattled us a little more.

"Not me," says Kathy. "I wasn't rattled."

"Really?" I say, tilting my head to one side.

"I knew they'd call. I knew they'd want us."

I look at Carole and then nod toward Kathy. "What do you make of this girl? Wasn't nervous? No doubts at all?"

Carole says to me, "She's always been pretty confident, but yeah, for the QVC thing, I think you were the most nervous. Of course you were—you're the baker. It's always your recipe and your execution up there on the judging stand. We're all invested, but for you, it's so much more personal, right?"

"Much," I say. "But I don't know, I think it's more than that. Whenever I have to wait to hear someone's opinion about a cake, I think I feel like a kid again, and I'm waiting for some snooty person in town to stop looking at me sideways. I know. It's messed up."

Twelve days later, we heard from Linda. "I'm sorry it took so long," she said, "but, ugh, that's just the way these things work. It actually might have taken longer, but the QVC decision-maker I happened to get an appointment with just attended a wedding, and believe it or not, he received a guest gift basket with one of *your* amaretto cakes in it! He loved it and asked why they'd never heard of you before."

All three of us squealed into the speaker phone.

Linda went on. "I've secured a spot for you on QVC's upcoming Holiday Food Special. You'll have just three minutes to show that your cakes make a great holiday gift. Only one of you can be onscreen. I'll be in touch soon with more details."

Now we had to decide who would go on camera to sell the cake.

"You baked 'em, you should pitch 'em," said Carole.

"I'm pretty sure any of us could speak knowingly about these cakes, ladies," I answered.

Kathy said, "You want one of us talking about the recipes however we see fit? In front of millions of people? Really? What if they ask a baking question?"

How was I going to argue that? In my fevered daydreams, the QVC person asks, "How do you know when the cake has been baked just the right amount of time?" and Kathy answers, "Don't you throw a piece of it against a wall to see if it sticks?" Carole says, "I ask Sue."

"Also," Kathy added, "you're the thinnest right now, so it has to be you."

Ha! Those two chickens would have said anything to stay off camera. Anyway, it was decided. I would be the one to face the audience. But before that, I'd have to make it past the orientation.

After months of preparing the QVC software to process the orders for shipping, printing all the paperwork required to be inserted in each shipment, and securing the approval to set up our display table on air, we were ready. Still, before I could be on air, I had to spend a full day at the QVC studio to learn how to behave on TV.

My training day was scheduled for the second Tuesday in October. This also just happened to be the final day of my 6:00 a.m. physical therapy following a double-knee replacement surgery six weeks earlier. I was told by the QVC scheduler to check in by 9:00 a.m. and expect to be there all day. She explained there would be a two-hour meeting to familiarize myself with QVC rules, then a test video to critique my TV presence. And I mustn't forget to bring some of my product to stage.

After rehab, I was all stretched and ready to go. I arrived at 8:30 a.m., leaving myself plenty of time to saunter into the enormous QVC facility. As I approached the front entrance, I met the Daisy Cake Lady who was there for the same training. She told me she'd been on Shark Tank and Barbara Corcoran had invested in her business. Now QVC was her first advertising mission. Both carrying bags of cakes, we found our way to the elevator and up to the third floor where businesspeople were hustling in to start their day. The space had a bright, pleasant feeling thanks to long hallways lined with glass-walled offices and a glass ceiling that let the sun in.

A handsome, blond, twenty-something directed us to a conference room with a long table topped with seven bottles of water and surrounded by eight chairs. The other trainees were already seated. There was an old guy selling some kind of little tool, a middle-aged woman selling kitchen gadgets, another young lady armed with brownies, and a stately woman with small oil paintings. The energy in the room crackled. For which of us would QVC be the big breakout?

At 9:30 a.m., instructor Jane, one of the show's seasoned hosts, came in, introduced herself, and asked each of us to introduce ourselves and describe what product we brought. The Daisy Cake Lady and I were the only two who said much more than the name of the thing we were selling, so in a few minutes we were onto the training itself.

Jane said each of us would be heading to the studio shortly

where we'd do a test tape, after which the instructor would review our performance and decide whether we were show worthy. I was moving pretty slow on two new knees, so I was sure all the young, sparky instructors must have thought I looked a hundred years old.

The mini-class about how to function on-camera consisted of little more than suggestions for how to stay calm and speak clearly.

"Be yourself and don't forget to smile!" Jane said with a big smile.

Class complete. It was time to hit the studio.

I was feeling fairly calm until somebody announced that since QVC is about the size of a football field plus two Costcos, it would be easier to walk down the three floors via the back stairway rather than take the elevator on the other side of the studio. Easier for who? But I made it, and there were no tears, just some very quiet whimpering.

The studio was quite a sight. There were several stages, each decked out like its own little universe. There was a full kitchen, a garden, a set that looked like a living room, and one with a Christmas tree in front of a fireplace. Each had a presentation table in front to display the products being sold. There were cameras, lights, cables, and gear everywhere, and there must have been fifty men and women moving them all around to take shot after shot for our practice appearances.

Each of us was assigned a presentation table with a host and camera operator ready to make us a star. Jane led me to my spot behind a table, and then offered a last bit of direction.

"Just smile, relax, and be yourself."

That was no problem until I heard that camera click on, at

which point I stumbled over my words. Then I took a big breath and relaxed through my take, and then it was over. I was relieved afterward to be able to cut up cake and serve it to all the workers. This was an activity I'm comfortable with.

After my big audition, I had to walk back up those three flights of stairs to the conference room. That was grueling, but I refused to show how much pain I was in. Patty, a sweet young woman with warm brown eyes and a calming voice, was there to critique my test. We watched my video together, and I winced the second it began to roll. I wondered, Who the hell is that old broad on the screen? It's like turning fifty, then looking in the mirror and seeing a seventy-year-old. Patty noted kindly that I seemed a bit stiff, which was perfectly normal for my first try, but that I spoke clearly and smiled. She suggested I practice a bit in front of the mirror and do my best to remain calm the day I would be on air. I'd passed! Finally, the day ended, and I did my stoic walk out to the parking lot without showing the extreme pain I was in.

As I headed to the parking lot, my partners were waiting for me but were visibly shaken at the sight of me breaking down in tears. I was in a lot of pain, but I'd made it through the day with a smile. I earned a few points for taking one for the team.

Eight weeks passed, and then it was time to sell some cakes, live, on-air. It was a holiday segment just three weeks before Christmas, so our sisterly trio was abuzz with excitement about potential sales.

Naively, I thought I'd just stroll into the studio on the day of the shoot and announce, "Okay gang, I'm ready for hair and makeup!" But no, I wasn't nearly important enough for QVC to bother with prettying me up. I found out a few days before showtime their version of primping the "talent" was to remind us not to wear clothes with busy patterns because they're distracting.

I started the day at my own hairdresser and then had my face done by a makeup artist at a salon close to the QVC studio. Our sister, Debbie, bought me a beautiful turquoise, cotton blouse for me to wear on the show, and with that, I was ready for my close-up.

QVC had agreed to let us set up and decorate our own display table for the airing, which wasn't their usual process. They charged a large fee for these setups, and we told them our little family operation didn't have much budget for such things but had an expert in-house designer who handled our aesthetics. Carole draped their four-foot-long table with white fabric, then created a lovely, layered display of polka-dot boxes, six of the amaretto in black and white and six of the limoncello in yellow and white. She added four plates with two slices of amaretto and two slices of limoncello cake, along with full-size cakes placed on doilies on top of beautiful glass-tiered cake stands. Because it was a Christmas holiday show, she also added lots of clippings of natural greens and beautifully handmade bows in red and green.

Finally, it was showtime. I was placed on my mark behind the table and told to relax for a few minutes. Sure, I thought. I'll do that. I tried to keep my mind busy by watching the seller for the next segment set up his table covered in holiday hams.

I took a big breath and waited for the stage director to raise his hand to signal we were on-air. Then, as if out of nowhere, the host appeared next to me, introduced herself (Don't ask me her name. I have no idea.), and then somebody shouted, "Everybody, quiet on the set. Action!"

The next three minutes flew by in a blur of seconds. I remember the host asking me about the cakes, flavors, and why we use liqueur, but I don't recall much else. I was stiff, so I definitely defied Jane's instruction to relax. Had I also rejected her direction to smile?

Later, Carole and Kathy told me that as the show aired, they watched from the green room screaming "Hell yeah!" each time the screen indicated another cake had sold, and that was a lot of shouting. They shouted their way through our selling sixteen hundred cakes in three minutes!

We were ready for it. QVC knew what they were doing and had directed us to have two thousand cakes ready to ship, so the bakery had prepared one thousand full-size amaretto and one thousand full-size limoncello cakes sealed and boxed. A small team of friends were ready to help us pack and ship, and the next day I went into our office, printed all the orders and packing slips, and ran them down to the bakery where our team waited to pack them all up for FedEx pick up the next day.

Even after that sales explosion, we still had four hundred cakes left over, but we had no trouble selling them within the next couple of weeks thanks to lots of orders still coming in from QVC.

John had taped the show so we could all watch it together that night. We gathered at my house with martinis, and I could barely watch myself. Oh man, I was stiff.

"You were greaaat!" said Kathy, in that voice she used back when her kids presented her with macaroni artwork.

"I was bad," I moaned.

Carole said, "You were fine. It's the host who was lame. She didn't ask anything interesting."

Okay, one point for Carole.

Kathy followed with, "*I* couldn't have done it. You did greaaat!" Again with the macaroni voice.

If we ever do QVC again, one of them will have to go on camera because I ain't putting myself through that again! I was a dud. I was a robot. I looked like the Tin Man before they oiled him. Without a live audience to interact with, I felt flat. *You* try being funny for dead air!

Despite that it outed me as a cyborg, the QVC appearance gave us credibility, which we saw reflected in countless comments on our website and Facebook page. For prospective buyers *As Seen on QVC* goes a long way. But the event wasn't a financial coup because of expenses related to order processing and all the other blahdy blah, which was why we didn't return to QVC when asked.

Carole got back on the beat and discovered our next delicious promotional opportunity: the New York City Meet the Media showcase, which offers entrepreneurs the chance to meet one on one with reps from the world of radio, television, newspapers, magazines, and blogs. Geez, New York can't get enough of us. Time for another Cake Ladies road trip!

We loaded Kathy's car with cakes, lots of promotional literature, and us—dressed to impress in our polka-dot shirts—and then it was back to the Big Apple, this time to present Full Spirited Flavours to the New York media.

The first attendee to show big interest was a writer for *Health Digest*. We warned, "Delicious as they are, our cakes might not align with your healthy eating guidelines."

The rep replied, "Some things are worth indulging."

That's our kind of girl! She wrote a terrific review of our

cakes and spun the recommendation with the message that sometimes you need to treat yourself, so make it worth the splurge.

The day ended with an invitation to appear on an episode of *Live Well TV* to describe our company and offer ideas for ways to serve the cake. Once again, we were being invited to present our goods on a show that wanted only one of us on-air, so this time I convinced Carole she could do it. She agreed, and yep, that would mean *another* trip to New York City.

Despite Kathy being adept at negotiating the city's mean streets, this time we decided to travel by train. The show's producer had directed us to arrive at the studio by 9:00 a.m., which meant we had to catch a train in Philadelphia by 6:00 a.m. Believe us when we say that getting *these* three ladies up and ready to leave anywhere by 4:00 a.m. is about as easy as lifting the front end of an F-150 with a sprained wrist.

The 30th Street Station in Philly was packed. People were hustling everywhere, and the three of us zipped and zagged through the crowds, lugging several pounds of cake in gigantic shopping bags. The station air was filled with delicious scents of fresh coffee and pastries, but we showed discipline by passing all treats to avoid missing our train. Fortunate for us, the train wasn't sold out because we and our bags of cake took up eight seats.

The train was barely out of the station when a very handsome elderly gentleman asked, "Ladies, what do you have in all those bags?"

"Glad you asked, good sir!" Carole said. "We're three sisters, and our business is selling liqueur-infused cakes. Want to try one?"

Now we had everybody's attention. A few young men lowered their newspapers and looked up.

One of them said, "Are you really giving out liqueur cake?"

And so began the train party. We opened a box, the samples started making their way through the train car, and within minutes the air was filled with the sounds of people calling out which flavor they wanted to try. By the time the train pulled into NYC, three lovely young men had offered to help us carry our bags to the cab line. We took their names and numbers and later thanked them with a cake. They've been regular customers ever since.

After a quick cab ride to the studio, we gathered our bags, paid the driver, and ran into the station with an hour to spare. As with QVC, for this presentation there would be no audience, just Carole and the hosts. Carole was calm and relaxed as she described our cake flavors, played up the fact that we buy booze in fifty-five-gallon barrels, and explained we actually love working together. Then it was a wrap. Not a terribly momentous event, but the train ride to New York had been unforgettable. Still, our television careers weren't over.

Our friend, Marie, who had worked on *Philadelphia Morning 10,* connected us with one of that show's producers, and we were invited to do our thing on the air again. This time we put a spin on the appearance by presenting how to "make" dessert when you're working with a cake that's already been made.

Once again, Carole was the star of the show. She was directed to a room for makeup as I prepared custard in the studio's little kitchen in the back of the green room and Kathy gave away amaretto juniors to members of the audience.

When the show was about to start, Kathy and I plopped

ourselves in the front row to watch. The teasers included a shot of me making custard in the studio kitchen and a shot of Carole opening the cakes, and arranging fruits, martini glasses, and the custard she'd need in her segment.

And then *action!*

The host and hostess introduced Carole, and she said, "Good morning. I'm here to show you how to build a perfect parfait using components you didn't make from scratch. But you can still feel honest when you tell your party guests, 'I made this,' because you will have *constructed* it. Hey, when you make chocolate chip cookies, aren't you using *already made* chocolate chips? When you make linguine with clam sauce, aren't you using *already made* clams? You get the idea. Now how about we see which host can create the best parfait?"

"Let's do it!" said the female host.

"Okay you two," Carole said, "whichever one of you makes the best parfait gets to take home an entire cake of your choice. I'll be the judge!"

At first, the male host appeared to have no interest in winning because he spent most of his time stuffing cake in his mouth. But eventually, both hosts crafted delicious-looking parfaits consisting of cake, fruit, and custard layered in polka-dotted martini glasses. Despite that the male host had spent more time eating than parfait sculpting, Carole declared him the winner because he did a more artful job of layering fruit and custard and cake than his opponent had.

As captivating as Carole was, Kathy and I were distracted by trying to figure out how to weasel our way to the green room to give cake to Kevin Bacon and his band.

With the competition's winner declared, the male host

walked off with a thirty-six-ounce amaretto cake, which he clutched and hunched over like he was trying to sneak a stolen Birkin bag out of Yankee Stadium.

"*What the hell?*" Carole shouts, gasping with laughter. "What the hell is a Birkin bag doing at Yankee Stadium? Hahaha!"

"I wanted people to be able to picture it, the way he was stooped over it, all protective and sneaky."

"Yeah, I caught the hunched part," she chortles, "but why didn't you just say he was sneaking out a fancy purse store, you goofball?"

"I wanted it to be relatable. People can picture Yankee Stadium."

"*Nothing* about a Birkin bag is relatable!" she says, still laughing.

"Do you want to do the typing? Be my guest. Here's my laptop." I turn my computer around and slide it across the table.

"No, no, that's fine," she says, dabbing her eyes with the hem of her shirt. "You just keep up the good work." Then she heads outside, and I can hear her calling, "Kathy! You're gonna love this one!"

CHAPTER EIGHTEEN

After trudging around trade shows for almost nine years, we began to accept that the "on your feet all day" part of our business was asking too much of us. Too much out of our cartilage, for starters. All three of us were wearing out our knees—that's six knees going to hell at the same time. Genetics probably started us on the road to knee replacement, and we'd all been pretty sporty for much of our lives. Years and years of playing softball, hockey, racquetball, and basketball pushed us even closer to the operating table. But we think it was the trade show circuit that eventually did us in. Fifteen to twenty trade shows per year ain't for sissies, and it certainly ain't for women of a certain age. So we were three tired women with six distressed knees that could no longer be ignored.

The three of us will do just about anything to avoid a surgery, but the surgeon I found made clear there was no work-around for our situation because all six of our knees were down to bone-on-bone—no brace, no pills, no shots, no exercises, not even changing our dessert-eating ways was going to fix this. We were going under the knife. Actually, given that it was going to be all three of us, let's say we were going under the knives.

"Yeah, let's make that plural," says Kathy. "I sure don't want him touching me with the same knife he uses on your dirty knees."

"And I sure don't want him using the knife he used on either of you two heathens," adds Carole.

"I'm going first, so haha to both of you *and* your bacteria-smeared knives," I say.

My research to find the best doctor led me to Dr. Nikos Pavilides of Pottstown. We all understood that having both knees replaced at the same time would be difficult, but we also knew we couldn't afford the time to recover twice, so two knees at a time it would be.

During the middle of my surgery, I woke up, took one blurry look at the anesthesiologist whose arms were covered in tattoos of leaves, and asked, "Am I in a tree?" Sounds kind of peaceful, right?

My surgery went beautifully and was followed by just three days in the hospital, five days in a rehab facility, and eight weeks of outpatient therapy.

One year later, Kathy was next, and her procedure also went exactly as planned. Back in her hospital bed, she awoke and asked, "What's for dinner?" Clearly, she was fine.

But Carole's wake-up comment—this one is the winner. After her surgery, she woke up, turned to a nurse, and said, "Who's in charge of the marketing at this place?" She explained to the baffled caregiver that, because the same doctor had performed all three of our double-knee replacements and because we'd all stayed in the same room afterward, we were fabulous candidates for a hospital marketing campaign. And not long after Carole had secured us as the focus of the hospital's marketing campaign, she also convinced the marketing director at Bryn Mawr Rehab that our triple, double-knee replacement scenario would make a great story for *Hospital Marketing Magazine*. Soon after, we appeared between the pages in an article titled, "Six New Knees Keep Three Sisters in Business." Finally, the centerfold exposure we'd all dreamed of.

In 2018, we reduced our line of cakes to include only the thirty-six-ounce rounds and the five-pound loaf cakes. The smaller products didn't prove profitable, so they had to go.

For the next couple of years, we made a profit and made people happy. Life was good. And then *dammit!* The world decided to roll around in the muck of a pandemic. Because our sales efforts had primarily targeted restaurants, COVID-19 smacked the hell out of our business, as restaurants had to scramble to survive in a sequestered world. As a result, our 2020 sales were reduced by close to 80 percent. Fortunate for us, because we also sell a lot of cake through our website, we survived thanks to a lot of shut-ins, who—Hallelujah!—wanted cake.

By 2021, many restaurants were bouncing back, retail sales were going back up, and even the barrel booze was getting easier to find again. So you might say that in more than a few ways we've come full circle.

It may sound like we're just three crazy partiers who spend most of our time trying to forget our rocky childhood by swilling martinis, but that's really not the case. We also spend time eating, and we pause for sleep and showering. And in truth, we're very responsible drinkers who almost always stop at two. With or without booze in the picture, we're always laughing.

We think our collective happiness is greatly based in, of course, the bonds of our sisterhood but also in our shared commitment to make the best of any situation we find ourselves in.

So where do we go from here? *Who* knows? But wherever it is, we know we'll be taking with us our friends, our husbands, *some* of our relatives (*you* get it), gratitude, laughter, and a case of Grey Goose. Wherever the next stop is, we'll be diving in full spirited. And we really hope we'll bump into you along the way.

"Wait," says Kathy. "Are we done? Is this a wrap?"

"Is it time to stick a fork in it? Done and dusted? Is this thing in the can?" adds Carole.

I decide to let them roll with this for a bit.

"Are we calling it a day?"

"Mission accomplished?"

"Have we crossed the finish line?"

"Put a bow on it?"

Then I realize this could go on all day. "Okay ladies, nice job with the completion idioms. I say it's time to put our feet up and toast to the future."

"That's all she wrote?" adds Kathy. Then her eyes light up. "Hey, get it? *That's all she wrote?*"

"I get it. And yes, that's all she wrote, for now. Let's have a martini."

Kathy dashes to the kitchen to help us seal the deal with a clink and a toast, featuring, of course, a round of her delicious, frosty martinis.

As we wait for our just rewards, Carole wistfully gazes out

the window and sighs, "Hard to believe we're done telling our story."

I tell her, "Yes, for now. But who knows what's next? We might even have another book in us."

Kathy walks in with a tray of martinis, sets the three glasses on the table, and says, "Don't scare the nice readers."

The End

Let's raise a glass to the eaters and drinkers,
The laughers, the jokers, the dreamers, the thinkers.
Here's to us all and the stories we spin—
Thanks for your time and for letting us in.

If we meet on the street, go on—give us *that* look,
And tell us you giggled while reading our book.
Or tell us you *loved* the damned thing, for God's sake.
(Until then, why haven't you ordered a cake?)

So everyone: Raise up your wine glass, your flute,
Your paper cup (really, no need to get cute).
Hoist those mojitos, martinis, and beers.
From the Crazy Cake Sisters,
God bless you and
Cheers!

ABOUT THE AUTHORS

Carole Algier, *Sue Katein*, and *Kathy Lanyon* grew up in Collegeville, PA, in a family of five girls, two boys, and two absent parents. Carole is an artist who enjoys gardening, gourmet cooking, and entertaining. Kathy is a no-nonsense, light-hearted mother of two whose strength is delegating with great organizational skills. Sue is a practical, sensitive mother of one who enjoys baking, writing, and entertaining. As partners, each of them brings something unique to the table: Sue, who has thirty-five years of experience in corporate small business operations development, is the creator of their business's cake recipes; Kathy, who has thirty-five years of corporate IT experience, and is the technical advisor who keeps them in the twenty-first century; and Carole, who has forty years of experience in the food industry, utilizes her art background for marketing and branding. All three sisters have a great sense of humor and value family time with their husbands, children, grandchildren, and friends.

Looking for your next great read?

We can help!

Visit www.shewritespress.com/next-read or scan the QR code below for a list of our recommended titles.

She Writes Press is an award-winning independent publishing company founded to serve women writers everywhere.